I0881370

There's Something that the Kop Wants You to Know

Keith Salmon

There's Something that the Kop Wants You to Know

A Dad, a Lad, and Jürgen Klopp: Following Liverpool FC's Return to Glory

pitch

First published by Pitch Publishing, 2025

Pitch Publishing
9 Donnington Park,
85 Birdham Road,
Chichester, West Sussex,
PO20 7AJ
www.pitchpublishing.co.uk
info@pitchpublishing.co.uk

A CIP catalogue record is available for this book from the British Library.

ISBN 978 1 83680 142 9

Typesetting and origination by Pitch Publishing

MIX
Paper | Supporting responsible forestry
FSC® C010615

Printed and bound on FSC® certified paper in line with our continuing commitment to ethical business practices, sustainability and the environment.

Printed and bound in India by Thomson Press

Contents

From the lad to his dad, this one's for you Bob Salmon.

You'll Never Walk Alone.

About the Author

Keith Salmon lives in the Isle of Man with his wife Nikki, his son Charlie and his daughter Izzy. *There's Something that the Kop Wants You to Know* is Keith's second book. His first, *We Had Dreams and Songs to Sing*, was originally published in 2009 and purchased in over 30 countries. After critical and reader acclaim, Keith has updated his story.

Here he tells his new stories with a passion for football, specifically Liverpool FC. It's a story about love, loss, a sense of belonging and, with an ever-changing world, the effect football, and Hillsborough in particular, has had on his life as he moves through his 50s and what lies beyond. He's now joined on his journey by his son Charlie, and the story becomes the ultimate 'dad-and-lad' football book. Going the match with your dad will resonate with so many people, something for everyone to relate to. Read about Keith's journey following Jürgen Klopp and Liverpool Football Club.

The Owen McVeigh Foundation

Message from Mark McVeigh

The Owen McVeigh Foundation was set up eight years ago after the passing of our 11-year-old son, Owen, who fought a brief battle with leukaemia. Our aim is to support children and their families going through a cancer diagnosis in and around the Merseyside area.

Over the last eight years we have supported well in excess of 2,000 children and families with the love and support shown to us daily at The Owen McVeigh Foundation.

A special thanks to Keith, a continued support to The Owen McVeigh Foundation.

YNWA

owenmcveighfoundation.co.uk

A portion of the book profits will be provided to the foundation to support the wonderful work Mark and the foundation do. Please check out the amazing work they do and, wherever possible, give them your support. If you could donate, gift or spread awareness, please do.

Thanks, Keith

Thank You

SO MANY thanks need to go to so many people that it's hard to know where to start. I want to thank every person who read *We Had Dreams and Songs to Sing*. Every time someone took the opportunity to tell me how much they enjoyed it was truly appreciated. You'll never know what that meant to me. For everyone who said, 'I can't wait until you write another,' or 'When's the next one coming?' this one is for you.

In the following pages I talk about loss, and the biggest has been the loss of my dad, who handed me down his passion and love for the Reds. I've followed them, like he did. I think he'd be very proud, and now my son Charlie is following in both our footsteps. Thanks from us both. My mum, who along with my dad, sold so many books back in 2009. Books would come out of her handbag at bus stops and north Liverpool social clubs at any given opportunity, and she's still championing everything I do. I can't thank her enough. My real brothers – 'Our Ian' and 'Our Kev' – who've been there on many steps of the journey.

My wonderful wife Nikki, without whose belief and support and telling me to follow my dream of book number two I wouldn't have made it this far. She drives me on, believes in me, giving me the confidence to believe in myself. She never argues about me following the Reds. She's fed up listening to all my stories now, though, and that's why I'm giving them to you. For my son Charlie, who when the first book was published was only a toddler. He's now an integral part in the story. Then my daughter Izzy, who rolls her eyes and lets the boys get on with shouting at the telly. You deserve every guilt-trip present I've ever bought you. I've always tried to make it up to you – I hope I succeeded.

A massive thanks to my companions on the journeys that follow with the Reds. Without you allowing me to tell your story, none of this is possible. These are real people, the best of people! I dedicate this to you, as many of my favourite times are the times I've spent with you, and a better band of brothers I could not wish for. I thank you all!

A special thank you to Richie Greaves, Damian Kavanagh, Kevin Sampson and David Conn, who did me the honour of reading 'We Climbed the Hill in Our Own Way', giving me valuable support and guidance – it's truly appreciated.

My thanks wouldn't be complete without saying a huge thank you to Herr Jürgen Klopp. Much of what you're about to read doesn't happen without him. *Danke schön*. But this book isn't about Jürgen, it's about a Scouse lad called Keith.

In memory of the 97 people who went to a football game and did not come home. We continue to climb the hill our own way. Justice for the 97!

We'll Be as We Are

'We'll be as we are when all the fools who doubt us fade away.'

THESE ARE prophetic words of the Liverpudlian musician Ian McNabb, he of The Icicle Works. There's a banner (actually two banners now) that proclaims those exact words, and it can be seen across European grounds nowadays, the original idea of Tigger from Twitter (X as it's now known, but I refuse to call it X, it's Twitter to me).

If you're going to have the greatest idea for a banner, then why not get it made by the best in the business, and that's what Tigger did. He asked Peter Carney, the supreme flag and banner maker, who has many of the greatest Liverpool flags on his CV, to make it for him. In my humble opinion it now sits alongside the greatest flags to adorn the Kop. The words still ring true to me. I don't feel like I've sold out, I still care about my fellow man and try to do my bit for the less fortunate than me.

Wednesday, 15 January 2020, a day of note for me. After nearly 31 years I finally sat in front of a professional therapist to talk specifically about Hillsborough. He said I had 'deep-seated trauma', no shit!

How did I get here? A man who has spoken openly about Hillsborough for years, a man who had the memories tucked in a box that he could open on command. The man who'd talk to anyone who'd listen, do lectures on his own experience. I even wrote a chapter in a book about it, for crying out loud. How could this man need help, now?

My life had been spiralling out of control, not that anyone except Nikki will have noticed. There was a moment in time where I knew. At Gatwick Airport in The Red Lion, and Zil said to me, 'How are you doing mate?' I'd normally respond, 'Sound, mate,' but not today. Today I just blurted it out, 'In a bad way, mate, I'm really struggling, to be honest.' He was taken aback, but he did what I needed him to do – he sat and listened and then gave me the support I needed.

All it took was 15 minutes. I needed to say it out loud and put it out on the air. If you keep it in your head, it drives you mad; say it out loud and you're sharing it, and it lifts the heaviest of weights.

To the outside world I was the same. The mask was on, the smiles and jokes were plentiful. I have everything: a beautiful wife, fabulous kids, loving wonderful family, great friends, more acquaintances than I can shake a stick at and the Mighty Reds turning themselves around. See, it's always linked to football. People who know me will read these words and probably not recognise this version of me.

Sometimes the tipping point isn't the trauma itself, it's numerous things that all add up and take you over the edge. Work, life, kids, or other things (and there were a lot of other things), take your pick. Whatever it was, I needed help. The hardest thing to do is admit that you need help. Here I was, the person who listened to other people's problems, always helpful, hopefully giving the right advice. Now I was the one who needed the advice, and it wasn't a 'pull yourself together' conversation.

You always put a face on for everyone, don't you? Now, though, the doors are open to the mental health discussion, it's no longer taboo. You still need to be brave to admit you have issues, and I now see myself as a brave man.

Luckily, I was working for a company that embraced mental health issues and the need to support their staff. They had a wellbeing helpline (step one on the ladder of support) where they analysed your issues and then provided the appropriate support. In November 2019, I took a deep breath and made the call. At the end of 30 minutes, the lady clearly knew I needed help, but she needed to take advice on the range of issues I had. She needed to take advice!

It was clear that basic counselling sessions were not going to be the answer. The answer was that it would need something like CBT (cognitive behavioural therapy) to help resolve my issues. I'd need to see a qualified professional, locally, to make such an assessment. Looking back, it came as no surprise that I fell over after the verdict at the David Duckenfield trial was announced. Hopefully, these words will help someone see that it does get better.

* * *

It's now over 15 years since I wrote my first book charting my first 40-odd years. This one will take you through what happened next, and it's been some journey. Writing a book changed my life and hopefully gave others the idea that everyone does have a book in them. We all have a story to tell. Some choose to tell it, while others keep it as personal memories.

There's no denying that I have stories to tell. I have more than most, maybe, but certainly not as many as others. Those boys and girls have brilliant books to write. Everyone has been asking me when I'm writing again. There's always someone asking, 'When's the next book out?' which is great, as they gave me the confidence to open my heart again. This is what happened next, and hopefully a glimpse of what the future holds. I did have a small focus group who I approached and asked them what they wanted to hear. With a loud voice it was more of the stories of the greatest trips, so that's what you're getting, and lots of other stuff thrown in for free.

In 2009, I was lucky enough to meet Paul Rogers at LFC TV (he ultimately went on to do amazing things at Roma) and he was looking to produce a show called the *Liverpool Library* where they'd interview authors about their books. Surprisingly enough, it was set in a library, the Central Library, an amazing building in William Brown Street, facing St George's Hall in Liverpool city centre. I got half an hour to tell my story to a lovely fella called Matt Critchley, who's now at ESPN. You used to see Matt sitting behind the bench on matchday looking at his notes, one of those guys who everyone wonders who he is and why he gets to sit close to Jürgen.

Before the interview, Matt walked me through the type of questions he was going to ask, putting me at ease and settling my nerves. The interview was going great, right until the end when Matt hit me with the sucker-punch question: 'What gives you the right to write about following Liverpool?' Quick as a flash, I answered that I had no more right than anyone else; anyone can write about it, I just did it. Everyone has stories like mine, mates like mine. I chose to write it down and get a book out there. There was nobody more amazed than me that I did that, by the way. But people loved it, except one fella who gave it two stars on Amazon; he totally missed the point of the book. The point is that it's not about the football, it's about the people, the camaraderie and the journey we go on together. If you're ready to come on the road with me again, please do. It was my pleasure last time and, thanks to my readers' compliments, companionship and interest, here I go again.

What I found after the first book was that people could relate to my story and it would remind them of their own adventures, so let's see if I've still got the touch. I've been blessed to have the stories to tell and pass down to my kids and bore the arse off anyone who'll listen. I've seen things that many people have never seen, done things many have never done and will never do, and I'm thankful to all the beautiful people I've met on the way. Football is about camaraderie, following the Reds doesn't start and stop at the ref's whistle, so don't let anyone tell you it does.

When you're still trying to get back from the middle of Europe two or three days after the final whistle, people don't see that.

I'm a big Liverpool fan. I don't profess to be the biggest or the best, a long way from it, but the passion runs deep and strong. The baton has now passed on to my son Charlie, who's driving me mad, exactly like I drove my dad mad some 50 years ago. I don't get to as many games as I used to, as it's much harder, living at a distance, with kids and a life to fund. Also, years of following the Reds has finally caught up with the cash reserves. This book should be called 'Following the Reds on the Never, Never', as, thankfully, Jürgen has cost me a fortune lately.

The first book, the writing part of it, ended with one child in our lives, Charlie, but by the time I was a published author I had a second child, a girl, Izzy (Isobel officially but she prefers Izzy). Having two children has certainly impacted upon the ability to write, adding a puppy (a lively jet-black Cockapoo) into the mix at the end of 2019. Add in bouts of redundancy and being self-employed and it has all delayed the book further, but changed it immeasurably, with many more stories to tell.

My first book was written in the long hours of travelling to and from work, when to and from work meant exotic locations such as Dubai, Johannesburg, Cape Town and Gibraltar. Travelling meant you either hit the bar or you wrote, so I chose to write. Now life is much more mundane, no business-class flights, no 4- and 5-star hotels. Writing at home was often difficult due to the children's demands for me to be interested in the things they do, then add in watching out to see if a puppy is crapping or pissing on the carpet under the table. It got that bad that I even said to Nikki, 'It's got to the stage, love, where it's either me or the dog,' to which her response was, 'Where do you want me to forward your post to.' Whoever said that a dog's not just for Christmas never met our Ringo; he was lucky to make his first Christmas!

The first book brought me all sorts of opportunities and I've met loads of brilliant Reds, from gracing the airwaves with radio appearances to podcasts and, as you've already heard, having the show on LFC TV. I found out that if you don't ask, you don't get, and if you do ask, you get to do some cool things. Living in the Isle of Man limits a lot of those things. From a literary landscape there were hardly any football fan books, other than hooliganism, to today where football writing is a career for many, but it's all bypassed me. Besides a couple of appearances on *The Anfield Wrap*, where my brother totally eclipsed me, I don't have a part in the modern fan media.

When my book was published, I was the new breed of writer. There was no fighting in my story, only lads enjoying the match, and the readers loved it. More people seemingly had my experience of going the match (we shorten everything in Liverpool, it's never going to the match) as opposed to the tales of fighting your way from a train station to a stadium on a Saturday afternoon. In fact, Saturday afternoon hardly exists anymore, as it can be anything from a Friday night to a Monday evening these days. Modern football demands that a game can be seen pretty much every day of the week, and while older fans like me miss the three o'clock kick-offs, we have an ever-diminishing voice and influence.

I have a presence on Twitter, and many of my followers are like me, more likely to be lads I shared a terrace with 30 years ago than the 'Liverpool Family'. A grand total of 2,300 followers now, and that will do me, as I don't want to be an account with tens of thousands of followers, as they won't like what I've got to say in 200-plus characters. There's not many likes for a tweet about the injustice of Hillsborough compared to someone anonymous behind a keyboard crying about Fenway Sports Group (FSG) and transfers. I love bits of Twitter but generally it's a cesspit of people hiding behind made-up names, trolls with a handful of followers winding up the Reds, and people biting. The world that harbours the hate of the likes of Katie Hopkins, Nigel Farage and Tommy Robinson only survives in this modern world where the likes and retweets and abuse thrown back gives them the oxygen to breathe and grow. Everything is true on Twitter, everyone has a fabulous life on Facebook, and everyone is gorgeous on Tinder (or so I'm told).

None of it's real, though. You never know who's real and who's not on Twitter, and those who aren't real can still influence all our lives because they can hide behind the anonymity. The hatred seen on Twitter doesn't always exist in real life, though, when it comes to football, but everybody takes it as gospel and this causes feuds with followers of City, Everton and Spurs. Living away from Liverpool, as I do, I breathe the same air as fans of clubs such as United, City, Everton and West Brom (loads of

Baggies here for some reason) and, do you know what? They're all sound, every one of them, they have a parochial view, of course, but when it comes down to it, we all love our teams and can have a good laugh at each other.

I said it's hard to know who's real on Twitter, but one way to tell is to meet them, and that's exactly what I've done, and every one of them has been boss. How do I know who to meet? I watch what they tweet. You can tell who's funny and who's decent by the tweets they send, and if they've bought the book, even better, that's a big tick in my book.

There are the boss boys from Barrow, and one of the funniest fellas on Twitter in Paul 'Bono' Hewson (no I'm not making it up). When I met him, he brought with him the White John Barnes, his old fella, and Sempy 'the sleeping man', who can sleep on a clothesline. You've all got mates like them. Paul had seen me on Twitter, and he'd liked the tweets and interaction, so we arranged a meeting in Manchester Airport on the way to Munich, via Stuttgart, for the Audi Cup. The rest is history. It feels like you've known them forever, but in reality it's five minutes snatched here, sometimes the odd pint, but these fellas are always pleased to see you. I like that.

There's Tigger, with the banner, a shared love of the same music. He follows Our Kid's plays. We met for the first time watching a Scouse play (written by Our Ian), but 30 years earlier in the 80s we'd have been sharing the terraces of England together. Tigger's a top man. What's his real name? Who cares! There's the Loves, Daz and Fiona. I love the Loves, what lovely people they are. Daz likes all my tweets, loves the book as it reminds him of the times I talk about. They were our times. We certainly stood next to each other in the 1980s on the terraces of Highbury, White Hart Lane and on the Kippax at City, but none of the youngsters can say this anymore.

There's the Big Red Fella, Carl's his name. I've seen him all over Europe the last few years. You can't help but see him, he's huge, about 6ft 8in. I first saw him on the way to Augsburg years ago, a friendly face in a departure lounge at Gatwick. Just five minutes here and there and an odd pint. There's Huw Jones OBE, none the less, a top man who I only met for five minutes on a never-to-be forgotten afternoon in Liverpool before we beat Dortmund, but it felt like I'd known him forever.

Then there's the younger crowd who I'm reliving my youth through while they're gallivanting through Europe living their best lives: Keifer, Jordi and all their mates. I stood next to Jordi in Madrid and became good mates with Keifer. When I first met him, I was just the old fella who liked all his tweets from my desk at work while they were sipping Peroni, Estrella and Mahou in the European sunshine.

And Vinny Banks. I can't forget Vinny. He follows Wolves, not like the Brexit Wolves, he's a top man. He took me for a pint in Birmingham before we played Wolves in the FA Cup and he paid the train fare (it was only a quid, but he didn't have to). I returned the favour in Frosts on County Road (classy, eh) for him and his mates. He has now chased Wolves around Europe, exactly like he dreamed of when we met. Friendships all formed over Twitter.

These are only some of the people I've met along the way, and there are many more. To anyone who bought the book, those who stopped to say hello, those who took time out to drop me a message saying they liked what I wrote, from the bottom of my heart, thank you so much. You'll never know how good it feels to hear from you. And to all the people who appear in this book who were happy to be named, the second part of the journey has been wonderful; it wouldn't have been the same without you. The journeys we shared and the bars we frequented were much better with you in them. Sit back and look at what came next. I've captured the experiences as I've seen them, and as a man in his mid-50s you see things differently now, maybe. If you've got a different version of events, keep it to yourselves, eh.

Come on the road with me and see where we went next, enjoy the ups and downs of following the Mighty Reds and see what it means to me now.

'We'll be as we are when all the doubters fade away.' Well, I'm still here and still the same, and the doubters who never thought I'd amount to much, well they went missing years ago. I'm happy being me, and I've been luckier than most.

Up the Reds!

Faith of our Fathers

AT TWO minutes past two on a beautiful sunny November afternoon, from a bed by the window in Fazakerley hospital in the north of Liverpool, in sight of his beloved Anfield, my dad had to give up his struggle to stay with us. He was never going to win his fight against the cancer that spread from his lungs into his bones, but my god did he battle; more than he ever said he would. When push came to shove, he really wanted to stay around.

Death doesn't define you, life does, and my dad had a great life. He never wanted for much, but he got more than he could have ever imagined as a kid growing up on the bombsites of Everton during and after the Second World War. The doctors reckoned playing on those bombsites may have accounted for the lung cancer – not to mention the cigarettes he smoked from the age of 21 until his early 60s. His generation generally started smoking very young, Dad was a late starter, his habit stopping on waking from a heart attack to be asked, 'Do you smoke, Mr Salmon?' and being told, 'Well, you don't now.'

The Blitz and its remnants, with god knows what substances blown into the air as the bombs fell on the city might account for the high rates of lung cancer in north Liverpool, with many people having moved from the devastated city centre to the northern suburbs. Outside of the Anglican Cathedral and the historic waterfront's 'Three Graces', which the Luftwaffe used as markers, much of Liverpool was razed to the ground in the German bombing campaigns which targeted the docks and surrounding areas.

Bob Salmon was his name, Bob, Bobby, or Robert (his Sunday name). Three of us are proud to be Bob Salmon's boys, it's a badge of honour, sons of a decent, kind and honest, gentle man is a great thing to be.

It was a tough world growing up after the war. His mum died in the early 1940s, of what we've never been sure. He was three or four when he lost her, didn't remember what she looked like, he certainly didn't know why she passed away, although he knew it wasn't related to the Blitz. His older sister, Winnie, died soon after 'from a broken heart'. He was far too young to understand. After he died, we found a photo in an old wallet of somebody who might have been my dad's mum, but we'll never know if it was now.

Dad spent the war being passed from pillar to post, being cared for by a succession of 'aunties', most of whom were simply family friends. Our grandad returned from war years spent in Burma to remarry, and Dad was the oldest of eight children with a lot of responsibility for the care of his siblings falling to him; if the younger kids needed anything, it was Bobby who got it sorted. It was only after losing my dad that we realised how fractured his relationship with his own dad had been. He'd never had the love we had.

That's why he hated talking about his childhood, why he made sure ours was happier than his had been. We were everything to him and he adored my mum. He always said that his life began when he met Mum; if it wasn't for her, he could have turned out bad. That's not true, he was always destined to be one of life's good guys.

He was one of those Scouse fellas who worked hard, got his pay packet on a Thursday, gave his wife a set amount for housekeeping and let her get on with managing life financially; never easy with three young mouths to feed on one poor wage. All he needed for himself was enough money to take my mum out on a Saturday night and enough to watch Liverpool play and have a few pints afterwards. Back when football was a working-man's sport, this was the thing that got the lads in the factory through the monotonous week, the thought of seeing the Reds in the afternoon, a few drinks before, a night out after. It was totally unrecognisable to the game of today.

He started going the match early, initially getting in for free at three-quarters time, then graduating to the feral environment of the Boys Pen, where only the strong and brave survived. He did all this alone; it wasn't something shared with his own dad. He graduated to the Kop as the 1950s arrived and was travelling the length of England by his early 20s. He was there in 1959, the day Liverpool were beaten by Worcester City in one of *the* great cup shocks, an embarrassing defeat that would ultimately mean the end of the manager, Phil Taylor, and the arrival of the greatest man to ever grace the football club, Bill Shankly.

My dad adored Shanks. He was the man who took the Reds from the old Second Division (now the Championship) to the First Division (now the Premier League), won the FA Cup for the first time in our history and brought us our first European trophy. Shanks provided the bedrock for many of us to travel across Europe and see places you could only dream of. My stories as a kid came from the Shanks era, and while my dad wasn't religious, he believed in one god; that god was Shanks.

When my dad met my mum, arriving in his life not long before Shanks did, he was travelling the roads of England watching the men in red. There were no motorways then, these were the hard yards those boys put in. It was the days of drinking in away supporters' clubs and leaving for home after last orders on the 'chara' (charabanc, Google it, it's more than an old word for a coach, it's an entire day out).

I came along in 1965. And what a year to be born, the year Liverpool first won the FA Cup. It was one of the happiest days of my dad's life ... not me being born, Liverpool winning the cup. This was the Holy Grail; the club had won leagues but never the FA Cup.

You can tell how much the cup meant to my dad; there's a great picture of him on the pitch at Villa Park after the 2-0 semi-final victory over Chelsea. It ran in the *Echo* at the time and popped up a few years ago on Twitter. Ian St John is being escorted off the pitch by a policeman and there in the background is my dad with his suit and tie on. Going the match in your suit? It was the 60s and the Scousers were taking over the world with their sartorial elegance. At the time of the photo he'd be 30 – 'grow up will you, Dad'. Nah never, he was already a dad of one and with another on the way, and there he was legging it on the pitch at full time. Winning the cup was huge and Dad was there to see it at Wembley in May.

There's another photo, taken the morning of the '65 Cup Final; Dad's in Trafalgar Square with my Uncle Jimmy (his brother, two years younger than him) and my Uncle Lenny (his brother-in-law). They're in front of the lions, surrounded by pigeons, wearing overcoats on a May morning, excited for what the day would bring, three young fellas living their best lives. And that's where we get it from. I hung on every word of these adventures as a kid. I wanted to be just like him. I've been lucky to do all he did and much more, but without the passion he passed down I'd have had none of it. I thank god he was a Red, and that I was. What a ride we've had.

He was probably still drunk from the final by the time I popped my big fat head out at the end of July. I was a big baby, and the home birth in Bootle, down by the docks, was no easy task for my slightly built mum.

When I look back, I think I was the luckier of the three brothers; I was the one who went the match with my dad the most. Money must have got a lot tighter when Our Kev was born, and my dad stopped going to away matches as much. Without those away games he still needed his footy fix, and we'd go to see the reserve team play most if not all their home games. The home games were played at Anfield on the same pitch as the first team; you sat in the same stands that the big boys did every other weekend and I loved it. I always remember getting the bus with my dad up to Everton Valley and walking from there, my dad having to listen to my banal conversation about who was playing and what the score would be. You could say I was a talkative child, but it wouldn't do justice to what dad's ears had to put up with.

We would sit in the Main Stand, towards the centre, behind the directors' box. You didn't want to sit on the sides as the wind would whip through the stand, and with only a couple of thousand people watching you would catch your death of cold. We'd enter through the turnstiles below the main stand in a dark passageway and climb the steps up to the concourse where the tea bar was. On the way we'd pick up a team sheet, or as I called it, the programme.

It was rare to see the big names play. If they were fit after injury, they often dropped straight back into the first team, it wasn't often that they'd play for the reserves. My heroes were people like Hughie Macauley, Derek Brownbill, Trevor Storton, Alan Waddle and Frankie Lane (the goalie not the singer). If you remember any of those boys, then you're as old as I am. They managed very few first-team appearances between them, but they were part of the Shankly rebuilding programme in the early 70s. He cast his net wide, not everyone turned into a first-teamer. I loved these lads though; they wore Red, and they were the closest things to my heroes.

I had my first taste of freedom at Anfield as a seven-year-old, as I could go the tea bar just before half-time. Obviously I was driving my dad mad with my incessant talking. He'd send me with a few pence to get a carton of orange squash and an Eccles cake or a packet of ready-salted crisps (the only choice), then he'd come and join me as half-time approached. I'd stand there and listen as my dad held court with all the old fellas debating the merits of the lads on the pitch, which wasn't always favourable. My ears were covered on more than one occasion. With football during Covid taking place in empty stadiums, you could hear every word the players yelled; it took me back to my earliest games in that half-empty ground.

Apart from the odd first-team game, I had to make do with being a reserve-team regular until the 1977/78 season when I got my first season ticket. My dad's match-going days were changed forever. As a father I now know how that feels; the match is no longer about you and what you want to do. You're secondary in the day's events; it's all about that noisy little beggar next to you.

My season ticket was in the paddock. I used to go in with a stool that one of the joiners in my dad's work had made for him (my mum still has it to this day, built to last). Kids either had a beer crate or a stool to stand on so they could see the game. I was always positioned in front of the bar (crush barrier but always known as the bar). If you fell off your stool for a goal, you weren't doing it right, as you had to hook your arm around the bar and keep your balance. If you lost your balance, the fella next to you was getting battered shins from your stool, and that wouldn't go down well.

Until I was 12, I got away with sitting on the barriers, but as a big 12-year-old that was no longer an option, especially as I couldn't hoist my fat arse up on to them anymore. My dad was in the Main Stand directly behind me, keeping an eye out. It felt a big thing, allowing me to go in on my own back then, although the paddock was safer than the Kop. These days it would be a much bigger deal. We're more protective of our kids now. I stayed in the paddock until I was 16 and then went on to the Kop.

I can see it now with how Charlie is growing up; the move away from your parents to a level of independence you need as you grow, and I had it. In football supporter terms, I was just growing up. As soon as the match was over, I was back with Dad, though. We'd meet by the wall at the end of the car park behind the Main Stand. That was the last thing he'd say to me before we split: 'I'll meet you by the wall.' And we said that for going on the next 40 years. Even if I was going my own way to town with my mates for the night, I'd always meet my dad by the wall after the match, even if only to say, 'See you later, Dad.'

In the later years he didn't go the pub after the game, he'd get a lift home, but I'd walk towards the car with him and Our Kev, his matchday chauffeur. It would be rare that I wouldn't meet him. The walk together might have only been ten yards, or it might have been all the way across the park to the streets around Goodison where a decent parking space could be found, but it was part of going the match.

God, I miss those walks.

In my match-going days with my dad, I always got the full experience. The 'going to the pub with the lads' experience was where I got a critical part of my education. Being around the grown-ups, listening and seeing what they did and how they acted was a wonderful part of my upbringing – you don't need to wrap kids up in cotton wool, let them see life. I saw life in the pubs around Anfield and what a life it was, one I wanted for myself. I remember sitting in pubs after the match with a bottle of coke, a packet of crisps and a matchday programme, what more could I need? Me and Our Tony – my cousin (Lenny's son) – would sit there and chew the fat just like our old fellas. We must have been funny to watch; we'd sit there drinking our cokes and, if the lads went the bar, we'd drink the dregs of their pints.

The taste of a Brown Bitter when you were 11 or 12 wasn't a thing you'd want to replicate at any point in later life. But I did when I started going to the pub at 16, hiding in the corner near a door in case the police came in. You drank what your dad drank, and mine drank Brown Bitter. For those who don't know, that's half a pint of bitter in a pint glass with a bottle of Manns Brown Ale (hard to get that now) poured on top. I can't remember the last time I saw anyone have one. My dalliance with Dad's drink didn't last long, for a few reasons. It would take you an age to drink it due to its awful taste; it was an old man's drink and people would look at you weirdly when you ordered; and lastly, the squits it gave you the following morning, carnage in the toilet. I gravitated to lager, nothing fancy, and by the time I was 18 I'd binned the ale off altogether (and for the next five years). My young man's body, now a slight frame, reduced dramatically from the chubby kid I was, didn't work well with alcohol.

Not drinking affected our going the match rituals, though, along with me saving every penny to go to away matches from the time I was 16. A paltry Youth Training Scheme wage of £25 a week at first, then a proper job working for the local council, meant every penny I earned was used to go the match, the rest to save up for driving lessons and my first car. Why did I need a car? Yes, you guessed it, to go the match.

Not drinking and being able to drive meant I became my dad's chauffeur. I'd be on call on a Saturday evening waiting for the 'can you come and pick us up, mate' call, usually around 8pm and usually with an inebriated Scouse slur. In his later years going the match, my dad and my uncles used to end up in the Park Hotel in Netherton in the north of Liverpool, not far from Aintree Racecourse. They went there as Our Dave used to know the fella who ran it, and it had the added benefit that Roy Evans used to pop in for a drink on his way home, and he'd enjoy their company with his mates. Mates like Ronnie Whelan and Sammy Lee, apparently. Drinking with the team after the match? Does it get any better?

My dad was generally supposed to be home early(ish) so he could take my mum out for the ritual Saturday night at the local social clubs. The Blessed Sac (the Blessed Sacrament Church club) in Walton Vale was their favourite, with a boss turn (entertainer, band, singer, take your pick) on a Saturday night. The sort of club where a band would play two music spots dissected by a game of bingo; the first spot would be their own stuff or some obscure favourites of theirs that no one listened to, the second spot was for dancing. The band would get everyone up with the big dance floor fillers from 20 years earlier (think now The Killers with 'Mr Brightside', these would use The Beatles and Gerry and The Pacemakers). It was a great night out at the Blessed Sac and sometimes I'd go along for the last hour and take them home again, to save them walking the mean streets of Walton.

Some nights my dad wouldn't make it to The Sac. He'd stumble in, mumble through his warmed-up tea (dinner if you're posh), talk nonsense and have 'a ten-minute snooze' before going out. A ten-minute snooze meant one thing; they were definitely not going out. My mum would put her jewellery back in its box and get a book out; it was a hazard after every home match. Funny, the first game back after Covid (Burnley at home) I turned into him. I went to the pub all afternoon, stumbled in, mumbled through my tea at Mum's then slumped on the couch and fell asleep like a baby. Dad always had the best of intentions, but 'one more pint' used to finish him off. That was all my dad did for himself, though, everything else was for my mum and for us. Mum never begrudged him the footy. If you find a girl who never begrudges you the footy and actively encourages you to go, hold on to her, she's a keeper.

As you get older and get on with your own life, your parents unfortunately fade into the background as you become all consumed with what you're doing. If you're lucky enough to keep your parents with you for a long time, you become friends, the relationship changes. You begin to recognise the pride your mum and dad have in your achievements, and they were always proud of me and my brothers; proud of how we turned out as men, as fathers and husbands. For me that's the real value of a life well lived. My dad was a great role model on that score; look after your family, love your wife, and give your kids the chances you never had. If I've followed that, which I believe I have to my best ability, I've done alright.

Trying to give something back to my mum and dad as a way of thanks was hard, as they didn't want anything. When I went to Peterborough United to work (you need to read the first book for that), they were proud of me going but disappointed to see their 'favourite' son leave home. I can hear my mum saying now, 'There were no favourites in our house.'

Peterborough gave me a chance to give my dad something back as a football fan; thanks to some decent connections I was able to wangle two tickets in the directors' box when Liverpool visited Blackburn Rovers. All I had to do was be a scout for the afternoon. Someone from a lower-tier club scouting a Premier League club, how did that work? Who cared? It was not all the thrills of a swanky box but there was a free cup of tea, a free programme and a warm welcome at the directors' entrance, not somewhere Dad had ever entered before.

It was an alien world to Dad, and to me too; we were only ten seats away from David Moores (LFC chairman at the time). If truth be told, we both still wanted to be behind the goal with the travelling Kop. There was always a great turnout at Blackburn, as it was within an hour's drive, and you were always back in time for your tea. The game stands out for one amazing moment that used to pop up on football 'blooper' compilations and is now easier to find on YouTube: ten minutes in and Stan Collymore, probably in his best form in a red kit, hit a shot from 25 yards in a central position. Now Stan could hit a ball, with pace and power, lots of his goals were screamers; this one, though, was a mishit shot, it lacked any power. Stan even turned away in disgust with himself, not seeing the ball heading towards Tim Flowers, a top-class goalkeeper, who casually dropped to one knee to collect it. As his knee hit the ground, the ball hit a divot, popped up over his right shoulder and into the back of the net, much to the delight of the travelling hordes in red.

Stan looked bemused, even embarrassed, as he started to celebrate and immediately stopped, looking almost apologetically towards Flowers. From our angle you couldn't see what had happened but that night on *Match of the Day* it was all too clear, destined for football comedy forever and a day.

Me and my dad sat there and laughed as the Reds went 2-0 up, while everyone else around us in the Blackburn directors' box fumed. Liverpool ultimately won 3-2 against a team that contained Alan Shearer, Tim Sherwood and Colin Hendry, a team that had won the Premier League the previous season. We slipped away as the whistle went, with smiles on our faces, the Blackburn contingent fuming about a penalty that was nailed on but not given. But a 3-2 win away from home when you hadn't even paid for your ticket was an absolute treat.

* * *

The only other experience I was able to give Dad of sitting in the posh seats was by a stroke of luck. I haven't won many competitions, but if you're going to win one, why not win two tickets in an executive box to watch Liverpool play Man City at Eastlands (before they started calling it the Etihad in 2011). What a prize!

There's a lovely Spanish fella who lives on the Isle of Man called Manolo, and he's never forgotten me giving him my season ticket for a derby match for his 50th birthday. He was always good to me and Nikki. Him buying my first book was just the start; he'd have it on the counter and push it to everybody who walked through the door. While his hometown team was Malaga, he'd left there so long ago that Liverpool was his big passion now. Manolo and his wife Gill provided authentic tapas, eaten as you would in Spain, little plates of food delivered to your table at regular intervals with wine, beer and sangria freely flowing; you never left the restaurant either hungry or sober.

My dad had met Manolo before, but not eaten his food. He wasn't that adventurous, he still hadn't tried pizza well into his 70s; foreign food didn't float his boat. Manolo had a customer who ran a betting firm in the Isle of Man, and they provided City's betting facilities back in 2010, only two years after the club was bought by the

Abu Dhabi group. Everyone who ate in the restaurant and supported either Liverpool or City went into the hat to win the tickets. Amazingly, my name came out of the hat. Who do I take? Well, there was only one person to take: my dad. He hadn't been to an away match probably since Blackburn; those days had well and truly gone.

The prize included two seats in an executive box, free drinks before and after the game and a six-course meal pre-match to set you up for the afternoon, or send you off to sleep. My dad was made up to be asked but how was he going to get there? Not the fact that he was getting a great opportunity to go to the match, but how was he going to get there?

Now, as I write this, I realise that he'd probably lost his confidence at travelling to new places. He was used to going to a small number of places now, namely Liverpool city centre, Anfield and the local social clubs. Anywhere else he'd be chauffeured by one of the lads. He needed certainty these days, so I sorted out train tickets from Lime Street to Manchester Piccadilly on the Sunday morning and I'd meet him at the station ticket office. I'd be flying in on the morning of the match from the Isle of Man. Easy enough, you'd think, but the winter weather decided to complicate things.

I also didn't realise that he'd lost confidence in meeting new people in strange surroundings. While he was confident in a local pub with a few pints in front of him, going into an executive box was way out of his league. He was anxious as to how to behave, who was going and, most of all, a six-course meal. He was a plain eater, and this was not his cup of tea. I wondered whether I'd done the right thing asking him. Had I read it wrong? Was it wrong to do? By the time the Saturday evening came, though, he was calm enough. He had his train tickets and I said we'd be there by noon, if the plane was on time, and we'd head to the ground from there. I went to bed confident things would be fine.

Sunday morning came and I woke to a thick layer of snow and the island had ground to a near-enough stop, all roads to the airport either closed or barely passable. The airport was still open, though, as it had only a dusting of snow. Planes were flying so I only needed to get there. We rarely get thick snow here, so when we do it naturally causes chaos. By the time I left home, two out of the three routes (the easiest two, of course) were already closed due to accidents and the advice was to undertake essential travel only. This was essential!

I rang home (that's still what I call Mum and Dad's house), told them the situation and that I'd update them once I got to the airport. Getting to the airport was bad enough, but knowing my dad was at the other end stressing about going in case I didn't make it only made it worse. After a drive that took three times as long as usual, with several precarious manoeuvres en route, I made the airport, only to find out the plane was delayed 30 minutes, but we'd definitely be flying to Manchester. I rang home to say it was all on and I may be a little late at Piccadilly, 12.30 as opposed to 12 noon.

That 30-minute delay became two hours, and by the time we took off my dad was already at Piccadilly waiting, with no mobile phone (as he hated them). I was relaying messages to my mum at home, who he was regularly ringing for travel updates. Manolo's friend had rung the hospitality team at City, so they knew we were coming and to keep our lunch warm. We needed something to mop up the pre-flight drinks. I was half-cut already after two hours' free ale in the lounge. As we landed at Manchester Airport, we were well behind schedule and as always, when you need to be quick, they parked the plane away from the terminal and there was no one to meet the aircraft, and then the shuttle buses went all around the world to get to the terminal.

Manolo and I jumped in a taxi to Piccadilly while everyone else headed to the stadium. As Manolo kept the taxi running, I ran into the station to find my dad, and there he was sitting reading his *Daily Mirror* outside the ticket office as arranged. How he made reading the *Daily Mirror* last so long was always a skill I could never master. A look of relief shot across his face, more the fact that I was alright and we'd get to see the match. The six-course meal being missed didn't matter as he wasn't that hungry, as he proudly announced, 'I've had a Gregg's sausage roll.' A simple man with simple tastes, that was my dad. His fear of six courses of fancy food was smashed away with a Gregg's sausage roll. Manolo greeted my dad like a long-lost friend. Manolo loved his simplicity and decency; he (my dad) was just like me, he said.

A quick ride to the stadium and we were at the entrance to hospitality, the one the City players now use when they arrive at the ground with that cringey team welcome off the coach. By the time we got into the executive box, the teams were coming out and we went straight out to watch the match. While everyone else was eating their six courses, I kept going in and out and grazing, so I didn't miss anything, food or football-wise. Not that there was anything to miss from the football as it was the most miserable 0-0 draw I'd ever seen. My dad didn't miss a second. That sausage roll did him no favours at all as he endured every second of the turgid 90 minutes. We'd been told that as away fans there should be no celebrating if Liverpool scored, but there was never a chance of us celebrating anything. Besides a quick cup of tea at half-time, my dad hadn't moved, and the sane members of our party hadn't even ventured out from behind the window. It was a typically miserable grey and cold Manchester afternoon.

At full time we headed inside. We had the use of the box until 6.30pm, so time to make the most of the hospitality. My dad was under the impression that everyone in the box (besides us) was mega-rich. Hand in hand with that impression was an assumption that they wouldn't talk to the likes of him. Wherever he got that from is beyond me. A mistrust of people with money is inherent in working-class culture, and the fact they were self-made men was irrelevant. Everyone was wonderful with him though; they were all interested in what he had to say and the stories he started telling when he loosened up. They were men, some with a lot of money, but only men interested in football. They weren't used to the football life that we led and the things we'd seen. They hung on every word of his trips to Rome and Paris. To cap it all off, one of them even called him Bob! Well, why wouldn't they? At 71 years of age, he learned a valuable lesson in life, that he can stand in a room with people of any stature and hold his own, and probably be the most interesting person in the room. No one was a better man than him, and all the fellas in that room to this day remember the day they met Bob Salmon.

He told me the bit about being called Bob when we were on the bus back into town to catch the train back to Liverpool. He was back in his comfort zone of the 'normal' match-going fan. Me too, it's where I feel more at home. The lounges or boxes are not for me, just give me a ticket in the ground to watch the Reds. I don't need anything fancy; free food and beer is nice but it's not really for me. I guess I'm my father's son.

* * *

My dad was still going the match until he was 79, only weeks before he passed away. He was still watching his boys in red. He'd been struggling to walk across Stanley Park for a while and the lads were dropping him off and picking him up as close to the ground as possible now, but it was becoming more and more difficult. Our Ian even tried to get him to see Liverpool play Real Madrid just a couple of weeks before he was hospitalised. It would have meant a wheelchair at the front of the Kop, but it was too wet and cold, and it didn't happen. I'm glad; imagine Liverpool getting battered 3-0 by that lot being your last game. He got to see some of his best football in years in

2014 with Suárez and Gerrard at the top of their games. That's a way to go, not getting beat by Real Madrid.

After every game I'd get the match report, whether I'd watched or not. In 2014, believe it or not, you still didn't get to see every game on TV. If I wasn't home, I'd get a message: 'It's only me, nothing to worry about, just to talk about the match, speak to you later.' He always started his calls with 'it's nothing to worry about'. I still miss those calls, I always will. It was our thing, me and Dad, talking about the match.

I remember when we found out he was extremely ill, and after years of him thinking he had something wrong with him, usually 'galloping kyanka' he'd call it, he was finally diagnosed with lung cancer. He reminded me of Spike Milligan, who has on his gravestone 'I told you I was ill' (written in Irish). Our Ian had done a sterling job, going to all the hospital appointments with my mum and dad and taking notes, so everyone was clear what was wrong. What was initially thought to be a pulled muscle at the top of his thigh, which caused him to collapse in the street one day, proved to be secondary cancer in his bones, with the primary cancer in his lungs. The words 'sorry we can only provide palliative care now' were met with resignation and disbelief. The big strong fella, our dad, our provider, was fading away, and this disease is cruel, it's cruel and quick, but not quick enough to feel no pain.

Nikki and I took the kids over a few times. We knew they were to be last special memories, but the kids didn't, they thought doctors were still going to make him better, they believed doctors could do anything. We knew it was only a matter of time, though, and before long he could no longer eat anything other than shakes, and thanks to the lack of funding for cancer patients in north Liverpool, he couldn't always get them. You had to fight for everything. Standing there at the back of the line waiting for what you should get doesn't get you anywhere. One day when I was in the chemist and I was fobbed off, and this was after my mum had been fobbed off for three days on the trot, I'd had enough. I told them in no uncertain terms that he was dying and that the shakes were not a 'nice to have', it was a necessity. They soon found a supply and, to be fair to them, he wasn't without again. They didn't know he was dying. You need to shout as loud as you can to get anything.

The end was both quick and painfully slow. There was no time for a hospice, nothing Macmillan nurses could do at home, and ultimately no chance to go and die at home. I'm glad, as those final painful hours are consigned to a hospital ward as opposed to our family home, where my mum continues to live. There was no Hollywood ending where he just passed away, every bit of it was painful for him and for us as a family, and while he always said he'd not hang around, he did, he fought with every last ounce of strength to stay as long as possible with his loving family. There were 16 of us around his bed in those final days. My boss at work had been brilliant with me, and for the last week allowed me to work out of a branch of the bank in central Liverpool. My days were behind a laptop and on the end of a phone, and my nights started with an hour at the side of his bed in Fazakerley hospital. The rest of the time I'd spend at my mum and dad's house keeping my mum company and on the phone to home lying to the kids about the doctors trying to make him better (I like to think of it as protecting them).

The call came at 2pm on a Friday afternoon, it was Our Ian: 'The doctors think you should come now.' Seven words that shatter your world and those around you. From Liverpool Central it was only 12 minutes to Fazakerley hospital, and from the bank to the hospital bed I was there next to him in 45 minutes. It was the right decision to be there, and I got some quality time with him. He was struggling to breathe now and was on constant oxygen but was still with us and able to talk. He was still talking about the Reds. Liverpool were playing Chelsea the following lunchtime, and he had it in mind to watch the match, not sure the gravity of the situation was clear to him. I hadn't even thought about the match, but surely if he went tonight, we'd go the match and give them a shout for him. There was no way we were going if he was still with us, and that goes back to my dad's experience. He did that with his dad, who was in hospital and supposedly not too bad, and he told my dad to go the match and he'd see him tomorrow. Tomorrow never came, he passed away while my dad watched Liverpool play. That wasn't happening to us, there are certainly things more important than football, and family is at the very top of the list.

I rang the kids at 7pm to wish them goodnight and Dad said he'd do his best to speak to them, and he did. He battled for his breath with every word, using up all the breath he had left. He had the most beautiful conversation with them, asking them about school and telling Charlie to look after Izzy. He knew this was his goodbye and so did I, it was heart-breaking and it still is as I write this. Charlie and Izzy didn't know at the time, they were just 'talking to grandad'. Charlie says now that he knew that was the last time he'd speak to his grandad. If he remembers that last conversation, he knows how much my dad loved him and Izzy. At eight years of age he was wise beyond his years. That was virtually my last conversation with Dad too, with one critical exception.

I'd been fighting with this for years, but I needed to tell my dad that I loved him. What do you mean, you'd never told him before? Well, no, I hadn't, it was complicated, my dad was complicated, the way he'd grown up I suppose; it was all complicated. We all knew in our house we loved each other, we're a very close family, but the words, those three words between father and son never happened. I'd watched the Channel 4 programme *24 hours in A&E* and I always remembered this fella from London, his dad was in a bad way. He was talking about trying to say the words and that he was going to say it so often, but he hadn't, and he was going to do it. But he didn't and his dad died before he said the words. It was one of the saddest things I'd seen on TV. I couldn't let it happen to me.

It was two years since the programme and I'd been saying to Nikki for ages, 'I'm going to say it,' but every time I started the conversation Dad dodged it. He was a master at avoiding the emotional conversation. But here he was, and he couldn't avoid me now, it was up to me to pluck up the courage and tell him I loved him, which I did. And his response? His response was my dad to a tee, 'Yeah, I know, I always knew, love you too.' He didn't need to hear the words, but I did, and I'm thankful I said it, as I'd have carried it as a burden forever if I never said it. I hope that fella in London realises his dad probably did too, it was just their generation, they were a different breed.

Now I think of them as the last words he said to me, which is lovely, and if there were more words, I can't remember. The Friday night was the last of the words. He asked us to look after Mum, got his priorities right like he always had. We all had one-to-one time with him and expected he wouldn't see the night through, but he did, and it was clear by the time Saturday lunchtime was upon us and Liverpool were kicking off that there were going to be three empty seats at Anfield. We'd been living through the night, minute by minute, there was no thought about football or anything outside of that ward and the bed in the corner.

He slipped into an unconscious state, and we spent the time around his bed. It was clear there wasn't long left. I sat at the side of the bed talking about Nikki and the kids and all the fabulous things me and Dad had seen together. Milk Cup finals in London, Leicester away in 1976 and the fabulous chippy in Ashby de la Zouch (Google it) after a magnificent 4-0 win, and our Friday nights across the river watching Tranmere under the lights at Prenton Park. Then his own glorious trips, of wonderful nights and days, Bruges and the UEFA Cup, Rome, Wembley and Paris and the European Cups, all his European triumphs. He could hear me, I could tell.

On the Sunday morning we sang a voice-breaking 'You'll Never Walk Alone' and told him it was alright to go now. And he did, at two minutes past two on a sunny Sunday afternoon in Liverpool he took his last walk to meet Lenny and Shanks.

My dad, Bobby Salmon, one of Liverpool's finest sons, a true ambassador for all that's good about where we come from, a fine role model and a man who never knew how good he was. A humble man, but a king among men.

* * *

His funeral was a true Scouse affair, carrying the coffin to 'You'll Never Walk Alone'; try listening to that ever again without that thought. He was carried by the lads he loved the most, family and friends, perfect. The funeral cortege stopped at Anfield to pay our respects to his longest love, not his greatest but his longest, while the real love of his life, his wife of 54 years, bravely watched on. This story may be about my dad and the football, but none of this happens without the love of a wonderful woman and that's my mum, she made all the magic happen. We took the flowers that spelled out Dad and Grandad back to place them on the Hillsborough memorial. The memorial serves as a place of remembrance for many of us, it's a beautiful reminder of life.

My dad was at Hillsborough and seated in the stand at the Sheffield Wednesday Kop end, watching intently at the lads carrying the makeshift stretchers. I know what he was looking for, he was looking for me and Our Kev, he knew we were in the Leppings Lane end. When I found him, and he knew we were safe, the look of relief on his face was undeniable. He didn't talk about Hillsborough for 20 years; he said we'd never see justice and the truth. One thing that disappoints me is that he left us before seeing the truth be told. Like many before him, they didn't live long enough to see the world find out what we all knew. He wouldn't talk about Hillsborough; he was scarred until the day he died.

The flowers were still there the following week when I took Charlie back to watch Liverpool play Stoke City. Our turnstile in the Anfield Road was the nearest to the memorial, which at that point was still on Anfield Road, and we stopped for a while on the way in and out. 'You'll Never Walk Alone' meant a lot that day.

We walk in the footsteps of our fathers, from toddlers to young men and beyond, and even now I catch myself sounding like my dad, acting like my dad, I've become my dad. No bad thing in my book.

God bless, Bob Salmon, miss you Dad, we'll meet you by the wall!

There She Goes

MY BIGGEST regret is that my dad never got to see what came next. It's special and as good as anything he'd ever seen following the Reds.

17 October 2015 was the start of a whole new magnificent journey, the Jürgen Klopp years (this is going to be fabulous). In his first press conference he described himself as 'maybe the normal one' and talked about turning the supporters from 'doubters to believers'. A 0-0 draw at Spurs started the ball rolling, but within months we were in a League Cup Final and progressing nicely in the Europa League. In a glorious, or maybe not so glorious (define glorious), four days in February we could see the Klopp revolution taking shape, giving us our hopes and dreams back.

The draw for the last 32 of the Europa League saw Liverpool play Augsburg. Who the hell are Augsburg? And, more importantly, where the hell is Augsburg? A small town near Munich; don't worry, you'll hear much more about Munich in the pages ahead, but for now a provincial town built on the foundations for Klopp's Liverpool. Its proximity to Munich meant I hit the websites and found a way to get there. Jürgen had given me something to get excited about.

For under £250, less than the cost of a normal European away-day trip, I got two days in Germany with my mates watching the Mighty Reds. A trip that tested you to the limits, weather delays, cancelled planes, lost hotel and train bookings, 4am trains and sleeping on airport floors, it had the lot. I loved it, as did the thousand hardy lucky souls who got tickets, of which I was one, as the gods (or my dad at least) sorted me out. It was the biggest night in Augsburg's history and they created some noise and thoroughly enjoyed themselves. We were all part of something fabulous and you could feel it. The game was awful, and alongside Oldham Athletic's Boundary Park in 1988, Augsburg's WKD Arena was the coldest place I'd ever watched Liverpool play. It was a relief to get out of there without frostbite. In just under 72 hours, with one false start, three countries, four plane journeys, three trains and numerous underground journeys, I got home.

Just in time to go again as the Reds headed to Wembley to play Man City in the League Cup Final. Once again I was ticketless until the last moment but my dad got me sorted again. Ticket in hand I got to watch the Reds go toe to toe with a fabulous City side. It gave us more belief than we could have dreamed of at the beginning of October; Jürgen was working his magic. The history books will show Liverpool got beat 3-1 on penalties after the game finished in a 1-1 draw after 120 minutes. We were back, four glorious days. We may not have won anything but we were on our way and Jürgen was turning us from 'doubters to believers'.

* * *

With Augsburg neatly dispatched in the return leg, all eyes were on the draw, and out popped Manchester United. We were going to have to win it the hard way. Unfortunately, both games had to be missed due to work commitments; at the end of the day it's what pays the bills, there's nothing you can do about it. The boys in red ripped United to bits at Anfield in the most one-sided 2-0 you've ever seen, and any hope they had at Old Trafford was snuffed out with an impudent goal from Coutinho just before half-time, which finished United off and sent the travelling Reds into raptures. That was the night when the pendulum swung. We could see our perch and we were climbing right back on it.

The Reds were in the draw for the last eight, and a return to Germany was on the cards with Borussia Dortmund and the great yellow wall our next destination. Jürgen's return was the game everyone wanted to go to and there was no chance of a ticket for the away leg. The second leg was a different story and, with no work clashes, all the Reds needed to do was stay in the tie in the away leg, ensuring the second leg was all to play for on 14 April.

The pilgrimage home was always planned for April 2016, as soon as I heard that the memorial on the 27th anniversary of the Hillsborough disaster was going to be the last official service, at the request of the families. Home always has a strong pull for me but no more than that week; the calling was stronger than ever. Before leaving Liverpool 16 years previously, I always attended the memorial service to show my respect and solidarity for the families of the 96. I went back to the same home I returned to 27 years earlier after the most harrowing of days following my beloved Reds. That slow painful return over the Pennines from Hillsborough took me into the arms of my family and friends and, with one notable exception, my dad, I returned again to them all.

In 30 hours I'd take a plane, a bus, seven trains, drink copious amounts of beer, topped off with a three-hour boat journey across the Irish Sea. It was probably the most exciting and emotional 30 hours I'll ever spend with LFC. From the massive highs of one of the greatest of European nights to the white doves flying high over the green turf, followed by one of the most beautiful yet rousing versions of 'You'll Never Walk Alone'.

Matchday afternoon was spent in town meeting up with those from the Liverpool-supporting outposts of Kent, Wales, the Isle of Man (more than me), Netherton and, last but not least, Maghull. At the Rubber Soul, Mathew Street, the party was in full swing and had been officially commandeered by Borussia Dortmund fans. The yellow and black mixed and swapped quite happily with the red and white. Before long nobody knew who was who and some random lad is shouting at me, 'Are you enjoying our city?'

'Yeah, sound lad, it's boss. I'm from Walton.'

I was sitting four seats away from the German fans behind the Anfield Road goal. A brilliant spec, 12 rows back and right behind the Anfield Road goal. The only problem was that all the best action was down the Kop end, but you can't have everything, can you? There's no point telling you about the match is there? There have been a million column inches applied to it so you probably know the score. Dortmund were fabulous in the first half. I had the obligatory 'if we get one, you never know' conversation at half-time. I had the obligatory 'if we get another one, you never know' conversation after we went 3-1 down.

At 3-1 down and seeing that I had the bladder of a 50-year-old, the size of a walnut, I needed the obligatory 50-year-old man's wee after losing an early second-half goal. There was a fella leaving, actually ordering a steward to let him out ... he made a huge mistake! The Germans made some noise, so much that I couldn't fully appreciate the noise of the Reds in the ground. The Germans' bullish and confident support gave way to a stunned silence as the Reds won late on. The Germans stood there bemused at what they'd witnessed.

Being low down in the Annie Road I couldn't tell exactly what happened down the Kop end and I was back in the pub by the time I fully realised Sakho and Lovren had scored. Having to watch the game again to know what happened is the sign of a great game. We'd been wrapped up in the match. We celebrated long into the night. The whole pub crowded around the flat-screen TVs, milking in every last bit of the highlights. This was one of the greatest of nights, my Saint-Étienne! I'd had great nights at Anfield: Auxerre (Google it, as it was amazing), Olympiakos, Juventus, but now I had my own Saint-Étienne. It was one of the greatest nights in our history and it felt great.

The Friday morning brought the 15th of April and for once it wasn't the most dreadful of days, the elation of the previous evening still evident. Before long, though, our thoughts turned to Anfield again. We headed up to the ground early and the crowds were different to the night before. There was a more reserved air walking back up Anfield Road in the bright afternoon sun. There was still a buzz about the night before. It seemed somewhat befitting that it would lift the day and tip a nod to the 96 and their families, football could still bring joy.

By the time we entered the ground and took the long walk up to the top tier of the Centenary Stand (now Sir Kenny Dalglish) all our thoughts were centred on those no longer with us and what the last 27 years had brought us. I was with my mum, Our Ian and Our Kev, and over 20,000 others. After a lovely service my abiding memories are threefold: the reading of the 96 names, which took over five minutes and makes you realise the size of the loss once again; secondly, 96 doves were released, the sight of which, flying above the green turf and up into the Liverpool blue sky was a thing of real beauty; finally, a beautiful version of 'You'll Never Walk Alone', sung with sadness, sung with hope, and sung with a real sense of community. It was our song, sung for our people and all those who have left us far too soon. This is my community, these are my people and I'm a real part of it.

* * *

I wasn't going to Basel for the Europa League Final. Honestly, but I couldn't keep away. Augsburg away was my cup final, two great days with my mates in Germany was enough. Who am I kidding? A cup final is a cup final. Augsburg being my cup final, and all that nonsense, had already gone in the bin as Liverpool pulled Borussia Dortmund out the hat, and Dortmund at home felt like a European away day. The afternoon saw the streets filled with Germans and Scousers and it was a wonderful combination. The evening saw a night that would stand alongside our greatest European nights as the Kop bounced with all its might and dragged the Reds over the line. The semi-final saw Villarreal of Spain pitted against the Reds. After a frustrating 1-0 defeat in Spain, the return leg called me home once again across the Irish Sea and I watched Liverpool ease their way to the final of the UEFA Cup. I'm not calling it the Europa League on purpose, it's still the UEFA Cup to me and holds a special place in our hearts. No need for the heroics shown against Dortmund as the Reds eased past the Yellow Submarine of Villarreal, a great night to be a Red, nonetheless. In the pubs around Anfield people were already making their plans.

UEFA, in their ultimate wisdom, chose a small Swiss city with the 119th-biggest stadium in Europe to host their second-biggest competition. The city only has 170,000 inhabitants, the infrastructure would creak with the expected influx of visitors, having nowhere to stay being only one of the issues. This was the competition they wanted to grow, the one they wanted to make more of, the one they want us (the fans) to love. The thing is they didn't want a big team to get to the final. Their thoughts were, Dortmund please don't get there, Liverpool, United and Spurs please don't get there, for all our sakes. We'd rather have an empty ground. They gambled on a team getting to the final who would only take 10,000 fans. Seville wouldn't even manage that, and 'the Suits' of UEFA could get there and back from their Zürich offices in the time you can say 'canapes'. Oh yeah, and they can box all their mates off with as many tickets as they want. Realistically, Liverpool could fill the ground on their own and still have thousands of fans wanting tickets. With tickets hard to come by I was resigned to watching from the couch with Charlie.

Following the magnificent victory over Villarreal, and the unadulterated joy that cascaded down from all four sides of Anfield, I'd spent the following days hoping against hope that a ticket would pop up, but once the distribution details were announced my heart sank. There was no chance!

But, say, if one was to pop up, just say one did, you needed to be prepared. I spent my lunchtimes travelling Europe from my desk, finding routes to and from Basel was all-consuming. All the cities and towns remotely close to Basel were already no-gos, flights were either non-existent or ridiculously expensive. I worked out that anywhere with a train line into Basel was an option, and it turns out that's a lot of places. Europe is so well connected that all trainlines seemingly lead to Basel, which I knew from experience gathered on my train travels around Europe some 27 years ago.

In that dark summer of 1989 following Hillsborough it took a while to see anything positive, but we started to see the light again as we (me, Our Kev and Zil) headed through Europe using the now well-known Inter Rail ticket. While usually the domain of students on gap years, we deserved a gap year of our own, and we took full advantage of the flexibility of where those steel rails could take us. We found Basel by mistake, heading up from Switzerland to Amsterdam on an overnight train from Milan in northern Italy.

A beautiful train journey via the stunning vistas of the Swiss mountains, sights to feast your eyes upon, you could be lost in life seeing such beauty. The train's last stop for the night was Basel, and at 10pm on a beautiful warm summer evening we drew into its station. Why does Basel stick in mind? Well, Zil got off and got a postcard so he could add another name to the list of places we'd visited. A postcard from every place would show off our adventures in the hottest of European summers. Basel was added to the list alongside Geneva, Milan, Rome, Paris, Monte Carlo, Cannes and Amsterdam. In truth, Basel was a cheat as we only stopped for ten minutes, and Zil nearly missed the train getting his postcard.

I love trains, it's a fabulous way to travel, freedom to get up and wander about while seeing the beauty of a landscape that you can't always appreciate from 20,000 feet. Trainline's European website showed me that for less than £50 you could go from Milan to Basel and back. A quick look at EasyJet and return flights from Gatwick to

Milan were less than £80. If, just if, a ticket was to pop up, that was my route in.

Our Ian got lucky in the ballot and it became route in. Unfortunately he was the only one. The ballot was a long-drawn-out affair and too slow for many travellers, and by the time his match ticket was secured all the trains from Milan were fully booked. He was going to have to drive on his own.

It was only a four-hour drive, like going from Liverpool to Wembley, but swap the industrial Midlands with views of the Alps … sounds much better doesn't it. Then Mongoose got a ticket, and he was looking for a way to go, so I put him in touch with Our Ian. At least they had each other for company now. I was gutted, but I was made up for them. I was, honestly, can you hear me trying to convince myself? But I was really pleased for them. Nah, you're not buying it, are you? I'd been lucky enough with Augsburg and Man City at Wembley, having fluked tickets for both matches when there seemed to be no chance. My dad had been looking after me from above and getting me boxed off; it was enough for one year. Maybe he could have a word with the big fella upstairs and get me sorted, one last favour? I wouldn't ask for anything again. Who am I kidding?

Nikki hadn't even asked me the question. The one where she asks me whether I'm going or not. She didn't know of my lunchtime European travels from my desk, but she knew, she always knows. One day she said to me, 'You know you've got a pass if you can get a ticket, don't you?' I didn't, but she knows I'll pay her back. I'm still paying for Istanbul, it's like a student loan, you never pay the bloody thing off!

Six days before the match and my phone buzzed on the desk with a simple message: 'How much will you pay for a ticket then?' I'd been looking at ticket resale sites, and I knew they were going for about £700 (including the rip-off service charge). With hands shaking I sent a message, cumbersome fingers misspelling the simplest of words: 'How much are you after?' A minute later (seemed like an hour): '£153, face value, do you want it?' One of the dearest tickets in the ground, but face value. 'What do you think? Of course I do.'

I'd been battling with the idea of paying the ticket site prices but I couldn't do that, I've never paid over the odds in my life (sorry that's a lie there was a ticket in Madrid for €180 but let's ignore that), so I wasn't starting now. I didn't have to, I was off to watch the Reds in Switzerland.

Now, how do I get there? All my preparation worked out, albeit more expensive than at the start of my travel searches, but suddenly with a few tweaks I had a travel itinerary. Flying from the Isle of Man to Birmingham, train from Birmingham to Gatwick via Euston (Gatwick gave me the cheapest flight to anywhere close to Basel), then Gatwick to Milan. Meet the others in some dosshouse hotel in Milan, jump in a car to Basel, snooze in car and return home with the cup. It sounds easy when you see it written down, doesn't it? It's much easier than doing it, that's for sure.

I could barely contain myself – 50 years of age, looking my age more than ever before on the outside, but on the inside I was 19 again, the age of my first European Cup Final at Heysel. My history with European finals was somewhat chequered. There was Heysel, covered in my first book and remembered for all the wrong reasons, followed by a trip to Dortmund that didn't happen because I was doing the right thing for an ex-partner (I thought at the time) and missing one of the greatest nights of a Liverpudlian's life. There was the glory of Istanbul, followed quickly by the chaos of Athens, which in retrospect I was lucky to miss, having a week's family holiday in Majorca, watching with my dad in a bar and with so little atmosphere that I might well have watched it on the moon. Now, though, for a glorious new chapter in Europe, Jürgen's Reds writing history, and before anyone thinks that I might be a jinx, Istanbul is on the list of European travels as are wins in the San Siro, the Bernabéu and the Camp Nou. Okay, they're not finals I know, but they are the most glorious of nights in Europe with the Reds.

Time was critical for this trip, as five days after my return we were due to be heading across to the United States for the holiday of a lifetime. Basel was an inconvenience, but what an inconvenience. Thousands of people had lost out and I was lucky to get a ticket. I knew many who hadn't, so until two days before the game I kept it under wraps, I kept a lid on my joy. I had great mates, great Reds who were ticketless. I'd do anything to get them a ticket, well almost anything obviously, as I wasn't giving them mine.

There were three of us in a car now, which cut the costs and added to the fun. Make that four! Out the blue, Mike popped up with a ticket and we were going to need a bigger car. Mike lived down south, and a ticket had popped up, and to save his friend's marriage Mike had bravely stepped in to help by taking the fella's ticket, removing the cause of strife between husband and wife. How's he going to get there? Via Milan, of course, happy days! See you in Milan, gentlemen.

And that's exactly what happened. From the Isle of Man via Birmingham and Gatwick and by the time I landed at Malpensa airport in Milan I was the last one to hit Italian soil. Our Ian had already picked up the car and found his way to the hotel that Mongoose had booked for the night. Mike had left Gatwick before me and was on the way to meet them. I was last to arrive. It was gone 9pm local time as I headed out of Milan Malpensa airport and headed for the coach to take me straight into the city centre. The driver put his foot down through the countryside north-west of Milan. It was obviously his last job of the night and he was keen to get home. We arrived at Milano Centrale (Central Station in Milan) 45 minutes later, an area I knew well from 2008 when we stayed there against Inter, and from our Inter Rail European travels in 1989. From there I jumped the metro a couple of stops to the Duomo, where I would meet the lads, who were already sampling the delights of the fancy bars in Milan.

As the coach screeched to a halt, I was first off, travelling light with only my backpack. On a warm night I headed towards the metro, exchanging Scouse welcomes with lads in Hat Scarf or a Badge T-shirts on, just like me. We stood out a mile, Scousers abroad. It's a nice feeling though, seeing people on your travels. I quickly worked out how to get a single ticket to the Duomo, it was surprisingly easy for a change. I was excited, only minutes away from meeting up with the lads in a far foreign land. It's a step up from saying, 'I'll see you in the King Harry.'

The station escalator took me up out of the bowels of Milan and slap bang in front of the Duomo, one of the finest buildings you'll ever see, absolutely beautiful. It was dark by now and, as I came out of the metro, the Duomo was lit up beautifully by bright white light against a crisp black night sky, a stunning sight. I reached for my phone to ring the lads. All I knew was that they were in a bar, and they were looking at the Duomo, but where exactly? It's a big square with lots of bars. The phone showed no signal, so I couldn't call them, and I didn't have a clue where they were. I started trawling bars, then finally went into McDonald's for the free Wi-Fi. Because I wasn't buying any food, the guys behind the counter wouldn't give me the password, so a bag of fries later I had the password and tried to message the lads. Lot of use those three were.

Me: 'Where are you?'

Them: 'By the Cathedral.'

Me: 'I know that, but where?'

Them: 'Looking over it.'

Me: (getting exasperated) 'But where?!'

Them: 'In a bar.'

Me: 'I know that, dickheads, but which one?' For crying out loud.

Them: 'The one that sells Martinis.'

Oh god give me strength. I might as well have gone into the Duomo and said a prayer. I knew Mongoose would be instigating this. They made me go to the metro and look around the square and said I'd be able to see them, they said the Martini bar was famous. It's famous only if you've ever heard of it, and I'd never heard of it. I drink bottles of beer, not bloody Martini. After about half an hour of nonsense they finally give me a clue and I stormed into this Martini bar fuming, only to find them wetting themselves, as they'd been watching me since I took the first step out of the metro. Looking from the ground it wasn't that obvious where they were, as it was about three floors up. The beer cost €10 a bottle, you're paying for the view, aren't you, and to be fair it was worth it. Ian and Mike were drinking Martinis, trying to act all cultured, muttering stuff like you can't come to a Martini bar and drink Peroni. Oh yes you can! A couple of beers on a terrace overlooking the Duomo, what a great beginning to the trip.

The seats were going up on the tables around us and we were the last to leave. As we headed across the now deserted square, we needed to take a tram to where the hotel was. It wasn't too far away, I was told, but could I trust these boys now? Amazingly, the right tram came along immediately and, as it shuddered to a halt, it was like stepping back in time to the 50s, a boneshaking ride if ever there was one. We always tried to avoid the trams while in Milan, as usually we were jumping out of the way of these beasts as they hurtled round corners, but now we were using it to head to the evening's accommodation. In a quiet residential area we found a perfect little hotel, which was 'ideal for couples'. The Hotel Rossovino was down a little side street off the main road, Viale Corsica, and it was cheap at £50 a room. Mongoose had booked it for him and Ian, then me and Mike booked a second room. If you Google it, I bet you think, *Be lovely for Valentine's night with the wife.* Either that or it was a knocking shop. All that mattered was it was £50 a night, clean, fairly central, close to the ring road so we could get away early in the morning, and close to a supermarket for supplies for the journey north the following day.

* * *

In what felt like no time at all, the alarm burst into life. We wanted to be on the road to Switzerland by 9am; any earlier you'd hit the morning rush hour. We took the opportunity to hit the local supermarket, the simply named 'Simply Market'. It had everything we needed: pastries, biscuits, crisps and a day's supply of Birra Mastro (local beer), enough to get us to Switzerland at least. A coffee for the driver and loads of cans for the lads. Our Ian is the driver, that's a result. We swerved the salami and the kebab sandwiches. For only €2 you could give yourself the wildies for days – no thanks, the pastries and biscuits would do.

There's always something that stands out about a trip, that one thing that takes you back, the one memory that will always make you think about that trip, the people you were with, and this was no different. As we left the supermarket in this nice suburb of Milan, there it was, in the gutter, a bag of piss, no word of a lie. A full (to bursting) bag of someone's urine. Obviously, they had a medical condition as it was a medically provided bag, not just a plastic bag from Tesco. It had tubes attached so was obviously attached to someone at some point, and it was full. Who would do such a thing? Leave a bag of piss in the gutter? The mind boggled and the stomach turned, and the decision not to get a kebab sandwich was fully justified, but every time you picked up your can of Birra Mastro the thought of the bag was never far from your mind. We still have the picture as evidence and ping it to each other randomly on WhatsApp to bring back the memories. There you go, I've just done it again.

Our Ian had upgraded the car and ignored the question 'are you taking the car out of Italy', but the upgrade wasn't a much bigger car, so god only knows what car we would have had. We had to squeeze into a cardboard box on wheels, a cardboard box with a Fiat badge plonked on the front of it. They marketed it as a Fiat Doblo. Ever heard of it? Nah, neither had we. I had to Google it again when writing this chapter, and let's say it's not one of the most popular in their range. It only had one job to do, though, and that was get us to Switzerland in time for kick-off. If it got us back again it would be a bonus.

Our kid had chosen to drive because he gets car sick sitting anywhere else in the car. Even though Mike was on the insurance, he was able to open his first can of beer at 9am. We slowly made our way out of Milan, and on these roads there were no rules, if you saw a gap you went for it. The other drivers didn't officially let you in with a nice thumbs-up or a wave, you had to steal the space. Our Ian wasn't used to this style of driving and struggled with the back-seat driver shouting, 'Go ed, go now,' every ten seconds. I should have shut up and let him drive. By the time we hit the motorway north towards Como and the border, he'd got the hang of it. I'd have loved to drive but, with a can in my hand and his travel sickness, he was on duty, all day!

As drives to the match go, you're not getting much better than this one. Once you leave industrial Milan, you're quickly into the most stunning scenery you're going to see on the way to a match. It's not the M6 stilts and Spaghetti Junction in Birmingham, that's for sure. The road followed the shores of Lake Como and the city of the same name on our right-hand side. Across the border and not long after Como, we were driving along the banks of stunning Lake Lugano, then past the town of Lugano and up towards the Alps. That description doesn't do it justice, but I can't. Go and do it yourself, take the drive.

The route to Basel goes straight through the Alps, and I mean straight through. You have to drive through the Gotthard road tunnel, which runs beneath the Gotthard Massif. It's exactly what it says, it's massive. There was no going around these mountains, you had to go through them. The tunnel is 10.5 miles long, and when constructed in 1980 it was the longest road tunnel in the world. Now, sadly, there are four longer than it. Yeah, you learn loads of stuff in my book, don't you. After driving in this tunnel, I can tell you now that I have no inclination to drive through any of the longer ones. Think about how you can't wait to get out the Mersey tunnels, and multiply that by ten. As we were approaching the tunnel some bright spark in the car decided to bang on about a massive accident in 2001 where two lorries collided, and a fireball killed 11 people. Why they had to talk about it as we were entering the tunnel, I don't know. They could have at least waited until we were through to the other side.

We were making good time towards Basel. The plan was to stay in a small town called Olten, 30 miles south of Basel and jump on the train. As with all European Cup finals, rooms were in short supply in the host city, and expensive as well, especially in Basel this time, as it was comparatively small as a host city. Olten wasn't too far off the motorway and our accommodation was a touch outside the town. It was the top floor of someone's house, more like a barn conversion, and it slept four. If you couldn't sleep, you could play pool all night as there was a table plonked right in the middle of the floor. It would have been a great place as a base for a week, but we were running short on time and were in and out in no time, much to the bemusement of the family who owned it. 'What? You no play pool?'

Fifty yards down the hill was a bar, and next to it was a bus stop. The sun was out, and the buses were every ten minutes, so we decided to have a beer or two in the sunshine. We'd broken our necks to get here and an hour in the sun, especially for the driver, was a welcome relief. According to the bus stop we were in Knoblauch (Knob lock), oh how we laughed, yeah; I know, I need to grow up. With no more time to spare, it was time to jump on the bus into town. From our research we knew that there were two trains to Basel each hour, one fast and one slow. The difference in the two was 30 minutes in travel time, so we were aiming for the fast train. Olten was a lovely town, set on a picturesque river and with plenty of hotels, and seemingly lots of Liverpool supporters were staying here, many gathered near to the train station sampling the delights of the town. The Reds were on the move. It was already past 3.30pm and, if we were lucky, we'd be in Basel by 4.30pm. It was going to be a great night.

After purchasing train tickets, we had a quick look at the river (and a beer) and we were back at the station and on the platform in plenty of time to see, with the famed Swiss precision, the on-time arrival of the 4pm train to Basel. With the last cans from this morning's tray of Birra Mastro, we were all sorted until Basel. The train was full of Reds off to the match, so the ground was going to be full of Reds as usual.

Within 30 minutes we pulled into Basel station and walked out the doors and into a different world. The calmness of the mountains, lakes and rivers of the Swiss countryside was replaced with a scene from a Hollywood blockbuster with a cast of thousands. There were people everywhere, all dressed in red and white, and it was already obvious this town wasn't big enough for this occasion. The bars were overrun, and street drinking had taken over. We caught up with Zil, who'd travelled from Liverpool overnight on a coach, taking the cheaper option, and he was with Gaz and Phil and the lads from the Kop. The atmosphere was a bit odd; the weather was starting to turn a bit moody, as was the atmosphere. It didn't feel right, but I couldn't put my finger on it. There was no bother or anything, it was just odd. Was it, yet again, people trying to reconstruct Istanbul? Were people trying too hard? Were people drinking too much? There was a strange friction within the support, it felt fractured. Basel was easy to get to, which meant there were lots of people without tickets and lots with tickets who weren't your usual support, it was strange.

There was no point trying to get into bars, maybe because we were right next to the train station. We moved on, via a supermarket to get some beer. Yeah, I know I said people were drinking too much and I've mentioned beer too many times already. We walked through the streets towards the central meeting point, probably the biggest square in Basel, and all the pubs on the way were full and the streets were full of people taking their own supplies and heading towards the square. This was dominated by a large church, the steps in front of it packed with Reds, as was the square itself, all overlooked by a huge gold UEFA inflatable football. Music was blaring, Bob Marley's song, 'Three Little Birds', on reprise. 'Everything's going to be alright,' the song said, but I had a feeling of foreboding. I wasn't sure why, but even before the game it didn't feel right.

The square wasn't fun. We were at the back in a roadway and had to keep moving out of the way of the riot police vans as masses of supporters still poured into the square. There was no trouble, but it never felt right, not the carnival atmosphere I'd hoped for. It was too busy, and the riot squad were getting itchy fingers on their batons. If there was going to be a problem, it would be here.

Sometimes it's the right thing to move on, and we all decided to move up towards the ground. The problem with the square was that it was on the path to the ground from the train station, so all those at the station had moved on to the square as a stepping stone towards the St Jakob Park Stadion. There weren't enough public spaces to split the crowds up. Everyone knew that you could walk from the centre of town to the stadium (which is unusual) and that's what most people did. Even though the stadium has its own train station, and you could get a tram, we all walked. Walking alongside thousands of Reds, the heavens started to weep. They must have known what was coming. The rain didn't seem to dampen the spirits of the crowd, though, as the procession of fans headed towards the ground with flags waving and songs getting louder as we headed under the bridges carrying roads and railways above our heads.

'Don't worry, every little thing's going to be alright.' It was this year's song, the song of the journey to another European final. As we got to the ground there were people everywhere and chaos was looking to be a likely outcome. The consensus among us was that it was time to get in before the inhabitants of the square a mile or two down the road joined us. Stories from Athens in 2007 were still in everyone's mind, so getting in early was a much better option than not getting in and being in the wrong place as the riot police weighed in.

Even with 90 minutes to go to kick-off, a mass of people were trying to squeeze through crowd control barriers to get through an initial ticket check. After 20 minutes of pushing, jostling and squeezing we were through the ticket check and into the stadium grounds. There was potential for chaos as all Liverpool fans had to enter the same way. To gain access to the stadium it looked like you were entering a shopping centre, and in some ways you were, as a shopping centre is attached to the stadium. From our entry point it was hard to see a football stadium.

I headed straight to the expensive seats, only to find my seat was low down, five rows back and right near the corner flag in the stand on the side. I was 50 feet away from Mike and Our Ian, who had the cheap tickets. What made this seat worth £153 I'll never know. Then again, if the Reds won it would be worth every penny. Every square inch of the stadium had a flag or a banner on it, Scouse flags from Tower Hill, The Kingfisher Kirkby, and the Huyton Baddies. It was a 'Keep Flags Scouse night'. If only the terraces were the same. There was a very odd mix in the stadium that night and there were so many people in red not actively involved in supporting their team. The Scouse heartbeat was fractured. It had been such a challenge to get tickets that everyone was split up. Apparently, money had won the day on the ticket sites, and it was obvious this wasn't a normal crowd. Personally, I think it was the worst support at any final I'd ever been to.

When I got to my seat, the team had come out to warm up and there was a real expectation that they'd win, as they'd done well to get there. They'd adapted to Klopp's way of playing, bringing his 'heavy metal' football on to the pitch. Liverpool could score goals for fun, but worryingly they could also concede at a heavy rate too. They'd beaten United, Dortmund and Villarreal on the way. Seville should be easier, ignoring the fact that they'd won the competition in 2014 and 2015, but they'd only beaten Dnipro from Ukraine and Benfica from Portugal, not the mighty Liverpool. They weren't exactly Real Madrid or Barcelona. If Coutinho turns up, we'll win. As the UEFA Cup trophy was paraded in front of us for photo opportunities, we were feeling confident. This trophy needed to come back to its spiritual home; it had been a while.

The first half went by quickly with very little happening, until the 35th minute when Daniel Sturridge showed his class and out of nothing with the outside of his left boot curled the ball into the corner of the net with a stunning finish. The Reds around the stadium celebrated and 'we shall not be moved' boomed out as half-time approached. As the referee's whistle blew to signal the end of the first half, we were 45 minutes away from European glory. The half-time will long be remembered for the playing of 'There She Goes' by Liverpool band The La's. The whole end was singing amid a party atmosphere.

I'm sure Klopp's last words were 'come on boys, keep it tight' but Alberto Moreno was obviously not listening, as within 18 seconds of the second half starting Seville (Moreno's old club) were level. Moreno had an absolute nightmare second half, and many declared he should never wear Red again. By all accounts he was a good lad, but sometimes if you're not good enough, you're not good enough. The first goal knocked the stuffing out of the team, and the fans as well, and then a quick second followed. Trying to get the support going to back the team was impossible. Maybe it was where I was, in the expensive seats (have I said that before?), but there was little or no backing as many watched on in stunned silence. There was certainly not the spirit of Istanbul. As Coke (his real name is Moreno) scored the second after 64 minutes, we never looked like getting back into it. He scored again, and any hope that it had been disallowed was quickly extinguished. The score was 3-1 to Seville and we were done. Oh yeah, and Coutinho didn't turn up. I constantly brought this up when he eventually claimed a bad back and a move to Barcelona. It was a huge disappointment, and it was time to start making the long trek home empty-handed.

As we walked back to the city centre under blackened skies, the rain started to pour down, and our mood matched the weather. It was a miserable walk back; Mongoose had already stormed off. We'd arranged to meet by the train station but me and Mike took a detour to a packed McDonald's to get the cheapest thing that you could eat in Switzerland. It took an eternity to get served but at least we were dry in there, as the heavens opened once again. I can't remember a time where I'd been so miserable going to a match. As we walked back to the station there was only Our Ian to greet us. Mongoose had a cob on (upset) and had already jumped on a train. He wasn't waiting for two 'dickheads' who were getting something to eat. He was already in Olten trying to get a pint, but to top it off all the local bars were closed and he had to make do with consoling himself with a couple of cans and waiting for us. Just a pity we had the only keys to the room … ha, ha, ha.

It was midnight by the time the last train to Olten departed, but we were on it. Mongoose was fuming now. He'd have been alright in a bar, but he wasn't, and he was fuming, which we all found very funny. The last train was a slow train as well, so it was an hour to Olten, and boy did it drag. By the time we got there it was 1am and nothing was open. Mongoose was in a mood, as were we, so we couldn't be arsed playing any pool tonight. We headed straight to bed after the worst cup final trip ever. And we still had the return journey to face, which was bound to be painful.

* * *

With early afternoon flights from Milan to varying airports, we had to be on the road early whether we wanted to or not, so there was still no time for a game of pool. On the drive up we had the excitement and beautiful scenery to keep us going. The drive home was terrible as we had nothing left, and a miserable day to go with our miserable mood. Our Ian, bless him, drove for four and a half hours in the middle of a rain cloud, inside and outside the car. It was a miserable goodbye to the lads. At least I had a once-in-a-lifetime trip to the US to come in five days' time to look forward to. The others had to put up with this all summer, and it was going to be a long summer.

It was meant to mean so much more. There's losing, but this was the worst sort of losing. I saw this as a year of transition on and off the pitch. Jürgen had seen what he needed to see, and he'd replace those players who didn't have the mentality to survive. He saw a lot that night, as did we. Off the pitch we needed to reclaim what we were. We'd been living off Istanbul for years, but you can't leave your support in the bars and squares of the host city, you need to take it into the stadium. Our response on the night as fans wasn't good enough, but we'd learn our lesson and walk hand in hand with Jürgen, and he'd drive us on to magnificent things. Maybe this was what we needed.

* * *

With the defeat in the back of my mind, we headed off for the holiday of a lifetime to the US, two weeks on the west coast and a week on the east coast seeing family. Why would you be thinking of anything as bad as Basel? I'd been pretty successful not thinking about it on the long trip out there via Dublin and San Francisco, and then for four days in San Francisco. We'd picked up a motorhome in San Francisco. Even out here the Reds were teasing me, getting in my head, though. As we drove out of the Bay Area, we were met with signs for Levi's Stadium in Santa Clara, the home of the San Francisco 49ers (the old home of Candlestick Park was well gone by now). Their 'home' is now 38 miles away from downtown San Francisco. It's like us playing at Old Trafford, and they were advertising that Liverpool would be playing AC Milan in a pre-season tournament. Charlie was most indignant that we were here six weeks too early.

Well, that was out the way, and there would be no more reminders of Liverpool as we headed inland to Yosemite National Park, one of the real wonders of the world, the most amazing place of natural beauty you'll ever see. But no, it wasn't the end of it, Liverpool always gets you when you're not expecting it, you can't escape the Liverpudlian influence for long. After the long drive to the park and our campsite for the night, the best was yet to come. Successfully reversing the 30-foot motorhome into its designated space in the dark without losing the insurance deposit was one of my greatest achievements in life. Tomorrow was a new day for new experiences.

And it was. I'd never met a Scouser in Yosemite before, never mind one who, like me, was still depressed about what happened in Basel a week before. I was minding my own business on an electric shuttle bus that transported you on the valley floor, electric to help save the planet. The kids were pretty much out on their feet after a six-mile walk, and we were heading back towards our campsite when a lady caught sight of my LFC cap and said, 'You should have a word with him,' and nodded towards a guy down the bus. Immediately he caught my eye as he had a massive Liver bird on his bicep. Nick, that's his real name, we're Facebook pals to this day, was standing there with his allegiance on show, and when we got off the bus together we talked about the despair of Basel. Everyone else left us to wallow in our own self-pity. I felt much better sharing my angst with a fellow sufferer, in a place that should leave you thinking about anything other than a miserable night in Switzerland. Getting it off my chest made me a better dad and husband for the rest of the trip. Meeting Reds in a far foreign land is good for the soul.

No matter the highs of following Liverpool, you're scarred by the losses. Basel still resonates to this day, but we'd seen the start of the Jürgen Klopp era. This was merely a blip. Strap yourself in, it's some journey.

Who Remembers the First Time?

WHEN YOU'RE a Red you always remember the first time. The first game, the first away game, the first cup final and the ultimate experience, the first time you travel to Europe and take on the elite of European football.

I never got to see the Reds in Europe with my dad, but I was brought up on his stories of his escapades to Bruges, Rome and Paris. The nearest we got to a European away trip together was Ashby de la Zouch. It may sound French, but it's 17 miles north-west of Leicester. I thought we were in France though. I was only 11. The chippy was boss, I remember that clearly.

I remember my first time on my own in Europe, unfortunately for all the wrong reasons. Heysel in 1985, but it never put me off and I've been infatuated with Europe ever since. I've had many amazing experiences, taking me to the Bernabéu, the Camp Nou and the San Siro, and my lad, Charlie, has read all my stories in *We Had Dreams and Songs to Sing* and heard them first-hand. Now we're writing about his first European adventures.

Charlie had been on at me for ages about going to Europe, so when I heard about the Audi Cup in Munich in the summer of 2017, I thought it would be a perfect opportunity to start his European football education. Easy for tickets, a great place to go and Liverpool would be playing some of Europe's greatest teams, namely Bayern Munich, Atlético Madrid and AC Milan (only for the latter to be replaced by Napoli). There would be world stars on show across the board and hopefully some new talent for the Reds too. Before the season had even ended, and having secured fourth place and a Champions League spot, we were planning our trip to see the cream of Europe. How do you tell a ten-year-old he's going to see the Kings of Europe?

Well, I typed it out on a piece of paper, popped it in an envelope and got him some fish and chips. Normally nothing stops him eating, but the words on the top of the page, 'Watching the Reds in Europe', stopped him munching away for at least a minute. He read the words and the tears came to his eyes, and then they came to mine. He couldn't quite take it in and, as his mum asked him what was in his envelope, he blurted out, 'I'm going to watch Liverpool in Germany, Italy and Spain.' Not quite. He didn't understand that it was actually all in one place and over only two days. All Charlie had to do, according to the paper, was to now book the flights and hotel!

He didn't know that I'd actually booked the flights and hotel. I'd booked them as soon as I'd got the tickets. As any Red worth his salt knows, you can't hang around booking the important stuff, as the cost of travel goes up as hotels and airlines clock on to what's happening. I don't always get it right, as you'll see from my moaning about other trips, but I do my best. I'd purchased tickets behind the goal on both days, with day one being €20 and day two €25, and for Charlie they were half-price. Charlie's task was that he had to find the flights, for which he was given the basic parameters of using Liverpool or Manchester airports to fly to Munich or Stuttgart, Monday outbound, Thursday home, and find the cheapest flights. Let's call it his education as a Red. Let's see how good he is on Expedia or Skyscanner.

I was at *The Anfield Wrap* do at Motel bar in Liverpool straight after the last home game of the season against Middlesbrough when I got a call from Charlie, and with the bash in full flow I had to step outside to speak to him. In one ear I had the music booming out of Motel and in the other Charlie telling me, in great detail, the flights he'd found, and details of baggage allowances and reservation charges. He'd done a great job and chosen exactly the same flights that I'd already booked. Give that lad an A*. He's either going to be a travel agent or following the Reds around Europe. He'd gone for 5-star hotels, while his dad had settled on 3-star.

* * *

On a bright and breezy Sunday afternoon, we were at the sea terminal in the Isle of Man, braving the Irish Sea for three hours, until we'd be landing next to the Liver birds at Pier Head. Charlie had had trouble sleeping since the Wednesday and there was nothing stopping his excitement, unless it was the Irish Sea. An hour out of the island and he'd gone awfully quiet, tired and hot, and the strategically placed sick bag in front of him was in his hands. 'Let's go and get a bit of fresh air mate.'

After 20 minutes outside in the force six breeze, with the salty spray a constant irritant, we were back indoors and it had worked a treat. The colour was back in his face and the excitement had returned as he was asking about Virgil van Dijk, as rumours were flying around that he was going to sign for us. Two hours later and Grandma's roast dinner had him well and truly sorted. Monday would see a flight to Stuttgart, train to Munich, followed by three nights taking in four games. Monday morning couldn't come quick enough for both of us, and to share in our lad's adventure we had 'Tommy the Butcher', my mate of 30 years. I've shared several fabulous European and English adventures with Tommy, so if we couldn't show Charlie how to do it, there was something wrong.

Tommy was unequivocal that the trip was all about Charlie, and he proved it at Manchester Airport at 10am as he ordered two pints for us! He didn't forget Charlie, though, he ordered him a full English breakfast and a coke. There were loads of Reds in Terminal 3, all heading to Stuttgart (our destination) or Nuremberg. The look on Charlie's face when one of the lads said it was only £30 a flight and the train only took an hour, and he whispered in my ear, 'Why didn't we go to Nuremberg dad?' I didn't even know you could. He only mentioned it every hour of every day in Germany (and still does). And every time we walked through Munich central station there were the signs taunting me, showing numerous trains to Nuremberg.

As we were heading to the gate, I managed to meet up with one of those decent fellas off Twitter, who stood out for his name, Paul 'Bono' Hewson, get it? And his funny tweets. You usually make all these arrangements and they never come off, but it was great meeting Paul and his mates, Paul and Sempy. Little did I know we'd see them every day of the trip, and for many years to come. Every time I see them, we always remember Munich, especially seeing that Sempy spent most of it asleep.

The delayed Ryanair jet landed in Stuttgart and our German adventure truly started. It was clear that the train I'd booked had been missed, but along with 30 others from our flight we headed on the metro towards Stuttgart Bahnhof, the main train station, and our ICE train to Munich. Finding our way to the main station was seemingly impossible, and platform 15 for our train was always tantalisingly out of reach. Confusing signage and poor understanding of German made life harder.

We just about made the next train to Munich, armed with some Tuborg (not seen or drunk that for years) and Mountain Dew for Charlie. Once we were on the train, we found a compartment that was designated as a quiet zone. Someone should have told Charlie, as there was no shutting him up until the train Wi-Fi kicked in and his iPad fired up. He was searching how we could get to Nuremberg.

Two hours later, as we stepped off the train at Munich, the heat hit us. We knew it was going to be hot, but the heat was fierce and the forecast for the following day was 37°C. Picturing the map from Expedia in my head (why didn't I use Google Maps, I hear you shout) I knew the hotel was out of the station on the left-hand side, and take a couple of lefts. Unbelievably, it worked, and within five minutes of leaving the station we were checking in, and greeted with those fabulous words you love to hear: 'We have upgraded your room sir.' Upgraded to a duplex suite, none the less, with a sofa bed and two singles upstairs. We gave Charlie the sofa bed and we took upstairs. Unfortunately, the air conditioning from downstairs didn't reach upstairs and the huge skylight in the roof would be the only source of ventilation on a night that didn't have a breath of air. Sleeping was going to be tough.

Charlie's stomach was telling us it was time for his tea, and Tripadvisor told us that the Italian restaurant next door was great, and it was. With pizza washed down with Peroni, and water for Charlie now, no more fizzy drinks as he was already bouncing off the walls, we were living like kings. It was 9.30pm and we were stuffed, so we needed to walk it off before bed. We headed to the train station, which was buzzing, and took in the sights and sounds of life in and around it, while checking out the trains for our adventures over the next few days. The sights and sounds of European cities at night are fabulous, the buzz of a mainline station, police sirens in the distance and the sound of chatter and laughter. The streets of Munich were alive. We had to keep an eye on the trams, which tended to creep up on you silently, and then there were the cycle paths, which you stepped into at your own peril. The sounds of warning bells coming a split second before they ploughed into you meant you had to have your wits about you.

On the opposite side of the station was an area where I'd stayed on a previous trip for the Augsburg game, where the shisha bars mixed with lap dancing bars and tourist hotels. Charlie couldn't believe his eyes. 'Remember lad, what goes in Munich stays in Munich.' By the way, he didn't go in, he waited outside for us to come out. On a sticky humid night, Munich was alive.

Back to the gaff and I needed to get him ready for the morning. His Liverpool kit was laid out ready for a very early morning start, as we were off somewhere special. We had an 8am train to catch to go to watch Liverpool train, the chance of a lifetime. In my 40-plus years following, I hadn't seen the Reds training. I told him earlier in the day, once I found out where Liverpool were training.

At 7am the phone alarm broke the silence after a fitful night's sleep, due to the heat. Even the air conditioning on full tilt had little effect. Charlie sprung up and his kit was on in seconds, unlike a school day. This was going to be 'the best day of my life' he told me. I was trying to manage his expectations in case it all fell flat, which was just as likely an outcome as it being brilliant.

Once again, my appalling German skills combined with the desperate need to get it right and the pressure to get his breakfast resulted in the comfortable time window of 30 minutes to catch the train reducing to seconds. The officious train conductor wouldn't allow us on without a purchased ticket, so back to the ticket office. Tickets in hand, we jumped on the train as the doors closed right behind us. It was all over if we'd missed that train. I was a frazzled dad, sweating profusely and breathing heavily.

I was guzzling water that was supposed to last for hours. Charlie was oblivious, though, and asking about whether we were signing VVD for the 20th time in two days. He was oblivious to the pressure I was under not to ruin his day (or his life); he was tucking into his chocolate croissant that, due to the already intense heat, was dripping on to his chin. I was desperately trying to keep the chocolate off his kit. Can't meet your heroes covered in chocolate can you? What would his mum say?

I knew that Liverpool were training in a tiny place called Rottach-Egern, 35 miles south of Munich. It was an hour's train journey to a town called Tegernsee, then a ten-minute bus ride to the town of Rottach-Egern. Twitter the previous day had shown us that you could watch training from outside the perimeter mesh fence, but they'd also held open training where fans got close to the players, so it was worth a shot. Fifty minutes in and Lake Tegernsee came into view and the train trundled through the edges of the town. It was stunning, a crystal-blue lake surrounded by beautiful alpine houses. The town is where the rich and influential of Munich spend the summer.

As we jumped off the train, we just about made the departing bus for Rottach-Egern, much to the frustration of the miserable bus driver, who'd already closed the door. There's always one miserable get, it's the same the world over. There was no way he was telling me where it was best to get off the bus, I had to guess when to get off. The centre of town had three bus stops, being clever I picked the middle one. As luck would have it, the bus stop was outside the tourist information office. I said, 'Here you go

Charlie, watch this lad, watch the master at work.' The young girl behind the counter smiled at me, and I said, 'Sprechen sie Englisch,' with a knowing smile, expecting a 'ja' in response. It had worked a treat in Munich, but not here, though. The girl's blank face said it all, this was going to be hard work. I reverted to the universal tourist language of talking very loudly and very slowly in English: 'Liverpool, football, training, FC Rottach-Egern.' This time a flicker of recognition and a smile followed by 'nien public'. Even I knew that meant no public. Yeah right, draw the place where the local football club is on the map, luv. I'll see if it's 'nien public'.

With a neatly highlighted route on the map, Charlie and I headed back out into the sunshine and towards the football club. It was baking hot now and the forecast of 37°C had come true. Even the mountains and the presence of the lake hadn't cooled this place down. We were heading inland towards the river when we were stopped by a driver who recognised Charlie's Liverpool kit. He told us that he'd tried to get into the car park, but it wasn't open to the public. He'd been able to articulate this in English. There was no way we were turning round. What sort of dad would I be?

I knew from the clips of training that if we got to the river, we'd find the training pitch, and so it transpired. A 15-minute walk down its banks and the training pitch appeared with a wire-mesh fence you could clearly see through. There was nobody on the path, and there were only a few people in the training ground, but no players or LFC staff. The one glimmer of hope, though, was that on the far side of the pitch we could see two coaches, and one of them was emblazoned with the red Liverpool livery. There was a chance.

We headed towards the entrance of the training ground past a builder's merchants and opposite a large wood yard, to where there was a security checkpoint on a single-track road leading into the football ground. The German lady on security once again spoke little English, but I confused her enough by babbling away in Scouse that she had to call her boss. By the time he came, I'd prised out of her that when the players trained, they came in convoy by bike (I knew that thanks to Twitter), and they came from the road to the right up past the wood yard. More importantly, they'd be training at 10.30am. Her boss came, who spoke much better English, which helps a lot when you're not telling the truth. He told me that only three players were training today, and they'd only be the ones with slight problems. No one else was training. Yeah right!

I thanked him for his time and headed off up to the right past the wood yard, out of sight, with a disappointed Charlie in tow. He'd believed every word the man had said. He was resigned to not seeing his heroes, at which point John Achterberg flew past on his bike. I told him that if John was here, more than three players would be training. Sitting out of the sun in a rare patch of cooler shade, I promised him we'd see some players, and even if it was only three, that would still be great. He didn't believe me. He'd tried hard not to get his hopes up, but it was tough. Tears weren't far away from his little face. Then after a long 15 minutes came the first sign that things might turn out just fine. More coaches in grey, then the first sign of the boys in Red, coming at a fair pace down the hill on their mountain bikes. Emre Can followed by Jürgen Klopp, Simon Mignolet, and with a special hello and waves from Jordan Henderson, Adam Lallana and Mo Salah. The result was the most excited little boy ever. This big boy wasn't far behind him.

It was time to head back to the tow path and watch them train. It was still pretty much only me and Charlie, there was no one else around. At the fence the team were only 50 yards away as they were put through their paces by Jürgen Klopp. Training was light and fun. They were playing nine hours later at the Allianz Arena against the mighty Bayern Munich. They put a lot of work in on corners, but they never scored from one during the session. Then again, they never conceded from one either. Within 30 minutes more people had come to watch, a variety of Scouse lads, German Reds, and random Romanian Liverpool fans.

Liverpool had their own stewards who'd travelled with them (what a job), and I asked whether there was any chance to get to meet the players after training. 'Unfortunately, not today,' was the response, but we were told that sometimes if you were lucky, some would stop. Sadio Mané, for instance, was one who'd stop and sign a kit if he saw you. Good job Charlie had Mané on his back on the new blood-red kit and the old toxic thunder (bright green) away kit in his bag with Mané on the back, so there was a chance. As the players completed their warm-down, we headed back to the security barriers and within minutes the players were flying up the hill on the bikes. Charlie with his toxic thunder shirt on show, shouted, 'Sadio, can you sign my shirt please?' and, even though he was on the way up the hill, he stopped and turned back for Charlie.

The next minute will stay with me and Charlie for the rest of our lives (there are tears in my eyes as I write this bit). Sadio Mané signed his shirt for him, and this humble man patiently waited for Charlie to get his phone ready and take his prized selfie. All I have to say is what a lovely man, who made a little boy's day, made his trip, his year and quite probably his life. He'll never forget the day he met Sadio, and neither will I. That simple act makes such a difference, all players should realise that, and clubs should make it happen as much as possible. As Sadio took to the saddle and wheeled away, Charlie grasped his shirt to his chest and stood in disbelief and then gave me a massive bear hug and said, 'Best dad in the world.' (Just got all dusty in here!)

In my desire to watch training, I'd totally ignored the fact of what time trains back to Munich were, or even buses to get back to Tegernsee to get the train, and with no Wi-Fi and an inability to roam (digitally that is), I was winging it. We'd missed a bus and had to wait another 30 minutes, which I thought would mean missing the hourly train back to Munich and would delay us further. After an agonising wait the bus came, and ten minutes later, after the sanctuary of the air-conditioned bus, we pulled into Tegernsee train station. I could see that there was a train on the platform waiting, ready to go. I dragged Charlie along, still clutching his shirt to his chest, up the platform towards the front carriages, and jumped on the train. As we got on the train, I saw a young lady, and, now running out of German phrases, I didn't even bother with 'sprechen sie Englisch'. I said, 'Munchen, ja?' to which she kindly nodded and said 'yes', quickly followed by 'are you Keith?'

How the hell did she know that? It was only Melissa Reddy, the now-famous Sky journalist and great friend of *The Anfield Wrap* guys, including Our Ian. I'd contacted Melissa the previous week to see whether she'd be in Munich. Never for a moment was I expecting to meet her. Melissa got the full Charlie treatment, his story of how he met Sadio Mané, and he showed the shirt as evidence. Funny, he never asked her about VVD. She'd have had more of a clue than me. The hour to Munich must have flown by for her with a inquisitive ten-year-old.

At Munich we bid our farewells and it was off to the match after a quick freshen-up at the hotel. In no time, along with Tommy, we were back at the station, feeding ourselves. A cheese and tomato panini, with all the 'stuff' (that's tomato and basil, by the way) taken out for Charlie, and a rack of ribs for Dad and Tommy. On the hottest day of the year those ribs were gorgeous. Eating at train stations in Europe isn't like the UK. Would you ever see ribs on the menu at Euston or Lime Street?

The move from the city to a stadium is usually a highlight of the trip after all-day drinking in a city centre, galvanised with pints of the local brew and up for a sing-song. No such thing today for us as we were heading off early to take in the first game of the four-team tournament between Napoli and Atlético Madrid. The metro was busy and full of football fans, many in Liverpool shirts from all over Europe, a fair proportion from Germany itself. The metro from Hauptbahnhof via Marienplatz and out to the stadium at Fröttmaning got hotter and hotter, and it was a real relief as we headed out of the station and towards the Allianz Arena, perched up on the hillside. As it was a ten-minute walk in the heat, you certainly needed your fluids on board, meaning pints of Paulaner beer, the local Munich brew, and very nice it was too. Obviously water for Charlie. The Paulaner sustained the old men as they battled their way up the hill. The Allianz is an impressive sight from wherever you view it, and photo opportunities are wide and varied. I'd safely wager money on it being the most-photographed stadium in the world.

We headed into the ground for the strictest search I'd been subject to at a football ground since I don't know when. There were no half-measures for kids either, it was full-on. All this for friendly matches, but I never saw a flare in that ground over the two nights. You enter the ground at an outer perimeter some 100 yards from the entrances to the stadium itself, and as is always the case, our entrance was right on the other side of the ground in block 128 behind the goal. The three of us sat there totally blown away by how good the Allianz is. The only thing you couldn't judge is what the atmosphere could really be like, as there was little in evidence over either of the days, bar pockets of Reds all over the ground. It was fairly quiet, definitely a pre-season crowd. The most interesting thing to me was that the Liverpool fans in our immediate vicinity were from the Czech Republic, Zürich, Germany, Transylvania, and Mike from Walton Village (Mike was with the Zürich Reds). They'd travelled some distance to watch the Reds and got behind them in their own little ways. One fan stood out, notably for his builder's crack that was showing, and his casual vomit on the way to the bogs, as if he was in the taxi queue in Liverpool on a Friday night.

The first match, Napoli and Atlético Madrid, was a tepid affair. The main event, Liverpool against Bayern, was still over an hour away. The beauty about having an outside concourse was that you could go outside the ground on to the concourse and escape the heat and talk to other fans. Being from Liverpool, we were popular, many fans from all over Europe wanting to talk to us, which was brilliant. Many of the fans were big fans of the Premier League and they'd often travel to England and take in Premier League games.

As the match edged closer, we returned to our seats with popcorn and beer (choose who had what?) and the stadium had filled up, obviously as Bayern were playing. At €20, whether you watched one game or two it didn't make much difference, and those who missed the first game still hadn't missed much. You could measure the interest in the first game by the Mexican wave count, and that was in the high numbers. As with any modern football match (or occasion), there's a ceremonial show that goes on beforehand. Today's show by Audi was noticeable because the men and women running with flags were as near normal as you could get, generally overweight and unfit, out of step and out of time, which was quite refreshing for an old fat man like me. There's hope for me yet. Watch out for my pre-match moves in front of the Kop one day soon.

Audi spent £12 million sponsoring the two days. I'm sure that they'll feel particularly let down by Bayern, who couldn't win on their home soil. Tonight that was mostly due to how good Liverpool were. Both clubs put out strong sides and there was no taking it easy, you could tell that as the German full-back decided to kick lumps out of Charlie's best mate, Mané. Charlie was fuming. To get his own back, Mané scored a fabulous first goal, then Mo Salah nodded into an empty net. Liverpool were cruising. The Czechs, the boys from Zürich, the Germans, the Transylvanians and especially us were having a great time. The Bayern fans surrounding us sat in silence as their team were picked apart on home turf.

The usual pre-season raft of changes at half-time made no difference as the Reds continued to pick at Bayern, and Ryan Kent especially teased their defence throughout the second half. Kent ultimately set up a disallowed Grujić goal, thanks to Adam Lallana standing in an offside position. While I was fuming at a pre-season disallowed goal, with a few pints inside me it was probably right. It looked like the referee was trying to look after Bayern and let them back into the game. The Mexican wave count increased again as the locals were restless. Daniel Sturridge put the wave to bed by scoring again, with a beautiful deft chip over the goalkeeper, then he went off injured. Only Daniel, eh, fittest he's ever been, he said!

Charlie's top was off, and twirling around his head, his European christening complete, watching the Reds tear Bayern Munich to bits in their own back yard. I know it's only a friendly, but Bayern and their fans weren't expecting this. Charlie's got this to look back on forever. Regardless of Charlie, both Tommy and I were loving it, and nothing to do with the Paulaner beer, the Reds looked special going forward, they were going to be a real joy to watch (how right that was).

As the final whistle went it was time to head back to the city centre behind 70,000 Bayern fans who'd left well before the end. This might take some time. It was still a warm evening. The thunder, lightning and lashing rain that accompanied some of the game had disappeared and left a balmy night. As we walked down the hill towards Fröttmaning station the Allianz was lit up in red and white at the top of the hill behind us – more photo opportunities. As we hit the back of the metro queue it looked like we could be here for some time, and a ten-year-old purely running on adrenaline, I doubted, was going to last too much longer. We'd been on the go since 7am, it was time to go home, and fortunately the queue moved quickly. As we hit the platform, with sporadic chants of 'Liverpool', the train rolled in. The doors opened and we crammed in for the 20-minute ride to Marienplatz, a quick connection to Hauptbahnhof and a five-minute walk to the hotel. Charlie wasn't out on his feet yet, proved by his dancing at Hauptbahnhof. He still had a spring in his step, that was for sure, and now he was going to be up all night long, and tomorrow too, as the Reds were to play in the late game again. We also had a full itinerary in the daytime.

As we headed back to the hotel, Tommy went for a pint or two to celebrate. It's what we'd normally do, but I got Charlie showered and to bed, asleep. Tommy asked me to set my alarm for 6am as he was off to see a Bavarian castle in the morning and had to catch a 7am train. With Charlie showered, in bed and asleep in minutes, I caught up on the feedback of the night's performance and updating Facebook for his mum with a selection of pictures of his day. What a day too, the day he met Sadio Mané, got his shirt signed and the Reds won 3-0 at the Allianz against Bayern Munich; not a bad day out that!

At 1.30am the silence was broken with the chairs from the table crashing to the floor. Tommy was home and trying to plug a phone charger in, drunk! Charlie was fast asleep, and as I helped Tommy plug in his phone and helped him up the stairs, he enquired as to whether I'd set the alarm. I had but I'd have put money on it he wasn't going to see any castles.

* * *

Wednesday morning came and at 6am the alarm on the phone burst into life. 'Tommy, it's six o'clock, mate,' I said, to which Tommy grumbled and staggered down the wooden stairs, went for a burst and staggered back up the stairs and went back to bed. 'I'll see the castles with Julie when we come back,' he said, and within seconds he was snoring again. By 8am, Charlie and I were ready for our morning excursion; we were going somewhere very important.

In a small corner of a little town on the edge of Munich lies a monument to man's inhumanity to man. Dachau concentration camp lay at the heart of the Nazi regime. The first of the Nazi concentration camps, it was initially designed to hold political prisoners, but ultimately held nearly 200,000 people and saw the deaths of over 40,000 (men, women and children). Putting that into perspective for a ten-year-old boy meant that nearly half of the people where he lived in the Isle of Man would have died there, and children as young as him were kept in there, many not to make it out alive. Some people might question why a ten-year-old should see such things, but Charlie isn't ten in his head. He's wise beyond his years and as a dad I thought it important to give him the opportunity to visit and understand what happened in such a place.

I'd asked people who'd visited Dachau what they thought, and the feedback was 'you know whether Charlie can understand or not'. Both Nikki and I trusted that he could, as he already knew about the Nazis. He knew about the Holocaust and now he had the chance to see where it happened. Nikki said I had to be prepared for the questions. Charlie never let me down, he took it all in. And the questions? There were loads of them, all well-formed, all to the point and all requiring answers, many to which I had no answers. The book purchased on our departure will help answer many of them over the years but as to the real question of 'why did they do it, Dad?' there's just no answer.

As you arrive at Dachau train station there's a bus waiting to take visitors to the camp. On the bus I met a lovely fella from Cork in Ireland, who was a tour guide at the camp. He gave me information for Charlie, and also gave me some valuable guidance as to what would be suitable for him and what maybe wasn't. After purchasing headsets, we were off at a fair pace. With a ten-year-old in charge, don't expect to stand still for long, as they're off to the next part of the exhibit as quickly as they arrived. Don't be fooled into thinking they're not taking it in, though. Charlie can recite virtually every board we read, and if you think he didn't take any notice, you couldn't be more wrong. To use the word 'amazing' for what we'd seen seems wrong, but yet right. It *was* amazing, and the name Dachau now means much more than before. The camp on the outskirts of this small Bavarian town holds the scars of a war on an undeserving people and should stand as a reminder of what happens when people's behaviours remain unchecked. Open your eyes. It's happening all around us, and in the years since there are signs that this could happen again, don't ever believe it won't. It's up to us to educate ourselves and fight the evil among us (originally written in 2018, prophetic maybe).

The return from Dachau was thought-provoking. As the bus headed back to the train station, the outlying area of this neat little German town showed no sign of the dark secrets a few miles up the road. What normal looked like now, so it did in the 1940s. The Allies who liberated Dachau and its prisoners made the locals go to see what horror was on their doorsteps. Many of them didn't have a clue what was happening down the road, or did they? Surely, they must have done. Was it that well hidden, or did people choose not to look past the gates or the transports that led past their doors. Back on the train that sped back to Munich and the old-world secrets gave way to modern life once again. Within an hour we were back to normal, but the couple of hours in the heat of the German countryside will never be forgotten.

* * *

The time taken going to Dachau had impacted upon what else to see in Munich, but we wouldn't change it. The Olympiastadion tour and the city of Munich will be there when we return. Before we headed back to the hotel, Charlie wanted to buy something from the Bayern Munich fan shop as a memento from his trip. As luck would have it, there was a club shop in the subway. Let's say it was a challenge to buy a memento, as the idea of a shirt went out the window quickly as soon as we saw the price. With a price tag of €90, it was never going to happen, and Charlie decided that it wasn't worth the money, especially as it wasn't even his team. Also, he had to buy presents for his mates, so 30 minutes (yeah, I know, he's like his mum when shopping) and €30 later we were off.

We quickly freshened up at the hotel, picked the old fella (Tommy) up and were back out, heading for Marienplatz. We were showing Charlie what the centre of Munich looked like, and we headed through the maze of streets towards the famous Hofbräuhaus and the surrounding squares. Last time I was here it was easy as

I had Mongoose as my guide and the streets were quiet, but now the streets were rammed and nowhere looked the same in the blazing sunshine as it did on that crisp cold February night. A quick bite to eat and some drinks in the sunshine and we'd be off to the night's matches. Not so vital that we see every minute of the first game this time around, Bayern and Napoli, as we were only interested in the main event. Charlie wanted to see the first game, though, so we'd be as quick as we could. A couple of pints, a coke and a ropey pizza later and we were heading back to the subway and on to Fröttmaning and the Allianz.

Walking past a couple of bars, I heard shouts of 'Keith, Keith'. It was Paul and the lads from the airport, tumbling out of the local hostelry. They'd obviously eaten better food than we had, you could tell that by the diners outside and their plates full of meat and dumplings, while we'd eaten a second-rate pizza from a kitchen next to the bogs. I only found the latter out after we'd eaten most of the meal, but I kept that to myself. I was glad Charlie never liked the pizza and left half of it. We caught up on our respective previous 48 hours with the lads. As a group with a young lad in tow we'd had 48 hours that was slightly different to the group without, but at least our livers would still be working when we got home. Well, Charlie's would. We were all in agreement that it was a fantastic trip, though.

Bidding farewell to our new mates we headed to the subway and the Allianz. There was no way we were making kick-off, though, but Charlie didn't seem too bothered. As we headed into the Marienplatz station we heard the distant sounds of 'Liverpool, Liverpool, Liverpool'. The

Liverpool boys were in town. Charlie was made up and his face lit up as we stood on the platform with a combination of Liverpool lads and all manner of nationalities. There was no way Charlie could miss this ride, it was like going away in Europe. The fans were running through their repertoire of songs: 'Fields of Anfield Road', 'Poor Scouser Tommy', 'We've got the best midfield in the world'. The locals on their way home from work were loving it. The train was bouncing all the way to the Allianz. At Fröttmaning the platform filled up with fans, and shouts of 'Liverpool, Liverpool, Liverpool' once again went up.

Entry into the ground was much quicker tonight, although still with the customary full-body search . The seats were only a few rows back from the previous night's, a fabulous view and nearer the bars and toilets. Things weren't going well for the hosts as Bayern were 1-0 down and the Mexican waves had already started. It wasn't even half-time. Artur Vidal was doing his best to liven things up by kicking anyone with a Napoli badge on their chest, but his team-mates looked much less interested. Bayern were well and truly beaten and I feared the interest of their supporters would dwindle and there would be a mass exodus at the end of their game, leaving Liverpool to play the final match in an near-empty stadium. However, while there were some gaps, most of the crowd stayed to watch the final, which was good to see.

Between games we once again headed to the concourse and had a little boy's tea of chicken nuggets and chips for all three of us. Food is food, and taking a chance on the types of German sausage on offer was not an option (still can't get the courage up for currywurst). Outside on the concourse there was a great mix of people, and we got talking to a man and his young family who'd travelled from Austria, and while supporting Bayern, it seemed that Liverpool was his 'English team'. There was some substance to his claim, though, as he loved Ian Rush when he was a boy, and he also got to see Liverpool play his local team when the Reds went to Sturm Graz some years ago. Over a pint and a chat, you get to meet some lovely people. I'm sure they'd say the same, no hint of malice anywhere over two days, so a perfect place for Charlie to start his European education.

With two games in two days in the heat of the Bavarian night, it was bound to take its toll, with the temperature still in the high 20s. The pace of the game was slow, and the vibrancy of the crowd low. The atmosphere was poorer than the night before and the Liverpool supporters around us were there to stare in awe at the Reds. Trying to get a song or two going after Liverpool went one-nil down was impossible. Charlie was getting more and more frustrated as he belted out 'Liverpool, Liverpool, Liverpool', much to the initial bemusement of a row of middle-aged Germans in front of us. I'm sure the bemusement turned to annoyance as he made me join in, and ultimately it turned into real admiration as he cheered his team on. The Reds were awarded a penalty in the 81st minute and Bobby Firmino slotted it home to bring unbridled joy to Charlie. I've never wanted us to score so badly. While Liverpool picked up the pace and searched for a winner it wasn't to be and we headed straight to a penalty shoot-out.

Now, to me and you it's a penalty shoot-out in a friendly competition over two hot days in Germany on a trip designed for fitness and preparation for the season ahead. To a ten-year-old boy on his first trip to a far foreign land it was the opportunity to win some silverware, and that's what he'd come for. As Jordan Henderson missed his penalty, the writing was on the wall and, while all the other Liverpool penalties were scored, Atlético (including Fernando Torres) calmly beat Danny Ward, so the cup, trophy, shield or whatever it was went to Atlético Madrid.

Charlie was devastated and burst into tears. He desperately wanted to win, he didn't come here to go home without a cup. There was no consoling him. He didn't want to hear his dad say that 'it doesn't matter, mate, it's only a friendly'. It wasn't just a friendly, we'd come all that way to win, and while he was later appreciative of Jordan Henderson tweeting that he was sorry, he'd ruined his trip. If Charlie's support could win us trophies, we'd be winning them all the time, but as you get older you realise you can't make them win. You can certainly help them along but there's no guarantee. The bemused Germans in front of us, what did they do? They queued up to give Charlie a hug and shake his hand, and mutter stuff in German that roughly translated meant 'well done lad'. We've all been ten once, haven't we!

The ground emptied rapidly, and after a final toilet visit for Charlie, which must have been about his 20th of the day, we were heading to the subway. The well-managed queue meant we were on the platform within minutes, and 25 minutes later, following a sardine-packed journey back to Marienplatz and the quick jump to Hauptbahnhof, we were walking towards our hotel for one last time. Charlie had finally gone quiet, the long days and heat having caught up with him. He admitted he was 10/10 on the tired scale. He rarely admits to being at that level so he must have been knackered. To bed, and in the morning the long trip home, the adventure nearly over. As always, the departure makes you wistful and wish for more, but besides the penalty shoot-out disappointment we couldn't have asked for more from Munich. Now it was time to go home and tell everyone about it.

* * *

Thursday morning came and it was time to go home. A late afternoon flight from Stuttgart back to Manchester meant we had plenty of time to make our way home. Charlie was exhausted on his bed, wearily waving his free Audi Cup flag like one final act of surrender. The European away trip had finished him off, a feeling many Reds have felt before, usually after loads of alcohol. If you're not out on your feet on the way home, you haven't had a good time. We had a great time, one to never forget, a dad-and-lad trip that will never be beaten (or maybe not). You always remember the first time, and this will never be forgotten by either of us.

With bags packed, we headed for breakfast, a full English at a café round the corner from the hotel. Tommy had found it the day before and highly recommended it, the California Kitchen it was called. I don't know what part of California it was supposed to be, but it was a

German representation of an English breakfast in an American-themed restaurant. Obviously, as full English goes, it wasn't up to the mark. It was fine, though, and Charlie's bacon butty looked like it had put him over the edge. He was yawning already, and it wasn't even 10am. It was going to be a long day.

We dragged him to the station for the ICE train bound for Stuttgart. He was still wanting a pizza, 'the best pizza in the world', according to Charlie, and he knows a thing or two about pizza. As we hit the station concourse the faces we'd been seeing for days since we sat down in Terminal 3 in Manchester Airport started arriving in varying states of hangover. These are the lads you'll be seeing around the ground for years to come, but you never know who they are, but you always know they were in Munich, though.

As the train slid away from the platform and headed to Stuttgart, Munich was gone, and Charlie was thinking about where we were going next. Hold on, mate, it doesn't work like that. I remember as an 11-year-old on my first away trip to Leicester with my dad; after that I was going everywhere with those Mighty Reds. I was soon put in my place that it wasn't regular, it was special, and it would be a few more years before away match number two. Charlie's dreams of the Bernabéu, Camp Nou and San Siro can stay dreams for now, but what dreams he'll have, and who knows what will come true.

Up the European Reds!

The Kings of Europe

'COME AND behold them, we're the Kings of Europe, oh come let us adore them'. A Kop anthem that gets rolled out at Christmas time, but it was true, we were becoming the Kings of Europe again. The Champions League campaign of 2017/18 saw Liverpool as a threat in Europe once more. Days of barely scraping into the top four for Champions League qualification were due to be a thing of the past.

The Audi Cup had come and gone, and summer turned to winter as the group stages concluded. Liverpool had walked their group with easy wins against Spartak Moscow and Maribor, the highlight being a 7-0 home win again the Russians, memorable in our house as it was Charlie's first competitive European game, one to remember. Riding on the back of the Audi Cup, he thought he was going everywhere to watch the Reds; I can't blame him for being greedy, can I. On the way home, at the airport, we shared security checks with the Spartak fans, and that was a real experience. It felt like a cage fighters' convention. I don't know what those boys had been taking (well I probably do, steroids!), but they were all huge, and thankfully rather subdued. I had visions of what a number of these fellas had probably been up to in Marseille in the summer of 2016, as they fitted the profile, and the police presence at John Lennon Airport showed they wanted to make sure they left Liverpool. The other team in the group was Sevilla, and we owed them one from Basel, but we ended up scraping two draws, even throwing away a 3-0 lead in Seville.

Many were questioning our credentials, especially our defending. As the draw was made for the knockout stages, as group winners we were going to get a weaker team, and as Porto came out the hat, we were all happy. Who fancies Portugal in February? The chance of some winter sun, Lisbon (with Benfica and Sporting) was a place that had been on my bucket list for years, but Porto would do.

Who was coming with me? Tommy raised his hand and everyone else kept their powder dry for what would come next, all fully expecting the Reds to progress. Bryan, Tommy's lad, fancied it as well if we could box off tickets. It was expected to be challenging after Seville, where tickets were like gold dust. The begging started. I was talking to a mate in the football world, who had a mate in Portugal, let's call him 'José' (well why not), who was an agent and could probably sort us out, and he put me in touch. What a fella José was. He promised me right away that he could sort two tickets out, and to give him a shout the week before to arrange collection. The tickets would be in the Porto end and probably not the cheapest, but having the confidence of travelling with tickets is a weight off your mind. José was as good as his word, and the week before he confirmed that two tickets were sorted, at €100 each. In the meantime, the ticket distribution brought us another two for the Liverpool section, so we were sorted – four tickets for three of us, and we'd be able to shift the other, no problem.

With the two Liverpool section tickets safely secured in our pockets, we met at the Premier Inn at Gatwick on the Monday night and had a couple of pints ahead of a Tuesday morning flight to Lisbon. I'd spoken to José and arranged to meet him at 6pm on the Wednesday night at a metro station close to the ground. José had hospitality tickets, but the offer didn't extend to us, not for €100 anyway. We were looking forward to a few days away for Valentine's – yeah, it was Valentine's Day, but if you can't tell your wife you love her every day, you don't deserve to go away watching the Reds. By the time I was booking flights, those to Porto were proving difficult, but Lisbon was cheap and only a couple of hours away by train. The plan was to spend the Tuesday in Lisbon and then make our way up to Porto on Wednesday morning.

Lisbon was great. If you've never been, you must go, I promise you won't regret it. We arrived as the sun was breaking up the grey February clouds, and by the time we checked into our hostel the sun was out. The locals had their heavy coats and scarves on, but we were in T-shirts, my Bill Shankly one raising a few looks. There was the odd Liverpudlian around but, being miles away from where the Reds were playing, Lisbon had a normal tourist crowd, and today we were tourists.

Our hostel was clean, even having an en-suite room to ourselves. We had no idea of what to see in Lisbon and the receptionist looked aghast when we said we only had three hours to see the sights and asked about the best things to do. Three hours doesn't give you long to see a beautiful city, but let's see what we can do. A ten-minute walk down to the Atlantic Ocean brought us to the bustling Praca do Comercio, one of the grandest and largest squares in Europe. The warmth of the afternoon sun meant there was no need for the jackets we were cradling. The evening's entertainment would be in the bars and clubs (if we lasted that long) of Bairro Alto, the famed nightlife quarter of Lisbon. It's a city that doesn't sleep.

The receptionist said that the Jerónimos Monastery was world-famous. We'd never heard of it, obviously, and you needed to jump a train to get to it, but we had a train ticket for the whole day, so we may as well use it. We found the train station, and its bar. The wait for the next train was 30 minutes, eased by a couple of bottles of Sagres (the local beer) at only €1 a pop; it would be criminal not to. The locals, a mix of Benfica and Sporting fans, wished us luck in beating Porto, as there's no love lost between them.

We took the train ten minutes up the coast to the monastery. From there you could see the mini-version of Rio de Janeiro's Christ the Redeemer, or a mini-version of the Golden Gate Bridge (San Francisco) – can't they have their own ideas for tourist sights? It was like the model village in Babbacombe in Devon we used to go to as kids. The monastery was incredibly beautiful, when viewed from a bar over the road, sat in the sun with a pint of Superbock (an even better local beer than Sagres). You didn't think we were going into a monastery, did you? With a second pint of Superbock, Tommy came back with a shot of some local liqueur, which came in a chocolate shot cup; it was beautiful. The sun was shining, we had liqueurs, chocolate and beer, so what more could you want from a Valentine's break?

'Get the bill, Tommy, and we'll go.' Tommy went to get the bill, and someone had paid up on our behalf, seemingly entertained by us as we were enjoying ourselves. They'd paid our bill and then quietly slipped away, lovely. As the sun went down, we took the train back to central Lisbon and straight back into the station bar for a couple more Sagres before heading to Bairro Alto for the night.

Google Maps showed us that we were just around the corner from Bairro Alto. As we walked towards it, we threw a right turn, and we were at the bottom of a steep hill. There are loads of them in Lisbon. The hill had cable car tracks running through the middle of a narrow street, with tightly packed buildings either side, framed by narrow pavements. You needed sherpas and mules to get you to the top, or you could get a cable car. One sat at the top of the hill, mocking us, there was no chance it was coming down. It looked like it was done for the day. We started the hike to the top of the hill. Two-thirds of the way up there was a sign advertising pints at €1.50 a pop, declaring that every fifth pint was free. The walk up the hill had given us a thirst. We looked inside what for all purposes was a hole in the wall, but the hole in the wall held hidden treasures.

A bar serving cold beer with beer kegs for tables, then throw in live Champions League football and we thought we might stay a while. We were there long enough to have a few free pints. The welcome from the hosts was warm and the Spurs game against Juventus was a cracker. We were scouting who we'd play next after Porto, but it was clear that neither of them would be good enough to take us on. The bar's clientele was an eclectic mix, and we were an oddity. It was clearly a locals' bar and not one that tourists would be expected to populate. The bar owner told us the reason that every fifth pint was free was that the local government had made him put his prices up to €1.50 from €1 a pint, and he wasn't having it, as it was killing his business. He said it was too expensive for beer! You want to move to Lisbon now, don't you.

Before we knew it the clock had hit 10.30pm and we were starving. The bar owner recommended a restaurant at the top of the hill where the locals ate, real Portuguese food, and cheap. As we headed into the night, the streets were alive. The night had only just started for many people, and the cable car had started running so we had to be careful not to end up under one. We walked into the restaurant and Tommy took control, assuming the role of dad. Well, at his age that was okay. Even pushing 11 o'clock the place was rammed, and we took a seat by the window where Tommy ordered us whatever he fancied. A huge fish for him and two big fat steaks drowned in garlic butter for me and Bryan. I was sure we'd be paying the price down the line for this, but you've got to do as your dad tells you, haven't you? There was wine to accompany the food, and I was getting slaughtered for drinking Mateus Rose – well it's a local brew, so why not? Tommy ordered three brandy chasers.

The food came to mop up the day's alcohol and there was enough on the plates to feed ten of us, never mind three. Tommy's fish came, he peeled it from the tail and the fish skeleton came out in one go, like a scene from *Tom and Jerry*. Tommy licked his lips like Tom the cat. Bryan and I looked at the steak, looked at each other and laughed, took a deep breath, and started to tackle it, man versus food. Besides some tapas and the chocolate shot cup, we'd had nothing since Gatwick. We demolished it. What a way to round off a magnificent day, one that will stay with me forever. If only that was the end, but little did Bryan know that his life was about to change forever, and for the better.

We headed back into the night as the clock struck midnight, and we were done for. Stuffed and full of ale, but we promised ourselves a quick nightcap by the hostel. Where's that map again? I got the travel map out and could see that we were around the corner from the hostel. All we needed to do was head down the hill opposite where a cable car was waiting to leave, so we jumped on. As we sat down, Tommy did what Tommy does when he has had a bevvy – he lit up a cigar and started puffing away. At which point the conductor went berserk, shouting at Tommy in Portuguese, much to our bemusement and laughter, which wound the conductor up even more. Then a lady opposite, in perfect English, told us that the conductor was saying it was a non-smoking tram and Tommy needed to extinguish his cigar. Wow, her English was amazing! As it turns out, the lady was called Monica and she was from London, so no wonder her English was amazing. She and her cousin were visiting her relatives in Lisbon. The girls had Brazilian heritage and also spoke perfect Portuguese.

We said thanks to Monica, as the conductor was all for throwing us off, and we asked whether the ladies fancied a drink as a thanks for calming the irate man. This area of Lisbon was closing for the night now and there was only one bar still open in the square by the hostel. They were moving their tables and chairs indoors and calling it a night. The bar staff's chance of an early dart had gone as soon as we sat down and ordered a round of Caipirinhas, a cocktail of Brazil, I believe. Quite apt.

An hour later and after having a great laugh, it was time to go, and 'Our Monica' was nearly part of the family. No matter how much Tommy tried to put her off, Bryan was getting her phone number to stay in touch. As the clock had ticked over into 14 February, it wasn't a bad start to Valentine's Day. We headed our separate ways, and all these years later Bryan and Our Monica are still together. Fate plays a strange hand in life sometimes, and a trip to watch the Reds led to two wonderful human beings connecting ... who needs Tinder?

* * *

The alarms burst into life; it was time to head up the coast to watch the Mighty Reds. A day in the sunshine drinking beer in a European square, there's no better feeling. The Portuguese weather had different ideas, though, and the further up the coast we got from Lisbon, the skies became greyer. By the time the train pulled into Porto's 19th-century Campanhã train station, the windows were splattered with rain drops, so we might as well put the shorts away. With the station to the east of the city centre, we had the choice of either a 20-minute walk or a quick metro ride and a three-minute walk to our evening's accommodation. The metro it was, an easy choice as the rain started to get heavier.

Our accommodation was a rather sleek apartment in an old townhouse in a narrow avenue. From the outside, in the rain, it looked a dump, but inside was great, and for €75 we had a smashing apartment. A double bed for the apartment booker (me) and a sofa bed for dad and lad, but we weren't planning on being in here for long. A quick wash and brush-up and we were out again, dodging the showers on a brisk walk down to where all the action was at, on the banks of the Douro river in the heart of Porto.

Under the shadow of the giant Luis I bridge, a standout landmark of the city, was where all the bars were situated, and the afternoon's meeting point for the Reds in town. It would be an amazing place to spend an afternoon in the sun, but there was no sun and certainly no shadow from the bridge. It was wet and cold, and we sought shelter in a courtyard bar opposite the moored pleasure boats, for which there were no customers today. Maybe the warmth of Lisbon was unusual, as in Porto it was coat weather and hiding in bars or under canopies all afternoon.

Bryan decided to go for the local delicacy, the francesinha, a ham and steak sandwich with cheese on top and a fried egg. I'd seen quite a few lads in Porto recommending it, and probably in top restaurants it was great, but in a shabby courtyard bar in the rain it was like a miserable ham and cheese toastie with a fried egg on top. After the previous night's drinking, I was still a little tender, and all I could slowly shuffle down my gut was a plate of chips, with a tentative bottle of Superbock to wash them down. The beer did the trick, or was it the chips? Who knows, but I'd come alive as we headed down the quayside.

We only made one more bar, which had a couple of hundred Reds outside, all huddled under the 'sun' canopies. The canopies were doing a pretty good job of keeping the rain at bay, but just don't get in between the canopies, where an icy river of rain cascaded down. I still had a spare ticket burning a hole in my pocket, but I wasn't the only one. Unbelievably, there were lots of spares floating around. Either loads of Liverpool fans are red-hot lovers and Valentine's Day means the world to them, or it was only Porto in February. It wasn't like we played them every year, it was 11 years since the last visit.

By 5pm it was time to head up the road into the centre of Porto and the main square, where more Liverpool fans were meeting. Dodging the showers was impossible as rain poured down. Legging it between shop doorways was pointless now, you just had to walk as fast as you could and only look up to avoid the trams as you crossed the roads. The 'main square' wasn't even a square, it was a couple of bars on the side of a busy road, the Avenida dos Aliados, and it was rubbish. Before anyone who has been to Porto says 'it's not, it's sound', after an afternoon in the lashing rain and huddled under some canopies fit to burst with the weight of the water, with a thousand Reds, it smelled of wet dog. Even though the beer flowed, it was miserable. It was a long way from sunny Lisbon 24 hours before.

The usual sing-song was going on, but one caught my ear that I hadn't heard before. It went something like this: 'Allez, Allez, Allez'. That's right, that's the one, it was brought to life in the lashing-down rain of northern Portugal. The song that was destined to shape our future was getting louder by the minute as people picked up on it. The concourse inside the stadium that night would give it to the masses, with videos filling social media. You can't underestimate how that song would take us all the way to Kyiv and ultimately become one of the key anthems in the history of our club.

I nipped out to meet José, getting even wetter, but there were still no takers for my spare ticket. However, after being so good, there was no way I could leave him €100 out of pocket and say I only wanted one of his tickets. After a nervy wait at a train station, one stop away from the Avenida dos Aliados, I finally got to meet José. I'd watched every Portuguese man heading my way to see if he was wearing a carnation and carrying a copy of *The Times* (you'll have to Google it), and finally José came around the corner with his mate. He was on to me, obviously I stood out like a sore thumb, I certainly didn't look like your normal Portuguese man, especially with my hair flattened against my skull thanks to the incessant rain.

Have I said it rained a lot? Have I? It was almost biblical now, and there was even a whisper that there would be a pitch inspection and the game might be off. We could have just stayed in Lisbon! José handed over the tickets and was off to his warm hospitality, while I was back out into the rain and hiding under canopies with Tommy and Bryan, and bottles of Superbock. There were still no takers for the ticket, so I said to the lads that I'd head up to the ground and I'd see Tommy inside and Bryan after the match, while watching out for the Porto ultras on my way. Within 15 minutes I was outside the away end looking for a buyer but there was no one looking to buy. I gave up the ghost after a horrible 30 minutes and headed inside with the stragglers. I was soaked through, and my jeans were weighing me down, my trainers sodden. I hoped the Reds would cheer me up, and boy did they cheer me up – what a performance!

As we were in with the home supporters, Tommy and I had vowed to be quiet, but that was in the afternoon, before the Superbock. As the match kicked off, the vow went out the window. The two of us started singing, 'Liverpool, Liverpool, Liverpool,' and several joined in. There were loads of Reds in this corporate bit and, as we found our voice, they all joined in. Gary McAllister was behind us, just shaking his head, laughing. It was a good job no one took offence as Liverpool, resplendent in their bright orange kit, took Porto apart with a great performance, ripping them to bits and winning 5-0. We had both feet in the last eight as the whistle blew, putting Porto out of their misery.

Being in with the home support, Tommy and I were allowed out as normal, but we had to wait for Bryan to come out, as the away fans were held back by the riot police, who had absolutely nothing to do. It was going to be a while before the Reds fans were allowed out so I took the chance to pop into the club superstore, where I could get Charlie something decent as a memento, as if he'd come with me. The shop was empty as the locals had nothing to celebrate tonight and everyone was heading home. On the sale rail was the current kit, and at a bargain price. Charlie would be delighted.

By the time I came out of the shop, the riot police were at the bottom of the stairway and were getting their protective kit on as the fans were ready to be moved. 'Allez, Allez, Allez' filtered down the stairs. Within minutes Bryan was with us and we were in an escort 100 yards to the stadium's own metro station, with half the fans heading into town and the rest to the airport. We were all in great spirits. As always, a few faces were recognised and acknowledged. Tony Acko was with his lad, Big Carl was towering over the crowd. We were all happy tonight, and it's always great to see people on your travels. The Reds had been mustard, and we were going to Kyiv.

As the train bounced back into town it was pushing midnight and, since a bowl of chips in the early afternoon, we'd consumed nothing, so the first stop had to be something to eat. Porto was pretty much closed after our win, this is often the case. We found a cool place down a back street, four floors of different foods, and we chose the substantial burger option. The fancy pizzas and stir fry wouldn't do it for us this time round. After a day in the rain, ending it with a big fat burger and chips and a couple of bottles of beer was just about right. We had a good couple of hours before our beds called us, but it wasn't long before our 5.30am alarm would be blasting out.

* * *

Whoever thought leaving Porto on a train at 6.30am was a good idea needs locking up. Come and visit me in prison, please! Flying out of Porto itself would have been a better option, we all agreed, as after a couple of hours' kip and a 5.30am alarm we were out the door for the 6am taxi. Bleary-eyed and running on empty, the chill of the morning woke us up and the taxi dashed through the wet deserted streets of Porto, and the start of the long way home. As the 6.30am train trundled out of Campanhã station, it was three hours to Lisbon then a 1pm flight back to Luton, leaving loads of time for any problems to iron themselves out. We'd be back in England by the time most of the Reds left in Portugal even thought about heading for the airport and home.

As we landed in Luton it was time to say goodbye after a brilliant few days with great people. Tommy and Bryan headed up the M1 and I headed south by train to Gatwick, knackered but smiling. Those lads and girls in Portugal were lucky to be flying home direct, but for me this was a long way home and it would be pushing 9pm by the time I plonked myself down on the sofa.

Sitting at Gatwick and just about keeping my eyes open now, Twitter was saying that nothing was moving out of Porto, so they were not as lucky after all. The storm that brought all the previous day's rain meant that most, if not all, flights out of Porto were being held and it would be days before people got home. Maybe our way home wasn't too bad after all. Even so, I wouldn't have changed anything. Days later people were still travelling home, even taking flights from Portugal via Germany to get back to England. One lad had two nights in a hotel in Frankfurt … two pairs of undies couldn't have been enough.

I arrived home as the conquering hero. I was done for, but Charlie loved his kit. He felt like he'd been with me and wore it with pride for a few weeks at least. His latest growth spurt rendered it unusable by the time Kyiv came around.

* * *

Kyiv was on everyone's mind, we were all having a quick look at flight schedules and transport connections. It was tough, but there would be some football obstacles to overcome first. With Porto brushed aside, who was next?

Give us an easy draw. UEFA did, Manchester City, it couldn't get any harder, could it. At home in the first leg, we believed that we could beat anyone. Anfield was becoming a fortress again. A new rivalry with the smaller club in Manchester was growing, and at home we had the better record, but at their place it was hit and miss, so this would be a real test. For the home leg, tickets were like gold dust. It promised to be a great night and that's exactly what it was. I had a problem with my auto cup ticket request that guaranteed my ticket, it didn't automatically renew, and my bottle went as I thought I'd lost my seat. Thankfully, though, I was able to secure a seat, not in the heart of the Kop as usual but on the edge of the box in the new Main Stand at the Kop end. It was pretty much where my dad used to sit, so I was hoping for some divine intervention from the old fella. I went to his stone outside Anfield and asked him to bring us luck, and that's exactly what he did. Not that Liverpool needed much luck as they blew City to pieces.

The teams walked out to a fervent Anfield, the crowd having brought a wave of emotion, from a stunning coach welcome outside to inside. Little did we know that the repercussions would be felt for years, all thanks to some idiot throwing a bottle of Kopparberg. A couple of idiots throwing bottles at the coach, what's wrong with them? A fervent wonderful coach welcome was overshadowed by some idiots. In the ground the noise was deafening, and as the first goal from Salah went in, you'd never heard noise like it, until the second went in, a stunning thunderbolt from the Ox, and then the third goal, a header from Mané. It was spine-tingling. After just over half an hour, Liverpool were 3-0 up, and City were shocked to the core. For the rest of the half, every time Liverpool attacked it looked like they'd score. The second half saw Liverpool settle for what they had, and while City huffed and puffed, they didn't produce anything of note. We bounced out of Anfield proclaiming the Kings of Europe. The following week was surely a formality, wasn't it?

City were a fabulous team, though, and they could do to us what we'd done to them. We needed to keep it tight in the first half and give them little encouragement, then they'd run out of ideas. City were used to blitzing teams but struggled the longer the breakthrough didn't arrive. We had our flags and banners, they had their plastic flags; we wouldn't be fearful of going to the Etihad. The teams were greeted with a mass of light-blue-and-white plastic flags around the ground, except for the packed away end. I sat myself down on the couch with my lucky Hat Scarf or a Badge T-shirt and dreaming of Kyiv.

It was far from the dream start we'd hoped for, and we had a nightmare first 45 minutes. We kept it tight for a whole minute, only one minute, and we were rocked by a goal from Jesus, the wrong type of divine intervention this time around. City pressed us, and we couldn't keep hold of the ball. All Liverpool needed to do was get through to half-time, but as it neared the break, within the space of two minutes City hit the post and had a goal disallowed. Liverpool were lucky with the goal, in the post-VAR world it would have been allowed. Pep went mad and got himself sent off, and we all breathed a huge sigh of relief.

Liverpool came out looking like a different team in the second half, and as Pep looked on frustrated from the directors' box, they took the wind out of City. Pep knew half-time had come at the right time for Jürgen and his boys. Just ten minutes into the second half and Pep and City were finished. Mo Salah fed the ball through to Mané, and he nipped between two City defenders and went down under the challenges of defenders and the goalkeeper. As we were shouting for a penalty, Salah took the loose ball and chipped it over Otamendi and into the City net, then headed off to the delirious away end. We went mental. Charlie and I were dancing round the living room, but the away end will go down in the legend of our fantastic club with the most amazing scenes of joy you'll ever see in an English football stadium. The pictures of Salah standing hands outstretched in front of his adoring fans will stay with us forever.

City had nothing left, and as the cameras panned on to Pep, neither did he. His face ashen, their race was run, and after 75 minutes Bobby Firmino put them out of their misery. Forcing a defensive error, he picked up the ball and strode into the area, opened his body up and curled the ball around the goalkeeper and in off the far post. The away end, and the Isle of Man couch, burst into life again with an outpouring of joy. The final whistle saw Liverpool into the semi-finals and all those doubters were now believers. Sleep didn't come easy, and I fed off social media for the rest of the night. The Reds were buzzing. Scenes of Reds at Piccadilly belting out 'Allez, Allez, Allez' played on repeat until the wee small hours. Right, who's next?

* * *

We eagerly awaited the draw, which was Roma to face the Mighty Reds next. The winners would go to Kyiv to face either Bayern Munich or Real Madrid, so there was real European royalty there. Meeting Roma in the semi-final was no formality, so there was no way you could firm up any travel plans for Kyiv. Day trips were already being talked about costing at least £1,000, possibly even more, so creativity was required for the cost-conscious. I was certainly in the cost-conscious corner, with a once-in-a-lifetime trip to the US the week after the final already booked, and needing to be paid for. So I needed to be creative, saving money.

Kyiv wasn't a place where you were going to see flights for £50 unless you'd been bold and booked flights many months before. There were virtually no flights into Kyiv itself and all gateway flights via the likes of Istanbul and Warsaw were sky high. We kept our fingers crossed that we'd at least have to face the cost of a trip to Kyiv. It could always go on a credit card. Roma had unbelievably overturned a 3-0 deficit at home to Barcelona to reach the semi-finals, but beyond an amazing goalkeeper and Eden Džeko, I didn't know a lot about them.

Another day off work was booked and I was in Liverpool by mid-afternoon. I was expecting to see lots of Roma fans enjoying the local hospitality, but around the central parts of town it was incredibly quiet. Mathew Street and the surrounding areas were ominously quiet. Seemingly, many Roma fans had stayed in the Albert Dock, and more ominously the Roma ultras had travelled in under the radar, arriving late at Lime Street from Manchester.

After having a few drinks in town with Mongoose, we took the soccer bus up to the ground and jumped off outside the Sandon pub. The Sandon was rammed and there was no chance of getting served quickly, so we headed over the road to a bar that was also rammed, but at least we got served from the bottle bar. Twitter was exploding with videos of the coach welcome, only a few hundred yards away, and once again it looked brilliant. If you can't play for these supporters there's something wrong with you.

The time was getting on towards kick-off, so we drank up and started to head to the ground. The excitement was building in the streets, there was real anticipation in the air. As we walked past the garage on Oakfield Road and towards the back of the Kop up ahead of us, there was a roar, and a group of black-clad Roma ultras were headed up towards the Anfield Road end, seemingly chased off from the back of the Kop. We didn't see what it was all about but quickly the word went around that someone had been attacked by the ultras outside The Albert pub. That someone we now know to be Sean Cox, an innocent man heading into the ground, attacked by Roma ultras. Sean and his brother happened to be in the right place at the wrong time. They were where they should be, outside the Kop on the way to watch their heroes play. It wasn't their fault a group of 60 ultras deliberately targeted innocent fans outside the ground. As always, the cowards were picking on the innocent.

The teams emerged to deafening roars, the belief that started against Porto, that had built against Manchester City, was now unstoppable and there was no way Liverpool were not winning. They promptly dismantled Roma and blew them away, even with a wonderful goalkeeper in the shape of Alisson Becker. Roma were lucky to even be playing on the same pitch as the Mighty Reds. Mo Salah, who only the season before was also in their colours, tore them to shreds and scored two wonderful goals. While he didn't celebrate his goals, the rest of us celebrated for him. And my how we celebrated. There were limbs flying everywhere, and 'Allez, Allez, Allez' got louder and louder. The soundtrack of the campaign roared us on, and wave after wave of Liverpool attacks brought them more goals, and Roma to their knees. The Reds were 5-0 up with only 70 minutes gone and absolutely cruising. We were Googling how to get to Kyiv for less than a grand. It could have been 10-0 with all the glorious chances we missed, and Lovren hit the bar with a header. It could have been very different as Karius made a mess of an early Kolarov shot, which fortunately hit the bar, but that type of shot and 'save' would ultimately ruin the campaign.

With the job done, Klopp took Salah off to what must be the biggest ovation ever given by the Anfield faithful. Even Gerrard, Dalglish, Fowler and Aldridge and their goodbyes didn't get roars like Mo did. Save yourself for the final lad, job done. No sooner had that thought crossed the mind than Liverpool shipped two goals, slack defending against Džeko and a penalty as the ball hit Milner's hand. They could have scored another couple as well.

We came out of Anfield deflated, if truth be told. No team had ever come back from 5-0 down, but now it was 5-2 and Roma had already scored three goals against the mighty Barcelona in the Stadio Olimpico, so we ended the night a little nervous. What a performance though, going forward we were mustard, but our Achilles heel, defending, was still there. And the goalkeeper? There was still a question mark in that position, as neither Mignolet nor Karius filled us with confidence, but then again the best goalkeeper in the world had shipped five against us. Going to Rome with our front three, there was no way we wouldn't score. It should be a walk in the park, hopefully not a dodgy one on the banks of the Tiber.

There was no way I was going to Rome. I'd always said so, ever since 1984 where hundreds of Liverpool fans were stabbed in retribution for winning the European Cup against Roma in their own backyard. The horror stories and the part that played in the following year's events in Brussels had made my mind up. I love Rome as a city but going to watch my team there, no thank you. I once had the 'pleasure' of being in the Roma end for a home game, and seeing what they were up to has always stayed with me. You can call me what you want, fair play to anyone going, but it wasn't for me. It was for my mates, though, and quite a few of them headed to the Eternal City to watch the Reds. As luck would have it, getting 5,000 tickets for the Stadio Olimpico, I qualified for a ticket and passed it on to Tommy, who was eternally grateful (like what I did there?).

I kept in touch with the lads all day long, happy in the knowledge they were having a great time in Rome and were safe. None of the expected trouble, for which I was relieved. As the day slowly passed in work, the messages from Rome multiplied, and by kick-off time I was happy they were all safely in the ground cheering the Reds on. What an away end it was. Absolutely wonderful to see and hear 5,000 of our lads and girls belting out 'Allez, Allez,

Allez'. From Augsburg a few years earlier, where it seemed our away support was getting older by the day, there was a real youthfulness as you scanned the away section in the Stadio Olimpico. Settling down on the couch with Charlie, we were in dreamland, hugging and cheering within 25 minutes as Liverpool took the lead, lost the lead with the strangest own goal as Lovren smashed the ball into Milner's chin, and then took the lead again and cruised towards half-time.

They only needed to take it easy in the second half, but this is Liverpool, and this was this Liverpool team, wonderful in attack and poor in defence, and they struggled to see games out. Roma needed four goals in the second half just to take it to extra time, and we were nervous. From being in total control we gave away a poor goal as Karius parried a shot straight into Džeko's path (he'd been doing the same all season), they should have had a penalty, and then with five minutes left they get one back as Karius just watched the ball go into his bottom corner.

I know it sounds like I'm picking on him, but it was obvious he wasn't good enough. Once again, all night he was all over the place, but throw in some great stops as well, and it was an erratic performance. Roma launched one last onslaught and, even though they still needed two, I was a nervous wreck, pacing the floor and going to the toilet every 30 seconds. I couldn't bear it. With two and a half minutes of the three minutes of added time played, surely it was all over, then out of nowhere the referee gave a penalty against Klavan. To be fair, he should have given one earlier against Trent. As the Belgian Nainggolan smashed it past Karius, thankfully it was as good as the last kick of the game. Another two minutes to play and you wouldn't have bet on us holding out.

As the whistle blew, we were the same as the players, on our knees, although we were in the living room hugging each other. The boys in red had 5,000 Reds roaring them on, who celebrated long into the night. WhatsApp was alive, and we watched the fans locked inside the Stadio Olimpico celebrate long and hard, and the players kept coming back for more, a real joyous night for our football club. Those scenes will stay with me a lifetime, and yeah, I wished I was there, of course I did.

A nice touch to end on was the players holding a red and white chequered flag emblazoned with Sean Cox's name and You'll Never Walk Alone in his Irish green. As the boys on the pitch and the fans in the stands serenaded each other, singing 'You'll Never Walk Alone', it brought tears to your eyes. All the best Sean, the Kop are always with you.

Up the Kyiv-bound Mighty Reds.

The Road to Kyiv

THE ROAD to Kyiv truly started in the lashing-down rain of Porto. We knew we were going all the way, but nobody knew how good this ride was going to be. This may be the greatest trip to any final ever. The fact we didn't win is irrelevant. If you were in Kyiv, you were possibly not as disappointed as those at home. Kyiv wins the competition for the most difficult Champions League Final to get to. You're probably thinking why isn't he calling it Kiev, it's always been Kiev. Everyone said we're going to Kiev, not we're going to Kyiv (now pronounced as Kee-eev). Kiev was commonly used internationally but is derived from the Russian language and following the Russian invasion it's more appropriate to use the Ukrainian version out of respect to the people of Ukraine. And Kee-eev sounds great in the Scouse tongue.

Istanbul in 2005 saw a few of us take planes, trains and automobiles, but most flew in and out on the day. Kyiv seemed to be the other way around, so you had to be creative with your travel plans.

Day trips were costing at least £1,000, but with the US trip to come, I needed to save money. By the time we played Roma away, after hours of research I'd found what I thought was a decent route. A city called Lviv, in the west of Ukraine, near to the Austrian border, looked a decent option, as you could get a fast train into Kyiv from there. The flights were not cheap at £400, but if we qualified this was my route.

To gamble or not to gamble? Before the home match against Roma, I said if we got to Kyiv this was the route. After Liverpool demolished Roma 5-2 it was 'when we go to Kyiv'. Until the ref blew his final whistle in Rome, though, it was a gamble, and I couldn't afford to waste £400 on flights.

One of the lads in work, Brads, was keen on going to Kyiv, and before I knew it the casual chat at the coffee machine about ways there meant my route was his route, and soon the route of several other travellers from the Isle of Man too. No pressure, it had better work out well. Luckily, Brads' mate is a travel agent, and on the day of the Roma away game he was able to reserve flights from Heathrow to Lviv, via Vienna, with Austrian Airlines. We couldn't do that ourselves, so the only thing he had to do was push the button to confirm the booking, and it had to be straight after the match, if we won. If you were in, you were all in, no messing, no dropping out, otherwise you took your chance that the price would go up or the flights wouldn't be available.

I'd become a master of booking train seats on the fast train from Lviv to Kyiv. It wasn't easy, it was a Ukrainian railways site, what do you expect? After 20 practices I was confident that I'd book successfully when required.

We had five reserved flights for those definite, and they'd get the price at the moment the travel agent pushed the button. There were no cheap ways into Kyiv, however hard you looked. If our man couldn't find one now, there were none left. Hitting lucky with that Roma ticket, I knew guaranteed me a final ticket. I was confident in saying yes, as you didn't want to be going to Kyiv without a ticket.

As the final whistle went in Rome and the fans celebrated long into the night WhatsApp burst into life. Within minutes all the flights were booked, as were the trains, but hotels could wait. Out of interest I looked at the Austrian Airlines site after the match and there were no seats left to Lviv, so the plan had worked. The other lads who couldn't commit pre-match were desperately looking for ways into Kyiv, while others followed us to Lviv via different routes. Mongoose was waiting on success in the ballot, which he ultimately got, and he'd go to Lviv via Warsaw, instead of Vienna, arriving in Lviv 30 minutes before us. Tommy and Bryan couldn't make the early start with us due to work commitments but would catch a later flight via Warsaw and catch up with us on the 6am train in Lviv on matchday, so we'd all arrive in Kyiv together.

Everyone was fast asleep in the house, but I was watching match highlights yet again, and as the clock struck 2am we were all sorted. There was just the small matter of hoovering up tickets for everyone travelling now, although easier said than done. While it was in the arse end of nowhere and murder to get there, thousands were preparing themselves for another European Red invasion.

I was putting quite a bit at risk here to go the match. It was money I could ill afford, and I'd be arriving back home four days before we were heading off to the US on a family holiday. I was warned that if I didn't arrive back in one piece and on time to help with preparations, I'd be in trouble. Nikki's very tolerant but there are lines not to cross. I needed to be considerate. I forgot I also had to square it with work. As luck would have it, I had to be in Gatwick for a meeting on the Thursday before the final, therefore my flights to and from London would be paid for and I'd only need one day off. What a result.

Brads booked the hotel, and a good job he made of it too, the Nota Bene hotel (not a very Ukrainian name, mind you, sounds more Italian), thanks to the wonders of booking.com, and we tagged along. It looked alright, to be fair, not far from the town centre and, more importantly, not far from the train station for the early start on matchday. There were no hotel rooms to be had in Kyiv for less than £1,000 a night, and there were stories of people having booked rooms early, only to be cancelled and told that rebooking would cost a fortune. Hotels in Kyiv had caught on to the fact that rooms that normally went for £50 a night could now attract hundreds if not thousands of pounds more, so accommodation providers were taking liberties.

UEFA had done themselves proud again, the Champions League Final at a venue that you couldn't afford to get to and, if you got there, you couldn't afford to stay. Fans' complaints as usual fell on deaf ears, as did the usual complaints about the distribution of tickets. Liverpool fans will always make sure they get there, though, even 'if there was a game on the moon' and all that. Getting tickets was going to be a real achievement for many. It was a double-edged sword, as you couldn't book your travel without a ticket, but if you waited for a ticket you couldn't book a flight for less than a couple of months' mortgage payments. Thankfully, this time none of those worries for me.

My ticket was sorted, mine and Zil's all paid for and to be collected. I had to give Zil my credit card and he could collect them, although he was named on the tickets, because I'd paid for them on my credit card so they needed my card for him to pick them up. At one point they even wanted me to come over from the Isle of Man to collect them in person. Can you make it any harder? At the last home game of the season, against Brighton, I handed my card over in the hope that he wasn't funding his family holiday to Mauritius on the back of my plastic friend.

It was a massive relief when the tickets were in safe hands. No way were we trusting the post on this one. Mongoose got sorted in the ballot, Our Ian and Kev didn't, Tommy and Bryan had to resort to paying exorbitant prices for tickets in the Real Madrid end from Ticketbis, trusting they'd arrive before their departure day. Mike even touched lucky in the final ballot. With only ten days to go, he too was looking for travel. Lviv was out now as there were no flights in and no trains out of Lviv on matchday to Kyiv, so he settled on flying to Lublin in Poland and then an overnight coach to Kyiv. Remarkably, he'd arrive only 30 minutes before us and 500 yards from the train station. He'd be hanging, but that wasn't a worry, no one was thinking of the way home, it was all about getting to Kyiv in time to watch the Reds win the European Cup for the sixth time.

There was a two-week gap between the last day of the Premier League season and the Champions League Final. It worked out well for me as I could get to the last home game with Charlie and then do the list of jobs, which allowed me to head eastwards at the end of May. The last home game against Brighton & Hove Albion gave Charlie his own 'Kyiv'. We went to Hat Scarf or a Badge (as you all must do) and he got himself a massive red-and-white chequered flag, and he sung 'Allez, Allez, Allez' all afternoon. On a perfectly sunny afternoon the Reds romped to an emphatic 4-0 win, which secured the next season's Champions League spot. The players competed a celebratory lap of honour and received a wonderful send-off. Finishing the season unbeaten at home, Anfield was once again a fortress, surely the start of great things. A Champions League Final to come, we'd come a long way under Jürgen, he'd turned doubters into believers.

As we headed to Frosts on County Road there was only one thing on our minds, Kyiv! Final plans to make, beer to be drunk and Charlie to milk in the celebratory atmosphere. He knew there was no way he was going to Kyiv, but he'd hoped beyond hope that I'd produce a miracle. After the Audi Cup he was ever-expectant, but he'd have to wait a bit longer for his day to come. A trip to Ukraine, where you didn't know what to expect, with no place to stay, no sleep, a tough travel schedule, no ticket, and a potentially hostile reception from local hooligans, it wasn't the place for my 11-year-old.

The departing shout was 'see you in Kyiv'!

* * *

Matchday was Saturday, 26 May, and of course I left home early, Thursday morning, 24 May. A 10am EasyJet flight to Gatwick was followed by a work meeting yards from the runway. Instead of heading back to Gatwick and a late plane home, I jumped on a train into central London's Victoria Station. A quick hop on the tube to Gloucester Road and then the Piccadilly Line for the 40-minute ride to Heathrow, and finally a bus to the evening's accommodation, the Park Inn. Zil and Mongoose were travelling down from Liverpool by train. I checked into the room, which was tiny, so finding Mongoose anywhere to sleep in the room would be problematic. Mongoose had drawn the short straw, but as he was jumping in with us after we'd booked, there were no arguments. It certainly wasn't worth him getting a separate room, as we'd only be in it for a few hours. That corner of the floor over there, that little bit, the little bit where the bin is, under the desk, that looked his best chance. We could rustle up a pillow and a blanket, so he'd be sound. We'd need to be up and out at 4am for our early morning flights, so it was no big deal (says he with the bed).

By the time I'd checked in and made Mongoose's bed (moved the bin) it was gone 7pm when I hit the bar. I was starving and thought a few quiet drinks would help with an early night and help me get up at 4am. Ha, ha, yeah right. Zil and Mongoose had only just left Lime Street, so I needed to stay awake. There was no early night coming. I ordered myself a Corona, a plate of chicken wings and chips, and I was set. Those two were guaranteed to be three sheets to the wind by the time they arrived, so there was no point me staying sober.

WhatsApp messages from Tweedle Dee and Tweedle Dum kept popping up. They were in the big smoke and on their way, drunker with every message. By 11pm I was under orders to get the ale in for the lads' arrival. I did as I was told and we propped the bar up until it closed at 2am; it was bedtime. Mongoose didn't even blink an eye at his bed for the night as he curled up and snored. Everyone had their phone alarms primed for 4am, and they were going off before we knew it, taxi booked for 4.20am, no time to waste.

By 4.45am we were at Terminal 2 and heading through security for our 6am flight to Vienna. Mongoose would be heading to Warsaw at 6.30am. It was that early that hardly anything was open, but we managed to get a coffee and a croissant. We had a cunning plan for Vienna and didn't want to fill up too much. At Heathrow we caught up with Sam (Samantha), Brads and Gilly from the Isle of Man, and introductions were made as we headed to the gate. I don't think they'd ever met anyone like Zil before, his match-going Tourette's in full flow. There were pockets of Reds all over the airport even at this early hour, all heading to different European outposts, all in great spirits. The journey had begun.

Two hours later, a little after 9.30am local time, we were landing in Vienna, where it was absolutely lashing down. It didn't matter, though, as we weren't leaving the airport. Remember the cunning plan for Vienna? Sam's brilliant idea was to use the Austrian Airlines lounge. For €30 there was a comfortable place to relax, showers, free food, free hot drinks, and most importantly free alcohol. We needed something to settle the cup final nerves. That's not true though, there were no nerves on show from any of us, as the run to the final had filled us with confidence and with Salah in the form of his life, he'd take some stopping. Surely 9.30am was too early for drinking? No, you're good to go, as long as you have a biscuit to line your stomach. Breakfast was vegetable curry and the local beer, unless you were Zil, who washed it down with a whisky, or as he did, finish the bottle. Drinking your own measures is dangerous. We got our €30 worth, and we all got to know each other, from passing acquaintances on the boat to firm friends. The quiet areas complete with beds and showers hadn't been used but they were tagged for our return on Sunday.

The exodus had begun, there was a red wave flooding east towards Kyiv. Planes, trains and automobiles were being utilised and it was clear that we were having an easier time than many of them. Heart-breaking news came for many with at least three direct planes from Liverpool to Kyiv being cancelled as landing slots mysteriously disappeared. There was now a rush on to find any way possible to get to, and across, the Ukrainian border. By the time we hit Vienna, Tony Acko and his two lads were on their way to Moldova, others to Belarus and Poland. There were going to be some tales from this trip.

At 12.30 the departure board was showing that our Austrian Airlines flight to Lviv was ready for boarding and the gate was closing. As we walked to the plane, Zil said, 'What the f*** is that?' It was a turbo-prop plane, that is a plane with two propellers. No problem for the Isle of Man gang as we fly on them all the time, but when you're used to jets, they're a bit of a shock. Not that the flight bothered Zil, as he was asleep for most of it thanks to his whisky breakfast.

An hour and 20 minutes later we landed in Lviv, 4.40pm local time, two hours ahead of the UK. We still felt energetic, and the plane snooze had worked wonders for Zil, who'd come alive. There was a distinct lack of airplanes at this seemingly new airport; the Isle of Man was busier. The airport was upgraded to an international airport in 2012. Along with a new football stadium, the 35,000-capacity Arena Lviv, the infrastructure was improved massively to host the 2012 Euros (hosting three group games). Usually, airports had energy but this one was dead, besides an excited band of Liverpool supporters. Passport control is usually a time to be quiet and take things seriously, not today, though, as the border guards were getting their photos taken with our scarves and flags. I thought Brads was going to get locked up, but no, he got a photo with a border guard and was wished the best of luck; they all knew why we were here. We were through passport control within minutes and on our way to exchange our money.

You couldn't change sterling before you entered Ukraine, it could only be changed within Ukraine itself.

As luck would have it, Mongoose had already arrived from Warsaw, and in his boredom he'd already changed his cash for the local currency, the hryvnia (UAH), where every UAH was worth 28p. He was keen to get into town for a pint or two and the taxis were on him. We could wait until town, where we were assured there were exchange booths and banks, as we'd been warned not to use credit cards during the trip as cloning cards was rife. We headed outside and caught a legitimate taxi from the rank outside, which had a meter and everything. Another warning for us was that taxis would try to rip you off. Everyone was on the make in the Ukraine, it seemed.

Even though I'd told everyone about Lviv, I knew absolutely nothing about it, other than it had an airport we could fly into, and a train station that connected to Kyiv. Lviv was a revelation, a city of over 750,000 people, the cultural heart of Ukraine and a seat of the last revolution, a place of beauty and learning. Not that our first impressions were that good. As the taxi pulled up at the Nota Bene hotel in the middle of a scruffy neighbourhood, a shiny new hotel plonked right in the middle of dusty roads, broken pavements and knackered old cars, it wasn't a good sign. Inside, the hotel was a different story, with the smell of fresh paint and new carpets. The rooms were fine, Mongoose had a two-seater couch for his bed tonight, a step up from the floor at Heathrow, whereas me and Zil would be sharing a king-size bed. Sleep would be easy tonight, after only two hours the night before.

Time for a quick change and we were out into town; it was nearly 6pm local time. While the others waited for a cab into town, we braved the 20-minute walk into the city centre. We threw a left from the hotel, walked a couple of blocks and were out on to the bustling cobbled main road into town. Not many main roads are cobbled nowadays, are they? Over to our left was a bus station. I gathered it was the station, as there were loads of knackered old buses blowing their fumes into the sky. The bodywork, more filler than bodywork, was just about holding them together, with people all looking miserably out of their windows. It was the end of a tough week by the looks of it.

Life looked tough here, even tougher when we saw what the local hawkers were trying to sell. There was a lady trying to sell lollipops from a tray around her neck, like a cinema usherette in the old days. There was one old fella, and in his box, one of those balsa wood boxes that hold mushrooms, he had a potato, a carrot and one piece of broccoli. He was selling that! He wasn't successful either, as from the looks of him he wasn't making ends meet. The people looked drab, exactly what you'd expect from a previously communist state. The way we're conditioned to believe people live is exactly how the people of Lviv were living. I'd never been anywhere like it.

Over to our left we could see the train station. You couldn't miss it, grand and unbefitting of its surroundings. From our local map we knew we weren't too far from the town centre and, as we neared, tramlines appeared. The first decrepit tram we saw was in keeping with the current surroundings. The second, though, was sleek and modern, something you'd see in a modern European city. This was a sign of things to come. To our right a big church bore all the scars of the Second World War, when Lviv was occupied by the Nazis, bullet holes of varying sizes all over the building. The occupation by all accounts was brutal, and a Jewish population of over 100,000 in 1941 became less than 800 by the end of the war and liberation by Soviet troops. Now the Russians are to be feared, after the latest invasion.

We walked along Svobody Avenue (try pronouncing it, you'll be here all day) and we entered a different world. Gone was the squalor of the outskirts, it had now become a city of grand buildings and huge monuments. A monument to Taras Shevchenko, a 19th-century poet, writer, artist and political figure, and the man who's the symbol of Ukrainian nationalism, dominated the main boulevard. Little did we know that within 24 hours his name would be written into Scouse folklore for ever, thanks to Boss Nights.

It had been a long hot walk into the city centre, and we needed refreshment. Within sight of the monument was a bar with a beer garden, as good a place as any to take stock and see what the city had to offer on a Friday night. We had menu in hand, thankfully with English translations, as Ukraine uses a Cyrillic script and there was no chance of us understanding anything it said. Three pints of Kronenbourg to start off with as we perused the food on offer, and it was quickly decided that we wouldn't be eating here. The savory (that's the spelling) wings, wings of what I don't know, followed by the crunchy pork ears, meant we'd wait until later. A couple of pints later, and there were Reds coming and going. Lviv was a starting point for their journeys tonight, overnight buses or trains their choice of transport. With a long day of travelling already under our belts, I was glad we'd be bedding down here for the night.

We fancied seeing what the city had to offer on a balmy Friday night, seeing what Ukraine was really like. Remember, tomorrow was going to be a Scouse takeover of Kyiv, which would make it feel very much like home. We wanted to see Ukraine for itself tonight. We followed the locals through an alleyway filled with bars and restaurants and entered a big square with the town hall at the centre of it. The place was teeming with people, a proper Friday night out, and the travelling Liverpool fans mixed well with the locals in the streets and bars as welcomed guests.

The early evening sun had a real warmth to it, and we found seats outside a small bar that had Wi-Fi, which was a bonus. I was incommunicado, as we'd been warned that mobile data costs were extortionate, and the advice was to only use Wi-Fi where it was available. That made communication difficult, but Wi-Fi allowed me to call home so Nikki and the kids could hear I was alright. It's a strange world we live in where we take communication for granted, the immediacy we have with messages, calls and videos. As we picked up our messages, we knew Tommy and Bryan were at Heathrow and Mike was on his way to Warsaw. Plans were made to meet Tommy and Bryan at the train station at 5.30am and for Mike to meet us off the train in Kyiv. Once everyone was in Ukraine, we didn't know when we'd hear from them again.

This was like the 'old days' when you'd tell people you'd meet them at a certain point at a certain time and god forbid you weren't there (you'll need to explain that to anyone under 20). Over a bottle of Jet Black Heart, a vanilla milk stout, we surveyed the scene, all wishing we'd chosen a different brew, as it was every bit as bad as it sounds. It came with a free glass of water ... must be to wash your mouth out. We held our nose, necked it quickly and went for a look around the square. Will we ever learn that drinking craft beers never ends well? The quick answer is no, we'll never learn. Never!

We walked around to the far side of the square, avoiding the ramshackle trams that plied their trade around the edges, as the good people of Lviv promenaded up and down the cobbled streets. There was a lovely feel to the city with people sauntering around with ice creams. It was like many major cities in Europe, different to our first impressions. People were dancing in the square, 'arty', 'bohemian', call them what you will, they were having a great time, old or young, it didn't matter that they were exchanging partners after every song. The music? A slow type of jazz, I'd say. Another couple of craft beers and I'd have been up for a dance too, but Mongoose and Zil are not the dancing types

We'd done a full lap of the square, and we went off to investigate the other side of Svobody Avenue. The clock was nudging nine as we stumbled into the Winston Churchill pub. We might find a drink we recognised in here. No chance, it was the local grog, craft ale again. Mongoose hates it but it has a strange magnetism to it. I picked the one that looked closest to normal lager. Looks are deceptive, though, and it tasted terrible. One pint was enough in the Winston Churchill, and it was time to move on, change some money and get some food.

Back on to Svobody Avenue, we'd seen an official exchange office and went to change our euros to hryvnia. We'd found out Lviv was cheap as chips and it was proving difficult to spend too much, but I assumed Kyiv would be normal football prices and a fiver a pint. You still needed your wits about you to not get ripped off, and knowing the going rates for taxis, etc. is always a good start. With the minimum of fuss my euros were changed for a fistful of hryvnia, and I paid what I owed Mongoose, who'd been bankrolling us in Ukraine.

We were unanimous in our choice of kebabs for tea. If we had one now, we wouldn't need one at 1am. There was a kebab shop 50 yards away, the wonderfully named I Love Kebab (Love being a heart), which looked busy and clean, always a good sign. Mongoose was in charge of ordering. Choosing a small kebab wasn't allowed, and not having hot sauce wasn't allowed either. Three large chicken kebabs with hot sauce it was. The place lived up to its name. While the kebab was the size of a horse's knob, the taste was sensational, and the hot sauce removed all lingering tastes of the stout and craft beers. We were ready to go again, or should we go to bed? Early start in the morning and all that. No chance, we could sleep on the train in the morning.

The *Liverpool Echo* had been telling everyone that the Lviv Liverpool Supporters' Club, yes there is such a thing, would be delighted to host travelling supporters for the night. It was the eve of the cup final, we'd done our cultural bit and now we were looking for something livelier. As we entered the bar, the Wi-Fi was found and messages pinged on our phones. Mike was on the bus from Poland, bedding down for the night. Tommy and Bryan had let us know that the plane into Warsaw to connect to Lviv was going to be late, but the airline would hold on for them. The next message told us that the plane hadn't waited for the 30-plus Reds on the flight and they were stranded in Warsaw and working on plan B. They wouldn't be on the train in the morning.

Wasn't great, knowing your mates were struggling, but we were here, and we were guests of the Lviv Liverpool Supporters' Club. They'd taken over a cellar bar in the Stargorad brewery, and it was obvious that the party had been going for a while. A mix of local supporters and travelling fans, the welcome was warm, and the beer cheap. They had the Istanbul 2005 game on a loop, and we were into the second half. Cheers greeted the goals and, as it went to 3-3, spontaneous choruses of 'Allez, Allez, Allez' bounced around the room in varying qualities of English pronunciation. From Liverpool to Lviv, we were all one.

The travelling fans started to drift off around midnight, as Saturday was going to be one long day, especially as most of us had nowhere to stay on the Saturday evening. We headed off too, discretion the better part of valour. We'd seen Liverpool lift the European Cup in Istanbul and tomorrow we'd be seeing it again, five hours down the train tracks in Kyiv. We headed off into the warm night air with 'Allez, Allez, Allez' ringing in our ears. We jumped into a cab outside and after a wild taxi ride were back in the hotel. A swift nightcap and we were away in the land of nod, sober enough to set an alarm to ring at 5am. Mongoose on his couch was snoring as soon as his head hit the pillow and we weren't far behind him. A night on the ale does that, but fingers crossed we wouldn't be paying the price in the morning.

Wine for my men, we ride at dawn!

See You in Kyiv

THE ALARMS all burst into life bang on 5am and it will have woken the whole hotel. Taxis arranged for 5.20am, there was no time to hang around. All kitted out in our matchday gear, it was going to be a warm one, shorts the order of the day along with a lightweight jacket just in case there was a chill in the night that followed. Depending on what happened, we might be scraping around for somewhere to spend the night, bars, cafés, McDonald's or even parks before our 6am train back to Lviv on Sunday morning.

In reception we found Brads, Sam and Gilly. We hadn't seen them at all on Friday night as the city was much bigger than we expected. The owner of the hotel had come down in his undies and wished them luck. The giant of a man was big mates with the mayor of Kyiv, none other than Vitali Klitschko, and he was raving about his mate, a guy called Oleksandr Usyk. We'd never heard of him, but it certainly looked like they'd been working out together. We could leave our bags at reception until Sunday morning, meaning we didn't have to lug them round Kyiv or find a safe place to leave them. Anything of value was with us – passports, and money – and travelling light was the order of the day.

We jumped into two battered old taxis and headed off to the train station. By 5.30am we were outside the grandest of stations and there were Reds everywhere. The 6am train was a sell-out; this was the only train that would realistically get you to Kyiv in time for the match. A five-hour fast intercity train, when was the last time you took a train journey of five hours anywhere? In Britain that length of journey would take you from London to Glasgow; it was a long trek we were undertaking. The train would get us to Kyiv at 11am, giving us time to explore and enjoy what the city had to offer.

The thermometer was nudging 17°C, and it was a beautiful morning as the sun rose over the grand railway station. Regardless of the early hour and long journey ahead, there was a real buzz around the station as Reds arrived in taxis or on foot from the surrounding areas. The pilgrimage was in full flow and surely replicated in many places within reach of Kyiv. Supplies, namely coffees, water and snacks, were purchased in preparation for the journey. The kiosks on the platforms dated back to the early 1920s by the look of them, and that included much of their stock. I took the opportunity to get a hot coffee, brioche and some snacks, a breakfast of champions. You never knew what you might get on the train, if anything, as it's not unheard of to have a train with no buffet car or service, so best taking no chances. Water was required as many of the passengers were somewhat dehydrated following the previous evening's escapades in Lviv.

We found our seats in first class, wider seats and free Wi-Fi that actually worked – take note Virgin, at £25 return it was brilliant value. With Wi-Fi we had confirmation that Tommy and Bryan hadn't made the train, and they were still trying to get across the border from Poland, but would meet us in Kyiv. Mongoose was delighted as he'd booked into cattle class but ended up taking Tommy's first-class seat next to us. The last message from Mike was that his coach was waiting at the border to get into Ukraine, but that was hours ago, and we didn't know where he was up to. There were definitely a few stories to be told when we all caught up; this was going to be a glorious day.

The station's electric clock's orange lights ticked over to 6.07 and the train slid gently away from the platform. We were off, the train was rammed and everyone was off to see the Reds – an eclectic mix of Scousers, Wools (non-derogatory term, before anyone shouts), Reds from all around Europe and then the drunkest of all, the Lviv Reds who'd come straight from the Stargorad brewery. Most people were thankful of the opportunity to have a bit of a quiet start, but not the Lviv Reds, who were already on the ale and telling everyone they were conquering all of Europe from their second-class lodgings. By 8am, Brads and Zil had joined them as well, taking the edge off their matchday nerves.

The outskirts of Lviv slipped away and we headed into the lush green countryside of western Ukraine, as the miles started to slip away from Lviv and closer to Kyiv. The countryside was dotted with grand gold-domed churches, in the middle of nowhere but a place to pray. By all accounts, Ukraine, especially western Ukraine, is very religious, with Orthodox Christianity being the most practiced faith. As with many churches, the money going to the church is often not in keeping with its surrounds – peasant villages with gold-domed churches doesn't sit too well, does it. From what I saw out the window, admittedly while travelling at 170 kilometres an hour, it looked a beautiful country, and there was so much of it. There wasn't much between Lviv and Kiev, and a country of 42 million people didn't have many inhabitants living between the two cities. Ukraine is, remarkably, the second-biggest country in Europe, after its neighbour, the mighty Russia.

As the miles rolled by and Kyiv got closer, the sense of anticipation grew. Now was the time to make those last-minute plans, as in Kyiv most of us would lose the ability to communicate, unless at a prohibitively high cost. There was still no word from Tommy, Bryan or Mike, other than they were trying to get across the border, but that was hours ago, and we assumed that no news was good news. As always, I'd made plans to meet people on the way as well, good lads off Twitter who were also travelling this route. It would be easy to meet up when you had five hours to spare. I was trying to meet up with Swifty, Andrew to his family, but all I had to go on was that he'd have his flag with him. I knew what his flag looked like but all flags were in bags or overhead bins, so I was relying on the 'looking lost' way of being seen, hoping he'd spot me stalking through the carriages. It was all to no avail, but on my way back to my carriage I did bump into Tony Evans, the journalist, author, real ale lover and Scouse raconteur. If you read my first book, you'll know it was Tony who was a big part of making it happen. He's always willing to support and guide and I know a lot of people are better off for knowing him. As always, we promised to catch up in Liverpool, but it's not happened yet, up to now it's been London, Milan and somewhere in western Ukraine.

The train rumbled through the outskirts of Kyiv, and we got our first glimpses of the city. It was pretty much what you'd expect of a city built in the communist era, even on a sunny day it was dark and bleak. Then again, in many cities in the world the train rumbles into the middle of the most marvellous of cities through urban blight. Try Rome or Paris, for instance, there's no sign of the Colosseum or the Eiffel Tower from the train tracks. What did Kyiv have in store?

Because of the short time between planning and execution and focus on travel and tickets, I'd paid little attention to Kyiv as a city, all I had was the information that came with the match ticket. The train lurched to a halt at Kyiv Pasazhyrskyi station (now to be referred to as 'the station' for obvious reasons) and we were off, a red tide flowing up the platform on to the escalators up to the overhead bridge. At the end of the bridge a pair of escalators took us down to a square main concourse. On the right-hand side as we looked was a huge arrivals and departures board, all in Ukrainian. The only thing I could understand was the numbers of the train and the times, which we'd all need for the following morning.

The train ticket had the Ukrainian translation for Lviv, so we'd be fine, even in an expected state of tiredness and potential drunkenness at 6am on a Sunday morning. Nineteen hours in Kyiv, let's get cracking.

And there he was, Telly Savalas, if you're old, or Ross Kemp if you're young; whichever one you choose, his baldy head was glinting in the sunlight. Mike had arrived and I shouted across the concourse, 'I told you I'll see you in Kyiv,' always a man of my word. I know that feeling of relief I had in Istanbul when I travelled on my own and you meet your mates in a far foreign land, there's nothing better. Where were Tommy and Bryan, though? We still didn't know, as there had been no word for hours. Brads, Gilly and Sam were off to meet the rest of the Isle of Man gang, heading to the soon to be legendary Boss fan zone at Shevchenko Park.

The huge central train station had a metro station attached, tramlines to wherever, and random buses, alongside hundreds of taxis vying for fares. Mongoose said it didn't look far on the map, maybe we should have a walk, as we'd been on the train for five hours. Stretching our legs wasn't such a bad idea. Facing the station was a long boulevard, Tarasa Shevchenko Boulevard, a road named after that fella's statue in Lviv. A huge park bordered the right-hand side of the boulevard, and we stuck to the edges of the park. The city had changed from dour to bright and beautiful and we were heading towards its centre and the Dnieper river, which runs all the way from Russia down to the Black Sea coast to the south, some 2,000 kilometres. The buildings were getting grander and more European, wide boulevards with fancy cars reminding me of France and Spain. Only the language was unfathomable, but this looked like a great European city.

At the top of the boulevard was Shevchenko Park, home to the fan zone. It was only mid-day, but it was already full of food stalls, portable toilets and drinks stands, and the little fountain in the middle opposite the stage already had people bathing in it, as it was much warmer now. I don't know who said it, but someone did: 'It's going to be a nightmare in here isn't it.' How wrong they were. Now, if you think I'm going to regale how Jamie Webster ripped it up, John Power had the crowd in the palm of his hands and the pyro was lit and there was a constant red mist, sorry, I can't, because I didn't see any of it! We planned to go back but, once we left the park, things didn't happen as planned. My Kyiv experience was different to many others and that's what probably made it great, but I still wish I'd seen Jamie and John.

We had a good look around the park and there was a statue of that fella from Lviv again, it was his park after all, and he was casting his steely gaze over masses of Liverpool banners. The authorities had put up barriers around the statue to protect it from over-enthusiastic fans, but by doing so they gave perfect hanging space for banners celebrating the journey to get here and even poignantly remembering Sean Cox. We headed against the red tide and down towards the stadium. Every other Red in Kyiv seemed to be heading towards Shevchenko Park.

Two hundred yards from the park entrance we turned right on to a wide boulevard. To our left were numerous pavement cafés, a place to remember for after the match. Then another right on to a boulevard that was closed off to vehicles, where people were strolling in the lunchtime sun. We walked down the boulevard, flanked on the right with bars and cafés, a place for pre-match drinks later. Halfway down the boulevard we turned left and there it was, the stunning Olympic Stadium.

It was already hot, so after a quick look at the stadium and our entry point, we decided it was time for a pint of the cold stuff. Only 100 yards from the entry gate and serving Belgian beer was the Belle Vue Belgian Beer Café (go figure). All the way to Ukraine to drink Belgian beer. We took the opportunity to use the Wi-Fi, and while quenching our thirst to see what Kyiv had to offer and how easy it would be to get around. An update from Tommy and Bryan said they were on the way by car and hoping to make kick-off at the very latest. Tony Fields had flown in from John Lennon on a day trip and was heading to Shevchenko Park, where Mongoose would meet him. Zil, Mike and I thought we'd head into the city for an hour or two before meeting them back in the park.

We headed across to the metro station, taking the escalator into the bowels of Kyiv. It was one of the longest escalators I'd ever been on, and what we found at the bottom was beautiful. A cavernous platform, adorned with huge chandeliers and ornate tiling. Where most metro stations worldwide are purely functional and clinically modern, Kyiv tips a nod to the ornate stations of Moscow (I believe). The ageing carriages on the train were from times gone by, it was like a bygone era (I guess the 1960s when the metro opened), and it was cool. The train hurtled towards what we assumed was the city centre.

Assumed, I say, as there was a lot of guesswork going on. The Ukrainian language doesn't lead to educated guesses as do Spanish, Italian and French. I've never felt that out of my depth anywhere in the world. Maps didn't seem to help, and asking for directions wasn't easy as the majority of locals we met didn't speak English, or if they did, they certainly didn't understand the Scouse accent. We guessed at our stop, hoping to be near the city centre and the UEFA Fan Zone with its huge Champions League trophy. We knew it existed from pictures we'd seen on Twitter the previous evening.

We headed out into the beautiful afternoon sunshine and looked for directions, but all the signs were in Ukrainian and there was no chance of us understanding, so we asked a policeman, 'Where is the centre, mate?' He didn't speak a word of English, he didn't have a clue what we were asking for, but he beckoned us to follow him, which we dutifully did. As he led us through the back streets and alleys, he could have been leading us anywhere, but thankfully he led us to a public square that housed a flea market and then pointed up a hill on the other side of the square and directed us towards a cobbled street. We walked through the market and there was little sign of a Champions League Final happening later in the day.

We headed up the cobbled street, not knowing what our ultimate destination would be, but we did know we now needed the toilet. Once Mike said that he needed to go, we all needed to go, and there was only one place to find a toilet, in a bar! We found a small open-air bar, opposite an 'Unofficial Chernobyl Museum'; honestly, it was identified by a head in a gas mask, obviously not to be confused with the larger 'official' museum. A table full of Reds were all in high spirits, and songs and laughter poured out the bar. We took our seats and ordered the local beer. We took it in turns to use the shed in the corner that doubled up as the bar toilet.

As the beers arrived, one of the lads from the table next door ordered us shots of vodka. He promised us we'd thank him later, it was 'wonderful'. What was it? Horseradish vodka was what it was – doesn't sound too appealing, does it? Hold your nose and lash it down your neck is the best advice I could give. As the thermometer hit 33°C, it sent a warm feeling through your veins, as if it wasn't warm enough already. At 20p a shot, the lad was buying us more. There was that much being consumed that the bar sent out for more bottles. It was the local brew, and in that bar, in that place, at that time, it was the best drink in the world. There was no way we were taking a bottle home, though. From a quick toilet stop we were here for the long haul.

As the afternoon wore on, visiting Reds from all over the world came to sit with us, and locals came to see what the fuss was all about. Sergei and his missus came and asked in decent English whether they could sit with us. It turned out that Sergei was a semi-professional footballer, a goalkeeper no less, with a team from Kyiv who were in the Ukrainian third division. Who were we to question him, the fact he was chubbier than me, which was some going, and under six feet, we let him crack on. Anyway, Sergei was much more interested in practising his English, talking about Liverpool, drinking vodka and telling us about life in Ukraine. Mo Salah came to join us for a picture or two. He was as close as we were getting to Mo Salah, his name actually was Mohammed and he was from Egypt. He was loving the attention, and he'd become a Twitter sensation overnight. He was more than happy with us serenading him with the Mo Salah chant, to the tune of the La's 'There She Goes'. He loved it that much that even after he left the bar, he'd walk past it again, knowing we'd strike up the song.

It was 4.30pm; where had the afternoon gone? We needed to look at heading back towards Shevchenko Park and meeting Tony and Mongoose. We decided that walking further up the hill in the heat wasn't a great idea, therefore we headed back down to the flea market and the metro station there. We found a Ukrainian groupie who wanted a picture with a Liverpool fan, and she chose Mike. She was 60 and had few of her own teeth left, so don't let Mike tell you she was young and gorgeous. She spoke not a word of English, but he made her day posing for a photo. I'm not sure the picture will find its way on to her mantelpiece, but you never know. As a ballerina pirouetted past us, we knew it was time to go. Man, that Ukrainian vodka was strong.

Ten minutes later and we were back at the stadium, where it was busier than when we left at lunchtime. We walked back up the boulevard towards Shevchenko Park, walking against a red tide. The events at Shevchenko Park were over and people were on their way to the stadium. Hunger struck us, and on the corner of Lev Tolstoi Boulevard was a chip van, which was all we needed. It served chips, chips with mayo, or chips with BBQ sauce. Chips it was, anything to mop up beer and vodka. How were we going to meet up with Tony and Mongoose now? Well, if we stand by a chip van, they'll find us, and that's exactly what happened, they appeared out of nowhere. Besides Tommy and Bryan, we were all together, which was amazing considering the communication difficulties.

We headed back towards the stadium and found a bar, but there was no chance of getting served. Luckily, there was a shop next door that sold warm cans of beer. We had a great spec by the side of the road and watched the thousands of Reds flooding towards the stadium. With every passing group a new chorus of 'Allez, Allez, Allez' would burst into life. From the flooded streets of Porto, the song had been our anthem on the way to Kyiv and now it was lifting the hope and spirits of thousands of Reds. Nobody was thinking this wasn't going to be our night, how could we not win it? Nobody was nervous, as our run to the final had shown that we were the best team playing knockout football in Europe, so we would not be beaten. No one was thinking about getting beat. We'd score, and with Salah in the form of his life our name was on the cup.

Time to move on again and head towards the ground, back to the Belle Vue bar, where miraculously you could get to the toilet and the bar. The early evening was still warm and at 8pm local time it was still two hours to kick-off. As we were standing outside the bar, who should pop up but Tony Acko and his lads, Anthony and Harry. They'd trekked all the way from Liverpool via Moldova and had some tale to tell, but it would have to wait for another day. The lads were keen to get inside, and who could blame them, it's not every day you go to a Champions League Final. We could see the stadium gates and it seemed orderly and well controlled by the authorities. There was no panic at the gates, and there was no need for us to panic either. We took our time finishing our drinks then headed past the bored squads of riot police, who had nothing to do. There had been no problems all day, and it didn't look like there would be either. Easy money for the robocop boys.

We headed to the gate, me checking my pocket for the hundredth time that day to ensure my golden ticket was safe. It was finally seeing the light of day. I scanned the barcode, and the light went green, I was in, the sense of excitement from all around me at fever pitch. There's no better feeling than being with your mates in a far foreign land going to watch the Reds play. This was the biggest game in years and the memories of Basel two years earlier had all gone, this felt different. As we entered, we met Gaz and Phil, who sit in front of us in the Kop. I've lost count of how many times we've seen these two and their compadres around Europe. It's not a European away without seeing these two, and as long as Phil's not farting it's sound, as some of his second-half deliveries at Anfield are disgraceful. We headed towards the concourse serenaded by 'Allez, Allez, Allez'. It's amazing that we weren't fed up with it yet, but it had spurred us on for months, so one last go and everyone was giving it loads. The noise was deafening.

We were on the cusp of greatness. As long as Salah, Mané and Firmino turned up, we should have too much for an ageing Real Madrid team with their fading *Galacticos*. When you're on the cusp of greatness you want the right people with you, and as always I had Zil by my side. Istanbul changed at half-time when I joined him, at winning cup finals I'm usually alongside him, and once again tonight. Basel? I was alongside Mongoose, and remember how that turned out. I've been going the match with Zil since 1985 and we've shared some amazing days.

We said our goodbyes to everyone else, arranged our meeting point for afterwards, obviously the Belle Vue bar, and headed for our seats. There was no surprise at how many Reds were in there. Officially we had 16,000 tickets but unofficially there must have been up to 40,000. In a stadium that holds close to 70,000, with half the tickets going to the 'UEFA family' and sold on the secondary market, the allocation to the clubs is pathetic. Now was not the time for complaining, though, as we were luckier than most and had the golden tickets. We took our seats, only ten rows back from the front and in line with the corner flag on the right-hand side of the massed Liverpool ranks. To give some perspective, our eye level was crossbar level, so seeing things down the far end of the pitch wasn't easy.

An hour to kick-off and the Reds were in great voice. This was going to be our night, our lads were in the form of their lives, just no soft mistakes, and we can score against anyone. 'Allez, Allez, Allez' rippled round the ground constantly, only to be interrupted by renditions of 'The Fields of Anfield Road'. The players were out warming up and their songs were being sung – Mo Salah, Sadio Mané and Virgil van Dijk all recognised the thousands of us who'd travelled so far, and many in such trying circumstances that these lads could never know. As the players left the pitch, they knew we were right behind them. After that night in Rome the bond had become ever closer, the love between the fans and the players there for all to see. As the players left the pitch, the ground staff prepared the stadium for the cringey pre-match show.

As an old man, I'd never even heard of the pop star singer (that shows I'm old, doesn't it), Dua Lipa, who'd be singing her number-one single, 'One Kiss'. I can't remember the last time I actually looked at the charts. I thought me and many others were ready to drown out whatever she was singing with our own songs, it's what football fans do. Much to my shock, as she bounded on stage and as the first beats of the music dropped, Dua Lipa sang 'One kiss is all it takes, falling in love with me,' and our end started bouncing, fists punching the air. Suddenly, I was old beyond my years and the kids had taken over. Everywhere I went during the summer of 2018 she was in my ears, and Scouse weddings for years to come will have it on the play list. It might even replace Freda Payne's 'Band of Gold'. As Dua Lipa shimmied off stage in her sequinned shorts it was our turn to sing our song, and an uplifting version of 'You'll Never Walk Alone' was belted out with real passion and feeling.

At 10pm local time and with the temperature still nudging 21°C, the Reds kicked off with a guttural roar from the massed ranks of Kopites behind the goal. The stadium was occupied by a majority in Red and there were pockets everywhere, even in the Madrid end, where many of the tickets on Stub Hub and the likes had surfaced. The view that Madrid fans wouldn't travel was unfounded, but the spares were generally in their end. Saying that, next to me were two Ukrainian fellas with their girlfriends. Not once did they crack a smile or say a word. The lads showed an interest in the football, but they didn't seem to support anyone until Real scored. It was annoying, as we were in the cheap seats that were sold by Liverpool, and it was obvious that Liverpool fans who'd qualified had sold them on, probably at an enormous cost, while there were loads of good people at home, including my two brothers. I nearly ended up fighting with the Ukrainian lad next to me, and anyone who knows me will laugh at that as I'm definitely not a fighter, I'm the peacemaker, but after a belly full of horseradish vodka I wasn't taking getting shoved in the back by a dickhead. Me shouting, 'Don't shove me, dickhead,' was obviously not being understood. Thankfully, Zil swapped places with me, and the dickhead sat down. That's as close to *The Football Factory* this book is going to get, sorry.

The first half started well enough, with Liverpool having the better chances and the Real Madrid goalie, Navas, keeping his side in it with some smart interceptions and a good save from Trent Alexander-Arnold. It was obvious that Real were targeting Salah, who they were clearly scared of, and he was on the end of a couple of rough challenges, most notably from Marcelo. And then came the challenge that changed the game.

In the 25th minute, Salah received the ball and wriggled past Sergio Ramos. As he was getting free of him, Ramos hooked his arm and deliberately brought him down. I'm not saying he deliberately put him out the game, but he knew exactly what he was doing. The referee didn't even give a free kick. Mo Salah was left writhing on the ground, holding his shoulder. The Reds' end of the stadium went quiet, and we held our breath. Mo received treatment and at first looked like he was going to play on, but soon it was obvious he was done, and he went off in tears. We all felt like crying as well. It knocked the stuffing out of us all. Lallana came on to replace Salah, but our talisman was gone. The Reds looked lost and Real Madrid took control. They had the ball in the net, but Benzema was thankfully ruled offside. It was a case of Liverpool getting to half-time, regrouping and letting Jürgen work his magic, and it was a massive relief to get to the break. I remember shouting at Karius to calm down and take his time as we needed to take the sting out the game, but obviously he wasn't listening.

The second half started, and they were right at us. Within minutes, Isco hit the bar and we were rocking, then the ball went over the top and ran through to Karius. What an experienced goalie would do is to hold on to the ball and calm his team down, but Karius wasn't experienced. In his naivety he tried to roll the ball out quickly but he threw it against the boot of Benzema. The ball rolled agonisingly into the back of the net. Were our eyes deceiving us? Even with a low-down view I could see right through the players and could see what happened, and the replay on the giant screen only made it worse. Karius was complaining, as were many of us in our end. Surely it must be a foul, but for what reason? There was no reason, though, it was just a really bad mistake. Again, the wind was taken out of our sails, and we couldn't honestly see a way back after the way we'd played since Salah departed the pitch. There was now little hope.

Within minutes, though, we'd changed our tune and with a real defiance we cheered the Reds on. Within four minutes, Sadio Mané had nipped in front of Navas and steered Lovren's header into the Madrid net right in front of us. The Liverpool end erupted. Out of nowhere we were back in it and the Reds had the stadium booming with, yeah you guessed it, 'Allez, Allez, Allez'. We were roaring the boys on; it wasn't the first time they'd had to dig deep this season.

Real were rocking and they replaced the ineffective Isco with the usually ineffective (against us at least) Gareth Bale. As substitutes go it wasn't one that I feared. Bale had been struggling at Real and there didn't seem much love lost between him and coach Zinedine Zidane. Then it all changed. We were level for a mere seven minutes, and with the Reds on top and pushing for the second, Marcelo put a hopeful ball into the middle, where Bale, with his back to goal, scored a stunning overhead kick with his left foot, beyond Karius's outstretched hand. There was nothing he could do about this one. Sometimes all you can say is, wow, what a goal. It was worthy of winning any cup final.

If that had been the final goal it would have been much more palatable, but it wasn't. With Liverpool going on to the front foot again, Mané hit the base of the post. We were right in line with his shot, and it looked like it might turn in, but to no avail. Then the hammer blow. Bale picked the ball up on the right-hand side and cut infield. From 40 yards he unleashed a left-foot shot. I looked down, as it was right at Karius. Next time I looked up, the ball was in the back of the net and those in white at the far end of the stadium were going mad. It had inexplicably squirmed out of Karius's grasp and into the back of the net. It had pace and dip on it, but he should be saving it. I wouldn't mind but he'd made a couple of great saves after his first error, but now unfortunately he'd handed the cup to Madrid.

And the dream was over. Liverpool huffed and puffed, Madrid drew foul after foul, Modrić controlled the game, and we sung, and we sung. We sung 'You'll Never Walk Alone' in support, but we knew the game was up. However, we were going nowhere tonight, it wasn't as if we were close to home, there were no cars to jump into and have a quick getaway. We all stayed to thank the boys. What a ride they'd given us, from creeping out the group stages to smashing Porto, followed by epic ties against Manchester City and Roma, some of the greatest nights that will live long in our history. A massive thank you to Jürgen and the boys in Red. Karius cut a disconsolate figure as the players came on to the running track before us. They actually get it, they get the sacrifices and the effort and appreciate the support. That's thanks to Jürgen.

For me it goes back to salvaging a point against West Brom and Klopp lining the players up in front of the Kop, German-style, bowing. We'd not looked back since and the love between the supporters and team was so strong. You win as a team and you lose as a team, but as a goalkeeper you'll never escape the criticism of bad mistakes and, ultimately, it was those mistakes that cost us. They'd also cost the young German goalkeeper his Anfield career.

* * *

What next? You're nearly 2,000 miles away and can't start the journey home until 6am in the morning. What are we going to do now? That's right, drink to our Mighty Redmen, we'll toast the magnificent men with the Liver bird on their chest. Don't let the result get you down, we'll be back stronger next year, this wasn't a one-off. There was disappointment, and I've heard lots of people say they were devastated at the result, but most of them were at home. Anyone who made it to Kyiv rarely says 'devastated', probably because of the overall experience.

We met up outside the Belle Vue bar but there was no chance of getting in, so we headed up the road towards Shevchenko Park. At the crossroads we threw a right, as the masses headed left towards the park and the awaiting coaches that were heading back to the airport for flights home. Fifty yards down the road and the first bar we came to had a bottle bar outside so we plonked ourselves there for a while and took time to understand what we'd witnessed, chewing over bad luck and poor mistakes and those seven minutes after Mané scored when the ground bounced, and we believed. Ultimately, though, we were resigned to the fact that we came up short, all while sipping our first bottle of beer. By the time the second bottle of beer had been bought we were laughing.

You wouldn't have believed only an hour earlier we'd trudged away from the ground; it was gone 1.30am and still warm enough to be outside drinking. Big Dave and his lads Tom and Matty had joined us. Then Tony attracted a couple of the local drunks, who for some reason wanted to show off their new Bluetooth headsets while drinking the Ukrainian version of White Lightning. These boys looked the worse for wear, they looked like rough sleepers, their clothes filthy and their skin not too far behind. They looked like they'd managed to make a few quid on the day from Reds throwing them a few coins. If you have nothing, you have nothing, and these boys looked like they had nothing. They did have enough to buy a couple of bags of cans, though. They were nice enough fellas and were even offering us a can of the local grog. Then for some unknown reason the local drunks had their shirts off, comparing six-packs with Tony. Tony took one look at the scrawny fella in front of him and gave him a new Liverpool T-shirt he had in his bag. That fella was made up and said he'd support Liverpool for the rest of his life. It doesn't take much to be kind, does it? Well in, Tony.

As the clocks ticked round to 3am the crowds started to disperse, as many made their way back to airports for early morning flights home. It got moodier with a few of the local idiots trying to rob flags from outside bars. As Dave and his lads moved on, it was also time for us to head somewhere else. Just a couple of hundred yards down the road a big shopping centre and its neon lights were inviting us in for a late drink. A bar in the far corner, attached to a VIP strip club, whatever one of them is, but it was good enough for us. The velvet doors protecting the strip club and its participants weren't getting opened by us, or by anyone else for that matter, as asking the local equivalent of £30 wasn't appealing to anyone. We settled for a seat by the window watching out over the shopping centre. We'd be fine as long as we had a drink in front of us until it was time to head to the train station for the 6am train back to Lviv. It wasn't long, though, before a few of us were taking the knock, me and Zil that is. The lack of sleep, a long hot day in Kyiv and the copious amounts of vodka finally caught up with us.

First it was Zil whose head went back on to the couch, and we roared with laughter, at which point he woke up and started singing. I wasn't laughing ten minutes later when my eyes gently closed and I drifted off, still hearing the noise around me but making no sense of it, until the big fella behind the bar started shouting at me in broken English, 'No sleeping, no sleeping, wake him up.' I woke from my slumber, got a beer in my hand and started drinking again. They don't like lightweights in Kyiv. Good job it was nearly time to go, and by 4.30am we were back off to Shevchenko Park. We walked through the now quiet park, the scene of a raucous afternoon just 12 hours before. Mongoose and Zil took the opportunity to use the portable toilets. They were brave men, especially while we were rocking them. Mongoose came out moaning about splashbacks, as we ran away to a safe distance.

The sun came up as we wearily made our way back down the main road to the train station. We were all starving now, but no kebabs tonight, the McDonald's at the station looked a safe bet. The walk down the hill had started the long road home, but Kyiv will be forever in my heart and mind. At 5am in the morning and the last thing we'd eaten was a tray of chips over 12 hours ago, so anything would do. The golden arches of McDonald's are every traveller's friend, usually a safe bet, you know what you're getting.

It was nearly time to say goodbye to our travelling companions. Tony was already on his way to the airport, and we were off on the express train to Lviv. Mike headed to the nearby coach depot for his 14-hour coach trip back to Lublin, it was a long time until he'd see a bed, but probably still before us. That left Mongoose, who couldn't get on the express train and had to make do with the slower train taking seven hours, leaving 50 minutes after us. I couldn't have asked for a better group of boys to do the trip with. Hugs and goodbyes and 'I'll see you next season'. With our goodbyes done, we staggered on to the escalator and rose to the gods and towards the platforms. One last effort to haul ourselves up off the platform and into the train, those first-class seats a welcome relief to our weary bodies.

* * *

The train was much more subdued than the journey to Kyiv 24 hours ago, the excitement replaced by exhaustion. No matter how young or old you are, what we'd done in the last 24 hours is enough to finish anyone off. We were back with Brads, Gilly and Sam. We hadn't seen them in Kyiv, but we were all too tired to tell them about what we'd been up to. By the time the train lurched forwards and the wheels turned to take us to Lviv, most of the train was asleep and the morning sun was starting to warm the carriage up.

I must have got about three hours snoozing on the train before I woke and headed to the café to get a morning coffee to take the edge off the tiredness. Once you've woken up, you're not going back to sleep, are you? I stretched my legs and walked down the train through second class and to the buffet car. As I did, who did I find but Tommy and Bryan. They'd made the train home at least and they had a story to tell. Not yet, though, it could wait until Lviv, where we'd catch a couple of hours with them before we flew home. The train ride was for sleeping.

I headed back to my carriage with coffee in hand and the others were all stirring by now. We caught up on our day's events, and Brads, Gilly and Sam regaled us of stories of an afternoon in Shevchenko Park and Jamie Webster ripping it up. All we had was horseradish vodka and a goalie from the Ukrainian third division. I still wouldn't swap it, we had a great time, just different. They'd met up with others from the Isle of Man who'd travelled various ways, day trips from Liverpool and trips via Belarus. We might be 80 miles away by sea but, man, we're passionate about the Reds. I'd said to loads of people 'I'll see you in Kyiv', but it just didn't happen. Blame it on the vodka.

As the clock ticked past 11am, we trundled through the outskirts of Lviv, and at 11.09am, bang on time, the train shuddered to a halt and 600 weary Reds hit the platform. I even caught up with Andy Swift from Twitter, but he was incapable of talking, his voice had gone after three days on the ale and cheering the Reds. We found Tommy and Bryan, who had a room booked in Lviv for the night, which they headed straight to, and we arranged to meet them in the central square. We headed back to the Shevchenko monument where there was a Ukraine national day being celebrated, and as the centre of Ukrainian nationalism it was a sight worth seeing. We caught up with Tommy and Bryan, a lovely way to finish our Ukrainian adventure, sitting in the sun, having a pint and catching up, and boy did they have a story to tell. A story of missed planes, dodgy border crossings, bribes and contraband, washing in wells, and vodka for breakfast, but that's their story to tell.

Unfortunately, we couldn't sit in the sun all day, we had a plane to catch. We headed from the square to the Shevchenko monument and found a taxi rank, where the first taxi driver asked for 2,000 hryvnia, when we knew the fare was only 200. He must have thought we only arrived yesterday, when in fact we arrived on Friday, less than 48 hours in Lviv, but we were no mugs. It was the difference between a real fare of £6 or an inflated one of £60. The next taxi driver told us it was 200 hryvnia, so we jumped in with him and, for being honest, we gave him 400 hryvnia. He was made up, a reward for not ripping us off. Twenty minutes later we were at the airport and, after ditching our last hryvnia, we headed through security and into departures.

You know that feeling when, suddenly, you're exhausted? It hit me just as I was putting all my gear on again and filling my pockets after the security check. I had this real urge to go to sleep right there and then. The initial boost of energy from this morning's nap was gone and it was going to be a long way home now, arriving in Gatwick at midnight then on to the Isle of Man the following morning. The airport was empty except for our flight to Vienna. There were about 50 people in this huge airport waiting for the turbo-prop plane to take us to Austria in time for the connection to London Heathrow.

At 4pm local time we were waving goodbye to Ukraine. What a country and what a warm welcome we had from the people, like nowhere I'd ever been before, and there's not often you can say that nowadays. As the landing gear was raised, our eyes closed and we snoozed until the bumpy landing announced our arrival in Vienna. Then it was straight to the Austrian Airlines lounge and a shower, bite to eat and a bit of a snooze before our 8pm flight to Heathrow. Getting an hour back in time meant we had a decent wait in the lounge, but the beer was much harder to get down this time round and they'd removed all bottles of whisky, which was probably good news for Zil.

Brads was first into the shower before anyone sat down, and the rest waited for their turn patiently. I must admit I've never felt so refreshed after a shower, as a wet wipe for ablutions over the last 36 hours hadn't made me feel fresh. We caught up on all the social media content from the last few days, and we saw how great Shevchenko Park had been. The descriptions from Brads, Gilly and Sam just couldn't do it justice, how could they? It looked amazing. We tortured ourselves and watched the goals over and over again, we relayed our stories of a fabulous Friday night in Lviv and our 24 hours in Kyiv. No one who travelled will forget Kyiv.

We finally got the call to go to the gate after further delays and headed to Heathrow. I then realised I still needed somewhere to sleep for the night, as my flight back to the Isle of Man wasn't until 8am Monday morning, so I needed a bed. I was officially too old for this nonsense. Ahh, I'll be grand at Gatwick, there's always rooms in the Premier Inn, never let me down yet. The flight to Heathrow was a blur as we took what's known in Liverpool as 'the knock', and we still weren't finished.

As the plane touched down at Heathrow Terminal 2 it was time for more goodbyes. Zil's next leg was a tough ask, needing to be back home for Monday morning, so he was on a coach out of Heathrow at 1am, which would get him back in Liverpool at 7am. The next leg for me and the Isle of Man Reds was a taxi from Heathrow to Gatwick where all bar me had a bed for the night. The taxi made great time and we pulled into the Premier Inn car park as the clock was hitting midnight. I'll get a room and have some decent kip. Wrong! There was no room at the Inn for me, but I jumped on their website, which

I should have done in the first place, and there was one room left at the Premier Inn at North Terminal. It didn't matter what it cost, so I tramped the quarter of a mile back to the terminal and the Premier Inn. By 1am my head hit the pillow, then at 6.30am it was off the pillow again, and by 7am I was in the terminal checking in and through security to departures. With a coffee and pastry in hand, I headed for the last plane of the trip.

The last goodbyes from a fabulous trip were said to the Isle of Man gang at Ronaldsway airport, where I'd be back in four days' time to head west to the US with the family. Nikki, Charlie and Izzy were pleased to see their wanderer return, as it guaranteed the holiday would happen. At least it was a bank holiday and there was no work, so we headed for a coffee in nearby Castletown to enjoy the early morning sunshine. We might not be European champions this year, but we see things others won't see, and you can add Ukraine to that now. Oh yeah, Mongoose and Mike were still in Poland, and they were still a good 12 hours from home. Next time you watch a match played abroad, just think it's probably going to be a few days before some of those boys and girls get home.

I still say for me this was the greatest trip to any final ever. The fact we lost is largely irrelevant, thanks to the people I was with and the experiences we shared. Many people will have very good memories of Kyiv and their journeys to get there. The disappointment did last throughout the long summer, but this was only the start of something. We all knew this was different to the feelings after Basel just a few years ago. We were all looking forward to what was to come next, and what came next would be glorious.

* * *

As a sorry footnote, on 24 February 2022, Russia invaded Ukraine and things would never be the same again. The places we loved and the Lviv Reds who warmly welcomed us were either under attack or wary of attack. The nightly news shows rockets attacking Kyiv and reporters using Lviv as a safe base to report from. I think often of those lovely people and places and what they face. Hopefully, they'll never walk alone.

Wunderbar

AT MY age there's not much I remember from being a kid now, not without photos to prompt the memory. Things are fading fast, too fast. As the hair starts greying, jowls fattening up, belly hanging over the belt, my gait is getting more pronounced and I strain every sinew just to get up off the couch. Old age was well and truly on its way as I rolled into my mid-50s. As you get older you can feel it, things start creaking and you need to start adapting. High blood pressure, low cholesterol and all manner of health issues are on the way. My childhood was so far from my memory, probably because of what I've packed in since I was 18 years old. There's little space left to easily recall childhood memories. Sometimes places and events can drag your memories right back.

December 2019, and Liverpool had crept out of their Champions League Group after a great performance against Napoli that was nearly undone in the last seconds. If it wasn't for the intervention of our new super Brazilian stopper Alisson, I'd be writing about the Europa League, and probably a trip to the arse end of nowhere. Making himself as big as possible, he denied Napoli a goal that would have sent us tumbling into the Europa League. As I jumped off the couch, I fist-pumped the air, hugged Charlie tight and danced around the living room. The last 16 of the Champions League beckoned. Who would we get in the last 16? There were some big names left, and some great trips to be had.

As the balls came out, there it was, BOOM! Big name, tick, great trip, tick, Bayern Munich! Massive ticks all round. Get in there. I'd been waiting since 1981 for this draw. In all my match-going years, never before had we got the chance to play them in competition. As you already know, I'd taken my opportunity to go to Munich before the Augsburg game and the pre-season Audi Cup with Charlie. Bayern away in the European Cup (let's not call it the Champions League and defo not the UCL), this was going to be special, EasyJet, Twitter and WhatsApp showed that everyone was off to Munich – boss city, boss stadium, just boss.

What about the memory? It was our back room, as in the back room of the family home, it was 1981, with me and my dad, him sitting in his armchair, cigarettes in hand, me pacing up and down, chatting incessantly. I must have been driving him mad. We were listening to the radio commentary coming from the Olympic Stadium in Munich, or if you prefer the Olympiastadion. The stadium, the shape of a bird's nest, is one of the classic European stadiums. A big bowl with a running track surrounded by huge stands full of 75,000 Bavarians, and don't forget there were thousands of Reds there too. They, the Munich fans that is, were expectant, believing they were certain to be going to the final in Paris. Bayern had actually printed directions to Paris, and recommended hotels to stay in for the final a few weeks later. They reckoned without the Mighty Reds, though. Paul Breitner, I believe, called our boys boring and unimaginative after a 0-0 draw at Anfield, where they came to stifle Liverpool, believing they could beat us on their home turf. A 0-0 draw in Europe at home in the first leg isn't always a disaster, the away goals rule meant that a slip from the home side in the second leg would leave them wide open.

Back to the memory. Our Kev and Our Ian kept coming in and out but I remember it being mostly only me and my dad, ciggies in hand (dad), more as a comfort than anything, his actual smoking waited for half-time. We were confident, we were Kings of Europe a few years earlier and we could take anyone on, with Dalglish, Rush, Kennedy, Hansen, we had quality everywhere on the pitch. My dad had a lot riding on it, as without saying anything, I knew he'd be off to Paris, why wouldn't he? He had been in Rome and at Wembley, it was what he did. Me, I'd be watching at home whatever happened.

Kick-off came and the noise was immense as it boomed out of the radio, and as only radios can do, everything was edge-of-your-seat stuff, and with Clive Tyldesley commentating on Radio City, even more so. With his evocative commentary you could feel the tension in the air. Soon it looked as though it wasn't going to be our night, as Kenny Dalglish, our King, was injured and the news was bad, he was coming off, with only nine minutes gone. Who was Bob Paisley bringing on? How light was the bench? And with real surprise in his voice and surprise in our house he brought on Howard Gayle, a local lad from Toxteth. This was the year of the riots in Toxteth and it was an area that was creaking under the weight of race relations, and police and community relations were at an all-time low. Howard, or as we knew him, Howie, had made it into the Liverpool first-team squad, and in an era where there were few black players, never mind from Liverpool, he stood out. He stood out as a beacon of hope for the community in Liverpool 8. Could one of our own be a hero, and that being one of our own who was black, it could move on race relations.

To put this in perspective, this was the 80s, and no matter what everyone says about our city now, it wasn't integrated in the early 80s. Being from north Liverpool there were few black faces on the streets this side of town, but the south end was a different matter. However, the two sides rarely met or mixed, south and north, never mind black or white. Many of Liverpool 8's community were second- or third-generation immigrants and many spoke with strong Scouse accents and were starting to get jobs in the city council, for example. A greater acceptance came as people became friends. Liverpool as a football club and fan base was still not fully accepting until the signing of John Barnes in 1987, and the inherited racism and disrespect started to dissipate.

Howie Gayle was unknown outside of Liverpool fans, and even many match-going Reds didn't know a lot either. He was a squad player, seemingly not trusted to hold down a position and only sporadically used as a substitute. There were questions about his attitude and temperament and he was never considered as having the ability to break into the team of superstars. Young Scouse lads had struggled for years as Liverpool bought quality players as opposed to created them. This was before Gerrard, Owen, Carragher and Trent Alexander-Arnold. We were a buying club, we often bought well, but local lads tended to ply their trade elsewhere and then came back, as did Terry McDermott, David Johnson and Steve McMahon.

In Munich, though, we had more home-grown talent than we'd had for a long time: Colin Irwin, Terry McDermott, David Johnson and Sammy Lee started, and Howie and Jimmy Case were on the bench. Now here was Howie coming on in the Olympic Stadium to face the mighty Bayern Munich. Could we hold out and take it to penalties, surely it was a damage limitation exercise. It was a masterstroke by Bob Paisley, though, as the Germans knew nothing about him either. Howie didn't care for reputations and he ripped the Germans to bits, he got battered, he was hacked down as the Germans couldn't cope with his pace, and he made them retreat towards their own goal as, all by himself, he kept all of their back four busy. There was the most blatant penalty you could ever see, obviously not given as the referee bottled it. We could only imagine what was going on from the descriptive powers of the commentator, but Howie was doing Liverpool 8 and the city of Liverpool proud, he was one of our own. He was taken off after 70 minutes, not before he'd torn the Germans to shreds for 61 minutes, but what a 61 minutes.

As the game edged towards the 90-minute mark the nerves got more frayed and my pacing up and down increased. Dad started smoking instead of playing with the cigarettes. He couldn't stay still, he stood up, then sat down, then told me to sit down because I was making him nervous. I've just realised that I've turned into my dad! I realised that it's me now watching the match with Charlie, kicking every ball, heading every corner away, going upstairs when the opposition have a corner, as they don't score if you're not in the room.

Get in there! Out of seemingly nothing, Ray Kennedy took the ball down on his thigh and, even though obviously injured, smashed a shot on the half-volley that flew low into the bottom corner, beating the goalkeeper's outstretched hand. Cue dancing and hugging and fist-pumping (wasn't even a thing then). That goal was worth two with the away goal, as Bayern now needed to score twice. Liverpool only needed to see it through, hold on for the last ten minutes. Bayern equalised very late but the Reds did see it through, and all our thoughts turned to Paris, and ultimately becoming European champions again.

One day I'd be going to go to Munich, like those Scouse adventurers who I could hear singing our songs through the radio in our back room. That one day took nearly 38 years to arrive. Every year you looked to the draw, kept your fingers crossed, and every year was a let-down, it just never happened. I was always gutted, but there are loads of great places to go in Europe aren't there? Yeah, but Munich, one day. As you know, I eventually got to Munich, playing Augsburg gave me the opportunity to at least have a night out there, and it didn't disappoint. I got to take Charlie too. While an amazing trip with my lad, it wasn't the same as playing Bayern in what I hoped would be a frenzied atmosphere with thousands of Reds painting the town red (of course).

Now to search for a favourable route. The match was to be the return leg and was due to take place on 13 March. Within days prices of direct flights to Munich from Manchester, Liverpool and Gatwick were already sky high, so I was looking at good connections. The beauty of Munich is that it's connected to everywhere. It's generally easier, and cheaper, for me to travel via Gatwick Airport, which has an amazing array of destinations to which you can fly, and EasyJet's main hub there should give plenty of options. Getting from outlying airports shouldn't be a problem. On the EasyJet website I checked Gatwick to anywhere for the day before the game and most of the German airports were already heavily booked and prices high. One airport did stand out, and I knew it was close enough to be an option. Innsbruck, across the border in Austria. A quick check on the Trainline website showed that there were over 20 trains a day and you'd be in Munich in under two hours from the centre of Innsbruck.

It wasn't even Christmas Day yet and Christmas had come early. Isle of Man to Innsbruck (via Gatwick) for only £130, not bad. I'd have to throw in a Premier Inn stay at Gatwick on the way out, but I'd be fresh to go and be in Munich for early evening the day before the game. Call it a Christmas present to me, from me; better than socks and undies isn't it?

March couldn't come quickly enough for the trip to Munich, and at the end of February I took Charlie across to watch the first leg against Bayern at Anfield. As we walked up from Kirkdale station to the ground, the streets below County Road were full of Bayern fans. They'd been escorted out of town early and stayed drinking around Barlows Lane, below the looming shadow of Goodison. They were loud and boisterous and many were clad in lederhosen. Charlie couldn't quite make out what he was watching, but they were all good-natured and considerate of Scouse passers-by, even if they were pissing anywhere they wanted (remember that). If only anyone had anything to cheer that night, but it was a poor game all round and ended 0-0. That would do us, we'd definitely score in the Allianz. Bayern couldn't sit back like they did at Anfield, their fans would demand more. With echoes of 1981, it felt as if they thought they'd done their job, and their home form would take them through. Let's see!

* * *

The momentous day came and I headed for the airport, much to Charlie's disappointment. I think he was still holding out hope of a last-minute surprise return to the Allianz, but this was for the big boys only, his time would come. By 10pm I was in the bar of the Premier Inn at the Gatwick North Terminal. I met my mate, Arthur, from Jersey, an old-school Red, been away from home for 30 years but every waking hour Liverpool FC is on his mind. He was with two of his best mates from Jersey, both exiled Scousers, Solly and Ricky. I'd never met these fellas before but over the next three hours it felt like I'd known them forever. None of them had tickets yet, but it was a trip to Munich, too good an opportunity to miss for a lads' trip away. We drank beer, ate pizza and drank more beer until there was no more beer. They had an early flight, but I could get a good few hours' kip as my Innsbruck flight didn't leave until 10.30am. They'd be in Munich by the time I took off. With the promise to meet them the following night in the Hofbräuhaus, we all staggered off to bed.

Tuesday morning and a decent flight time to Innsbruck, fully refreshed and a Premier Inn breakfast smashed, I headed through departures at Gatwick Airport. I was looking to catch up with a Scouse lad, Gary Shaw. I'd met Gary on a show called *That's What We Call History* that I did on *The Anfield Wrap*, a review of the double-winning season in 1985/86; there's not many of us who remember that season. I went to every game, home and away, seeing every minute of the double-winning season, not a bad thing to be able to say. Gary and a lad called Mike Nevin had written a book on the period and we had a ball recording the show. We'd hooked up on Twitter and, as luck would have it, Gary was taking the same journey I was, so it would be good to catch up. A plane doesn't hold that many people, does it? But trying to find him at the departure gate at Gatwick was like finding a needle in a haystack. There were quite a few Reds on the flight and, as I got on, I caught sight of him right down the front. I'd catch him in Innsbruck.

If you ever want to fly into somewhere really special, try Innsbruck, the flight path gave me the most amazing flight I've ever taken. On a beautiful sunny day we flew in over the snow-covered Alps and then back up a valley bordered by mountains to land at the head of the valley surrounded by snow-capped mountains. I've never seen that many people interested in what lay outside the plane's windows. As we stepped off the plane you could taste the alpine air, mixed with the whiff of aviation fuel on the gentle afternoon breeze. I caught up with Gary on the short transfer to the terminal. It was a short bus ride into town and, with a decent mix of Reds, there was an excited babble on the bus about what lay ahead of us tonight and the match tomorrow. As it turned out, the rest of the Reds were staying in Innsbruck for the night and sampling the delights of the Austrian city before heading to Munich in the morning. It was a new place to visit for many. Why not have two cultural experiences in one trip, one German and one Austrian. I needed to get to Munich, where Mongoose was waiting for me. He'd travelled down that morning from Berlin, where he'd spent a couple of nights.

Innsbruck is a beautiful place with a real old-world feel to it, but plonked right in the middle of it is a modern train station that's so out of place. Think Euston as opposed to St Pancras. There was still over two hours until our train and I had a job to do, while Gary was going to refuel in the station restaurant.

What sort of job could I have to do in a provincial train station in Austria? In a month's time Nikki and I were taking Charlie and Izzy on an Inter Rail tour of Europe. Something that Nikki and I had both done in our youth and thought would be a great trip for us as a family.

Europe by train, there's no better way to see it. Most of the trip was planned to the minutest detail and booked thanks to the internet, but there were some things you couldn't do online. I kept hitting a brick wall with the most crucial part of the trip, an overnight train from Venice to Vienna, with the Austrian train company OBB. The overnight cabins could only be booked directly at a train station in either Italy or Austria, now who would be able to do that? Hold on, I could, it would only take five minutes and I'd be back next door having a pint and some schnitzel.

How wrong could I be. Finding the booking office wasn't hard, finding the right queue wasn't that easy but making yourself understood was nigh on impossible. There was only one man in there who could speak English and he wasn't too keen to help. Ultimately, I was being such a pain in the arse for the whole booking office that he had to help, while muttering Austrian expletives under his breath. It took him five minutes to do what was required, but 45 minutes to try to avoid doing it. I said, 'Danke, mein herr,' to which he looked somewhat bemused, as I mumbled on the end of it 'knobhead'. Don't think they know what a knobhead is in Austria.

By the time I got back to Gary he was already a couple of pints in and nicely full after a plate of the local grub. It was less than an hour until the train. Gary said the service here was painfully slow and you couldn't guarantee your food would arrive before the train, so it was just a pint of the local brew for me. 'I'll eat later.' Famous last words. Another pint and we were ready to go, heading to the platforms via the station shop for Pringles and a few bottles of the local brew, Gosser, a lovely beer. As we hit the platform up to our right-hand side, at the end of the platform (that went on forever) was a huge ski jump. It was still cloaked in snow, a reminder, if the air temperature hadn't already told you, that it was still early March and the ski season was still running. I might check that ski jump out on my return on Thursday.

Somehow Gary had wangled a free ticket from the train guard to go to watch Munich 1860 play that night, but he was cutting it fine to drop his bags at his hotel and get to the match. However, with all the Scouse confidence in the world, it was happening. Munich 1860 no longer played at the Allianz, which they had previously shared with Bayern, they were now back in the much smaller Grunwalder Stadion, holding 15,000. They sell out regularly, so getting a ticket was a result. I had other plans with Mongoose, Arthur and his mates, and warmer venues than a football stadium.

As the train rolled into Munich Hauptbahnhof we said our goodbyes and I headed towards Goethestrasse and our evening's accommodation. Mongoose had sorted the room out again and hit gold, as he often does. I sauntered through the concourse to find him waiting for me. He'd been on his own for two days now and wanted company and to 'get right on it'. The accommodation, the Hotel Andra, was a real find, clean, centrally located and breakfast thrown in. A huge room suitable for three, as Zil, currently in Berlin, would join us on matchday. A five-minute walk from the station, a quick change and within 20 minutes we were back out into the chilled Munich night air. Good job I brought my big coat.

We threw a right out the hotel and a quick left and were on our way towards the Hofbräuhaus. It was quicker walking than going to the station and catching the metro. Arthur and the lads were standing outside the Hofbräuhaus. They'd closed the door to football fans already, 'Zu voll,' (too full) according to the bouncer who was taking no reasonable argument to get inside. People leaving didn't agree with the bouncer's version of events, though, saying it was pretty quiet, but we were the 'wrong crowd' tonight. It was only half-seven and many places were already refusing entry. It wasn't the only place saying no, the Irish bar over the road was the same, so we headed away from the main tourist area.

As we were darting in and out of the busy evening traffic, Arthur was with me and Mongoose, then all of a sudden Rick and Solly were gone. We didn't know whether they'd found a bar or not as none of Arthur's calls were returned, so we decided to get in the first bar that would accept us. The first to let us through the door was more of a restaurant, but it had a bar area where you were expected to wait for your table. It was full of Reds waiting for beer without the food. Every time anyone in the bar burst into song, which they were regularly prone to do, the restaurant staff were shouting for quiet. It was a losing battle, especially as the steins were being sunk with regularity. They closed the doors behind us and no one else was allowed in. The diners had long given up on having a quiet night out and waited for the rowdy Reds to leave for pastures new. After a few steins it was time to go. We were still tickled that Mongoose and Arthur looked like father and son, and even though Arthur gave Mongoose a 20-year head start, it was Arthur who looked like the son.

We got a message from the lads saying they were in Kennedys Irish bar, a ten-minute walk away. The fresh air would do us good. Oh yeah, and I needed something to eat soon, as I'd had nothing since the Pringles in Innsbruck. We got to Kennedys and there was absolutely no chance of getting in. It was rammed and the sweat dripping off those leaving supported that fact. The bouncers were allowing no more people in. 'Zu voll.' It was the story of Munich. There was a bar/restaurant a few doors up the street and we nipped in there, where they were showing Champions League football, so we thought we might stay a while. Once again the bar area was rammed, and the diners, mainly Reds, would have to put up with the noise from the bar. The staff weren't too happy, though, even though they were making a fortune. One waitress took a particular dislike to the customers in the bar area and was constantly ramming the stoneware steins into our backs. One of the lads put a stop to that as he slide-tackled her on her return. VAR would have ruled it a certain red card. She went mental, he protested his innocence and it looked like the barman was going to sort him out, then he realised there were loads of us spending our money and he took her out the back. She came back with a slightly different attitude. Arthur took this as his cue to leave and get an early night, as he'd only been on the ale for 12 hours. Must be his age.

It was time for us to go too, 20 yards to Kennedys, which was still bouncing, but you could get in the door now. The lad who'd slide-tackled the barmaid was now leading the singing, and the songs were bouncing around the room, the Reds in full voice, until the local police decided we'd all had enough and closed the bar down at just gone 1am. The bar staff looked relieved, it looked as if they'd been on the go all night long, but the owners must have been laughing. With some slight cajoling from the security staff and the police, there was no need for any truncheons or any bother, we slowly edged to the exit and out into the night air. Funny, it didn't feel cold anymore, maybe it was that thick beer jacket we were wearing.

It was definitely time for something to eat on the way back to the hotel. Thanks to Mongoose's early afternoon scout around he knew that if we walked from here to the central station and threw a left we might get a swift nightcap and a kebab. He was spot on as usual. At the top of one of the side streets near the station was a sports bar, and the crowd was spilling out on to the street. I was told in no uncertain terms it was my round, regardless of how hungry I was. I said to Mongoose that he must be starving too and then he told me he'd had a pizza while he was waiting for my train and he didn't need anything. He hadn't mentioned it all night when I was going on about being hungry. It wasn't the first time he'd done that, made me starve and getting me hammered.

Off I toddled to the bar, and some 20 minutes later he comes in with a face on him. 'Where's the ale, knobhead?' he shouts, but I couldn't hear him over all the singing.

I was enjoying myself singing with the lads, and I'd decided that I didn't mind if everyone got served before me. Mongoose shouted to the barman and got served right away. Sound, I was still singing 'Si Señor, give the ball to Bobby …' We'd picked it up in the back streets of Pigalle in Paris before playing PSG and it had grown on its way to Germany. Outside we bumped into the guys from *The Anfield Wrap* and Charlie's mate, Melissa Reddy. I think we must have been too drunk for a proper conversation as she made her excuses and left, sorry Mel.

It was definitely time for a kebab now, I couldn't hang on anymore, and 50 yards down the road I could see a kebab shop. I stumbled off, leaving Mongoose to his beer. Lemon's Kebap shop in Munich, get it on your list of late-night places to eat, it was spot on, a massive chicken kebab (kebap in Germany, by the way) and I was sorted, no need for any more beer. It was gone 3am and time for bed. Mongoose was ready and we were off. We'd walked virtually all the way back to the hotel on a pub crawl, so the bed was a welcome sight. Roll on matchday.

* * *

Matchday came along with a booming headache and a sensitive disposition. The free breakfast pretended it was helpful but not sure it was going to stay where it was for long. Right kids, it's not big and clever to drink as much as we did the night before. It's brilliant, but certainly not clever. The only plan we had was to be at the train station for 12.30pm to meet Phil and Gaz, who were on a train coming from Nuremberg. They had a spare ticket for us, and Tony Acko could have it for one of his lads. Zil's train from Berlin was due in at 3pm. The great thing about Munich train station is that the food is great and I was looking forward to some ribs for lunch, even in my delicate state.

We decided to have a walk to clear the cobwebs, and a fair old walk it was too, up to where the Boss Nights fans event was taking place later that afternoon. There was nothing going on, it hadn't even opened yet, so we turned right round and headed back to the nearest metro. As we were leaving, the Isle of Man guys turned up looking considerably fresher than I felt. It wasn't hard, to be fair. We had a quick chat but we were running tight on time now to meet Phil and Gaz to collect the priceless ticket. As we were heading back to the station the weather took a turn for the worse. There had been rumours that weather may affect the match. As we stepped foot on the station platform a mini-tornado hit us. That may be a slight exaggeration but it was windy as hell and the rain started lashing down as we dived for shelter, yet within seconds it was over with and spun off towards the city centre. We jumped on the next metro and followed the tornado's path to Munich Hauptbahnhof, five minutes down the line.

Munich station is a sight to behold, a cavernous building serving the whole of Europe. One look at the arrivals board and you'd see trains due to arrive from Italy, Austria, France, Belgium and obviously Germany itself. The trains we were interested in were those from Nuremberg and Berlin. The station concourse is a treasure trove of food, many dishes originating from the countries the station serves. I had my eyes on something specific, though, a rack of ribs was calling my name, alongside spicy spiral fries and accompanied by a spicy BBQ sauce. It was time to eat as my body was craving it, but whether spicy was a good path to take only time would tell. It wasn't beer time yet, as last night's escapades were still having an effect. All I needed was water to stop dehydration, beer could wait until later.

The station was buzzing with people arriving from all over Europe, not just Liverpool fans. Bayern have a huge following and they come from all over Germany to watch their team. It was still early in the day but there were lots of Bayern fans out and about already, and it made for a lovely atmosphere in the city. Gaz and Phil arrived from Nuremberg bang on time and with hugs and tickets exchanged they were on their way to check into their hotel and get out to see Munich. With a bit of luck we'd meet up with them later, but trips don't always go according to plan. Even with the advent of smartphones, Wi-Fi and data roaming, visits to different bars at different times often means you miss each other. One fella we couldn't afford to miss was Zil, as he had no clue where our hotel was and after four and a half hours on a fast train from Berlin, which is over 300 miles away, with strong German beer as a companion, it would probably mean he'd be somewhat disorientated upon arrival. It was still a couple of hours until his train was due and I had enough time to do another train-related job. As with my stop at Innsbruck, I took advantage of the fact that I was at a train station and could do things in person at a booking office that were proving impossible online.

I'd been trying to book the last leg of the family Inter Rail trip, which would take us from Munich to Paris. You'd think it was pretty straightforward with two cities renowned for their links to the rest of Europe, but no, it was the hardest leg to book. Every time I got close online the booking systems would throw me out, whether it be from the German side or the French; nothing worked. Armed with the remains of my hangover and a large bottle of water, I headed to the booking office and took a number from the dispenser. There were about 15 manned booths and about 40 people in line in front of me. It can't take that long, can it? Of course it could. Every time anyone completed their transaction it seemed the booth would close for lunch and the wait would go on. It was quite clear that many people in the queue had given up, or died, waiting.

When I finally got to the front and it was my turn, the lady didn't speak English. She understood enough to point me in the direction of an international window, and to join the back of another queue of bemused travellers. The hangover was still at the same levels but the water was running dangerously low. If I didn't get seen soon I'd wither and die, or create a real spectacle of myself – I was fighting a terrible urge to go! You know, to go. The day-after shits are nothing to be messed with and this queue was messing with them. The last thing I wanted to do was leave the queue after what was now nearly an hour's wait. As luck would have it, the last three in front of me must have had the same conundrum and couldn't hold out, as their numbers were called and went unanswered.

As I went to the booth, the guy was speaking fluent German and I didn't have a clue what he was saying to me. The trusted phrase of 'sprechen sie Englisch' was trotted out, and much to my relief he smiled and said, 'Yes, of course.' He was a Canadian guy who'd lived in Munich for ten years and obviously spoke fluent German, and he was also very good at his job. Much to my relief he found a way to get me from Munich to Paris on the day we wanted, in good time and with the relevant reservations. It seemed that because we would be travelling on Good Friday there were very few seats left on trains anywhere in Germany. After exchanging a large amount of euros for the reservations, our trip planning was now completed, everything was booked and I could look forward to the rest of the day. Obviously that was after a quick run to the spotlessly clean toilets on the lower concourse. It's amazing what you get for a euro, a place where you don't worry what you're catching when you're dropping the kids off at the pool.

It was with a huge feeling of relief that I headed back to the concourse to find Mongoose. I was greeted by a 'where the f*** have you been?' He'd been waiting hours. He was nearly as miserable as he was the night before while waiting for his pint that never came. I tried to explain, but he was in no mood, he just wanted Zil to get here and then we could sample the afternoon delights of Munich and its beer halls. The Berlin train was due in any minute and his wish would be granted.

There he was in all his glory! Zil was sauntering down the platform, full of the finest German beer. Mongoose's mood didn't put a spring in Zil's step, only a cackle in his voice as he buzzed off our moody mate. We were off to the hotel. Zil, not having been in Munich before, was taking in the sights of the train station and its vibrant surrounding streets. Mongoose muttered, 'Get a move on, soft arse.'

With the bags dropped we were out again in no time, the first stop being the famous Augustiner beer hall, the oldest in Munich. The beer hall, which is still in the original building where the beer was brewed, was beautiful inside and the beer was brilliant. It was their own brew, and many variations of it too, with service at your table by waiters who were dressed for the part. There was a brilliant atmosphere inside, with Bayern fans mixing with the visiting Reds. There were no Bayern songs but they were entertained with renditions from the Kop song book. If you're ever in Munich put this one on your list, the Augustiner beer hall, the one in the original building, that's the important bit. After a couple of beers it was time to move on. It was getting close to 5pm now and we still had to meet Tony and his lads; he'd be sweating on the ticket.

Not far from the beer hall was Marienplatz, which is probably considered to be the centre of Munich life, and home to the world famous Glockenspiel in the Rathaus. We met Tony and his lads outside a coffee-house-cum-bar on the opposite side of the square. It might be famous but I'd seen the Glockenspiel before and it was boring (watch it on YouTube). As the chimes started and the figures moved slowly, I went the bar for the drinks. That was a mistake, as the seating area outside it had the best view of the Glockenspiel show, so there was a premium paid to sit there, but hey-ho, you're only here once aren't you.

The coffee and the cokes for Tony and his boys cost more than the beer, but I was more than happy to put my hand in my pocket for these boys. The songs were rippling around the Marienplatz and it was time to make a move. Even though kick-off was at 9pm local time, by 6pm people were starting to head towards the metro entrance in the corner of the square. Tony headed off with the lads so they could take in the atmosphere, while we swerved the metro for now and headed down a side street to find another bierhaus for 'one more'.

And find one we did, in the form of the Schneider Bräuhaus (thanks to Google for helping me with this one), a great find and another one to put on your list. We were past the food stage, but it looked great and the beer was excellent. Even I was on steins of the stuff and I'm usually a bottle-only man. We got talking to some people from Russia who were impressed that we'd travelled all this way to see the game. Hold on, they've come all the way from Russia, it's just as far. Father and son and respective wives. Father and son were going to the match, the son's treat for his dad. The son was the only one who spoke English, and it was a great conversation with him interpreting our drunken gibberish. We probably sounded more Russian than English at this time of day.

On the way for the pre-match pee I met two Scouse lads, probably around the same age as me, and they were looking forward to the match but also a few days skiing tagged on at the end of it. They were also heading to Austria tomorrow. Now why didn't I think of that? It would have been a great end to the trip. Not sure I'd have the energy to ski though, and breaking my legs on a black run wouldn't be cool.

We needed to be making a move now. It was still 25 minutes on the metro to the stadium train station, and don't forget the ten-minute hike up the hill to the Allianz Arena. It was half past seven by the time we hit the platform at Marienplatz, and before long we were enjoying a boisterous trip on the metro to Fröttmaning station. Surrounded by all nationalities and fans of both teams we had an absolute ball, no hint of bother, just people having a great time together. As we spilled out of the train at Fröttmaning it was an hour to kick-off. We'd been having such a great time we almost forgot there was a match on. We climbed the stairs from the platform alongside thousands of others drawn like moths towards the brightly lit stadium high on the hillside, perfectly lit in a vibrant Red tonight, perfect for both teams. To help us up the hill we got another drink. This was guaranteed to be the last one, but the metro ride had made us thirsty. It sounds like all we did was drink beer all afternoon, doesn't it? Well, we sort of did, but remember the culture we saw. Now it was to the football and the Mighty Reds doing what they do as the Kings of Europe.

The normal nonsense awaited us at the turnstiles, and it was chaos getting though the first security check, where as I arrived at the ticket check I was frisked and stopped for being in possession of a power bank for my phone. You were never lasting all day with one charge on your phone and the power bank was perfect, but it was now taken off me. After loads of arguing in broken English, I was promised I could have it back at the end of the match. I had to leave the queue, take it to a portacabin and get a ticket. I thought I'd never see it again. Taking photos and videos inside was now restricted to how long my battery would give me. It serves me right for being such a tourist. 'Put your phone away, lad.'

I bounded up the steps three at a time. To be honest, after the first six steps it became one at a time. The Champions League music started and, as I entered the seating area, I was met by the teams walking out of the tunnel to deafening roars. Bayern resplendent in red and Liverpool stunning in grey! I always thought it was a washed-out kit. The orange kit of the year before meant everybody could tell the Reds were swarming over their opponents, but in grey? Who was going to fear them in that? I soon changed my mind.

The atmosphere was everything you hoped it to be, every fan playing their part, the green pitch, the flags, the noise, it's what it's all about. I took my seat alongside the boys from the Isle of Man. Tristan had helped me with the ticket and he lives 50 yards from me. All the way to Germany and you're sitting next to your neighbour. Then there was Ryan and Jack. Jack was lucky to get in as he was smashed. The German beer had taken control of his legs and they wouldn't work properly. Ryan had said to the steward he was his carer and the steward waved him though. By the time I got to him he was already on his third coffee, which had worked a treat and he was compos mentis by the time we took the lead.

The grey must have been like camouflage because Bayern didn't see them coming. In one of the all-time great European away performances Liverpool swept them aside and silenced not only Munich, but Bavaria and the rest of Germany, while the rest of Europe sat up and collectively shouted, 'Oh shit, we've got no chance against these boys.' All except Evertonians, City and United fans, as according to them Bayern were finished, well past their best. But it was pretty much the same Bayern side that stormed the Champions League the following year, the same voices lauding them on the way, strange that.

The 3-1 scoreline didn't really do justice to Liverpool's dominance. You'll have seen Sadio Mané's goal countless times, making a mug of Neuer and the Bayern defence, sending us at the far end of the stadium into raptures. From that moment onwards it was never in doubt. A Matip own goal was a mere fly in the ointment as a thumping header from Virgil and a superb header from Mané, from a delightful ball from Salah, silenced 95 per cent of the fans in the Allianz, with most Bayern fans heading for the exits long before the final whistle. The other 5 per cent? Well, we were celebrating like we'd won the thing already. These are the nights you remember. 'We see things they'll never see.' Don't we just! The police didn't even bother keeping us in, but no one was rushing away to Fröttmaning metro as we stayed and sung our hearts out, before heading back into Munich.

Before the match we'd picked a meeting point outside the security fence that surrounds the stadium, where miraculously Mongoose appeared with beers in hand. Paulaner, the local brew, had a concession stand, and as usual Mongoose was at the bar first, with his hand in his pocket. Every home game it's the same, we hang back knowing he'll get the round in and then moan about it. Zil rocked up, and then Tony, Harry and Ant, so you knew this would be one of the famous nights you'll tell your kids (or the world in a book) about. What happens when you're excited? That's right, you need a wee, and the boys and the old men did. Where do you go by a football ground? Mongoose uttered the immortal line, 'You can piss where you want in Germany, no one's arsed.' And it's true, you can, and they do, and they're not arsed. No wonder they behaved like they did in Liverpool. True enough, there were loads of Germans and now Reds queued up, whistling and peeing against the wall as they looked down into the car park below, and no one batted an eyelid. I asked Tony about what the lads remember most about Munich and it was, you guessed it, 'You can piss where you want in Germany.' That's one of their greatest memories, and having a great time with your dad and his mates, it's special.

Tony and the boys were heading back to their hotel near the airport, while we were heading back into the city centre. You couldn't move on the train but we lurched towards Marienplatz and the carriage was filled with joy and song. Even Bayern fans were smiling, as they'd seen the new champions of Europe tonight. As the metro dropped people at the central city stations, the carriage thinned out and we waited to jump off at Marienplatz. This is often where your night ends, as the bars have usually closed and the police have decided you've had enough enjoyment. After the previous night when it wasn't that hospitable, I didn't hold out much hope.

We headed towards the hotel and towards the sports bar we were in the night before. Thankfully they were open and doing a roaring trade. No bother, loads of beer and loads of singing, people would come and go, have a pint and leave, but we were out for the duration, the early morning start to head home forgotten about. With the match highlights on a loop in the bar all you could hear was 'ooohhs' and 'aahhhs' as the goals kept going in. What a night to be a Red.

By 3am it was kebab o'clock and we stumbled along to Lemon, my new favourite kebab shop, and my friend behind the counter shouted 'chicken kebap'. What a memory. I was amazed he remembered. That's a proper skill, to remember every customer's order from the night before, or is it? Did he just have a 50/50 chance of getting it right? It's either doner kebab or chicken kebab, isn't it? But with a day's beer on board I was impressed. As we weaved our way home, the ladies of the night were asking for a bit. No chance I was giving any of my kebab away. I think that's what they were asking for.

By the time my head hit the pillow it was 4am. What a day we'd had in Munich. Surely it can't have been much better in 1981. I know we reached the final then, but today we restored ourselves to the very top of the European game. I was dreaming of a final in Madrid!

* * *

It was sweet dreams until 7am, when Zil stumbled around collecting his bits and bobs before heading to the station for a train back to Berlin. Come 8.30am I was on my way too, leaving Mongoose to lock up and leave. I said my goodbyes and was met with grunts from Mongoose, who wanted to get his money's worth out of the bed and some peace and quiet.

Coffee and pastries, the breakfast of champions for the long journey home, 12 hours if all went to plan. There was a sombre air to the train station. Bayern's heroes had been taught a lesson, and Reds like me starting the long journey home were the worse for wear. Raising an eyebrow and anything more than a smile was a real effort. Good job my smile was permanent this morning.

The 9.34am train to Bologna was waiting for me. I know that's Italy but it takes the scenic route around the base of the Alps, and Innsbruck is on the way. Due to arrive in Innsbruck at 11.18am and expensive at £65 return for less than two hours' journey. Don't let anyone tell you it's dirt cheap for trains and hotels. What you save on flights, it often costs you elsewhere, but then you don't have the story to tell.

Coffee in hand and pastries finished before we even left the station, I'd conquered yet another European giant. Adding Bayern Munich to the illustrious list of

Real Madrid, Barcelona and Inter Milan, the Reds were the toast of Europe and here I was on a train bound for Innsbruck while my comrades were heading back to destinations across Europe – Phil and Gaz via Vienna, Zil via Berlin and Mongoose back via Frankfurt. With the wonders of Wi-Fi and WhatsApp you're never alone these days, and the stories and pictures kept me entertained all the way back to Austria.

Before I knew it Innsbruck was within sight and I had a challenge at the end of the platform, the ski jump. I was going to walk to the ski jump to see it in all its glory. Never been this close to one before, I wasn't missing the chance. Who am I kidding? Tired and the effects of two days on the lash, too much beer, too many kebabs and little sleep finally caught up with me.

Straight to the airport to catch up with Gary, Arthur and the lads, and that was all the energy I could exert. As the plane rumbled up the runway, the snow-capped Alps were on my left and I nodded off as the plane was flying over mountains. The next thing I knew the announcement declared. 'Cabin crew prepare the cabin for arrival.' Howard Gayle must have felt the same the night he ran the Germans ragged. Me and Howie were knackered, but happy and dreaming of Munich for the rest of our lives. Now he has a mural in Liverpool 8. I wonder if I'll get one as an adventurer from Liverpool 9.

Until we meet again, Auf wiedersehen. Wunderbar!

There's Something that the Kop Wants You to Know

THERE'S A lot that the Kop wants you to know. Let's start with the fact that Liverpool are now six times European champions. Look at that again, six. Six (English), or *sechs* (German for Jürgen). Whatever way you say it, that's just wonderful. The journey to our sixth European Cup is a thing of wonder and a more personal and emotional journey than I ever expected.

As the referee raised his whistle to his lips one last time in the centre circle of the Wanda Metropolitano in Madrid on a sultry June evening, he will never realise what his shrill whistle released. A torrent of salty tears and the emotion of my journey let loose. I needed this!

I wasn't in a good place on the road to Madrid. Two weeks of illness had triggered a depression I hadn't seen for some time, and here I feel is probably not the right place to analyse exactly what was causing the depression, but it was important to recognise that I needed help to address it, sometimes you can't help yourself.

The referee's whistle released the tears of relief but Jordan Henderson lifting that big, beautiful, shiny trophy high above his head brought tears of joy. Every time one of those glorious boys in red lifted it above their head, the tears came again and again. All I could think about was my dad and how special a connection that European Cup gave us. My dad had three cups to his name, Rome in 1977, London 1978 and Paris 1981, and now I have two. He always had it over me, in all the years I'd been watching the Reds.

He always had the European Cup over me, until 2005 that was, and I struck gold that year. I remember ringing him at some ungodly hour from Istanbul, as I waited for a bus outside the Atatürk stadium. I rang him to share the experience. I knew what he felt in Rome, I knew how it felt to be champions of Europe, and not many people know the feeling, it's wonderful. He was buzzing for me. His son, his middle son, had single-handedly conquered Europe and he was coming home with the European Cup. Forget the Champions League, it's the European Cup! He said I'd seen the greatest-ever European Cup victory, so at long last I had one over on him. Then just before he put the phone down, he said, 'It wasn't Rome, though, Rome was the first. The first is the most special. Safe journey home, lad.' He'd done me in one sentence, and he was probably right, the first is special, but Istanbul was my first and it was special. Madrid will always be special, but it wasn't Istanbul. However, it was magnificent in its own right.

Why was this so important to me? It's complicated, and at the time I don't think I understood why. The sheer weight of history, Liverpool's history and my own history, was weighing heavily on my shoulders. In the three and a half weeks between the magnificent Anfield night when the Reds unbelievably sent Barcelona packing and the journey to Madrid, I'd fallen apart. I went from elation to depression within a week and I didn't know why. It started with my stomach being off. I put it down to over-celebrating getting to Madrid, but it quickly moved to full-on shitting through the eye of a needle for two weeks, and not being able to eat. My physical health deteriorated, as did my mental health, and the demons I'd been fighting on and off since I hit 50 were back.

Tickets were sorted for the final, as was the travel, but I certainly wasn't, and with only 48 hours before I was due to go, it was touch and go, as I was still 'touching cloth'. I couldn't trust my body to not let me down. I was seriously considering not going, as I couldn't trust that I wouldn't embarrass myself on my travels. To the outside world I only had a stomach upset, but in my head I was thinking it was much worse and going through the 'what if' scenarios. I was only 53 with two young kids, great wife, lovely life, and it was all falling apart. It wasn't, but that's how it felt in my head. I needed to do something about it and quickly, but what?

Nikki said, 'You've got to go, it means that much to you. Take the Imodium [the traveller's friend], you'll feel better if you go and be with everyone else.' Thanks to that gentle push and a day on the Imodium I was going, and once that positive decision was made, mentally I started to improve. Positive thinking helps, who'd have thought, eh!

I was meeting the lads, Zil in Gatwick late Friday afternoon and Our Ian in Alicante train station at 7am on Saturday morning. Everyone else we'd see at some point in Madrid on Saturday. Thursday night came and my backpack was tightly packed with all my worldly goods, additional undies (just in case), passport and euros. Zil had my ticket so he could be the one sweating, checking that he still had it every five minutes, until he passed it to me.

Friday morning came and for the first time in weeks I had a spring in my step. Maybe not a real spring but I could put one foot in front of another, and the food from yesterday had stayed where it was supposed to, so I was confident of my travels. At 8am I took the first step out of the door, and I walked 50 yards to the bus stop. It was the furthest I'd walked in two weeks, and I was knackered, so god help me over the weekend. By 10am I was on an EasyJet plane heading to Luton Airport and the doors were closing. No turning back now. Twenty minutes later with a cup of tea and some biscuits to 'firm me up' I was feeling much better. This is what I do. This is what I've done for ever, and I was lucky to be doing it again. Just 45 minutes later the wheels hit the runway at Luton, and I was feeling much better. Now on to Gatwick. In a few hours' time I'd have company.

The WhatsApp group burst into life. Zil was on his way from Lime Street and Mike and his lad Josh were already on the ale in the Red Lion at Gatwick, before their flight to Madrid. Zil's message read: 'Got the match tickets Keith, surprisingly they were in the same place as the last 37 times I've checked this morning.' Told you he'd be sweating until he handed mine over. I took the connecting bus to Luton Parkway (train station) and the 90-minute train journey to Gatwick Airport; I always forget how far it is and how long it takes to get from one side of London to the other. Sounds easy, doesn't it? Fly to Luton and then go to Gatwick, but it took me nearly eight hours before I was sitting down with the lads in the Red Lion. Within five minutes, Mike and Josh's flight was called, so it was now just me and Zil with a pint of lager and a bottle of Corona. I dropped my bombshell. I told him how bad I felt, how I nearly hadn't made it. Shocked is not the word. I was always the one who listened and made sense of stuff, but now my mate listened and listened intently. Then I went to the bar.

When I got back from the bar we started talking about the Reds, the last 30-odd years and what was to come this weekend. We didn't need to talk about me anymore. When people say talking helps, it does, even better when someone listens, like properly listens. Please always have the conversation, though, no matter how hard it is, if you're on the receiving end. The person saying what they need to say isn't looking for you to provide solutions, they just need to get it off their chest and start moving forward. I'd moved on and was now looking forward to the next few days. It was amazing how the beer settled my stomach, or was it my mental state? The two are intrinsically linked, I firmly believe.

We were heading to the gate in no time at all for our 7.40pm EasyJet flight to Alicante. Flight costs to Madrid had been sky high. I had cheap flights reserved to Alicante prior to the first leg of the semi-final against Barcelona. I reserved them with a £5 deposit. After the 3-0 defeat, though, I decided to cut my losses and lose my fiver. What an idiot! I was obviously still one of Jürgen's doubters. I needed to be a believer and save myself a fortune. By the time we won the second leg, flights were at nightmare prices. The steps we had to take to make the trip affordable are laughable, and wait until you see the way we go home. The flight to Alicante sent any depressive thoughts out of my head, as the two-and-a-half-hour flight was a dream. With the sun going down on the right-hand side of the aircraft, everything was good, and tomorrow was the only thought on my mind.

As always, when you want to get away quickly from the airport you end up having to bus to the terminal from the plane, with the bus taking the longest route. The number of customs officers went from four to two as a queue formed, and everything took twice as long. By the time we arrived at our accommodation it was approaching midnight. Our accommodation for the evening was the delightfully named Guesthouse Central, not very Spanish, but it was more than adequate. Twin beds, clean and tidy, no frills, shared toilet but spotless (god help those who follow us in the morning). The Guesthouse Central was ten minutes' walk from the train station, important in the morning, and only £20 each. We checked in, using our best Spanglish, then swiftly dropped our bags and headed out the door looking for a bar. As the clock struck 12, we were sitting outside a bar, populated mainly by locals who never batted an eyelid as we toasted each other and the

Reds with pints of Stella Artois and bowls of nuts. The evening air was a lovely temperature now, not too cool, T-shirts were fine and al fresco drinking, how European. Outside of tourist Alicante it seemed like this local bar was the go-to place. People would come and go, staying for one drink and moving on. Everyone knew everyone else; we were the only two people who never said *ola* to everyone who walked in the door.

Mongoose, Mike and Josh were in Madrid, and the temperature had hit 37°C. Oh my, it's going to be a hot one tomorrow. Alicante was closing for the night. It was June, but it was dead, so we headed down towards the port and found a disco bar. Yeah, as bad as it sounds. By 2am we were done for, no point killing ourselves as we were up at 7am to catch a train to Valencia. I'll tell you about that in a minute. I was starving now but nothing was open to get something to eat. By half past two, Zil was snoring like a Walrus and our alarms were set for 7am.

* * *

The iPhone alarms went off in unison and even our deafness wasn't going to stop us hearing them. The rest of the guests must have too. Wine for my men, we ride at dawn! Well sort of, it was more like coffee at dawn. We sauntered up to the train station and, as booking.com promised, within ten minutes we were at Alicante train station, and it was already full of Reds. Most were on the fast train to Madrid, but not us, as we were taking the scenic route, via Valencia. Twice the length of time but a much better story for this chapter. The initial plan was to get the fast train to Madrid, taking just over two hours, but by the time everyone had agreed to go by train, the fast train had sold out and the cost of all other trains had gone up. The only other travel choice was a five-hour coach journey and there was no way I was going by coach, and certainly not coming home by one.

The train may have cost over £100 but what I shaved off the flights would subsidise it. It was still cheaper than a day trip from John Lennon, and you got the adventure thrown in. We met Our Ian in Alicante train station and a look of relief shot across his face as we walked through the doors. Ian had taken the opportunity to take a week away in a 4-star resort near Alicante with his wife, but she was staying at the resort. Being a Blue she had absolutely zero interest in what was happening in Madrid. She was looking forward to having a peaceful day in the sun. Ian was relieved that he could now be excited and talk about the match, as he'd been holding it all in since they left Manchester Airport.

It's amazing how much better I felt than 24 hours earlier. My stomach had eased after a load of beer the day before, my head was clearer as I had lightened the load and we were on the way to the Champions League Final. What more could I want, today was going to be a brilliant day. There was no hope, it was expectation. Madrid was going to be amazing, and the big shiny thing would once again be glistening on the banks of the Mersey.

Coffees and pastries in hand, we headed through the security check and boarded the 7.55am train to Valencia, as most of the assembled Reds boarded the adjacent fast train directly to Madrid. By the time we got to Valencia they would already be in Spain's capital city. What do you do with two hours on a train? Well, I lightened the mental load further and shared my thoughts with Our Ian. He wasn't that surprised at everything I had to say, some of it yes, but not all. The half conversations we'd had over the last couple of years gave him enough of a clue to know that I was struggling, but as with loads of fellas the detail was always lacking. This time he got it all over a strong coffee, and boy did he need that to listen to some of the stuff. The shadow of Hillsborough, which had been kept at bay over 30 years, was now darker than ever, and the loss of my dad nearly five years before. They were both issues that needed addressing. Once again, though, by uttering the words 'I'm not in a good place', it really helped. As the saying goes: 'It's okay to not be okay.' And it's true. The first step on the journey to getting better is admitting you need help, and today was the day. When I look back now it's clearly the first major step on my journey to being well and becoming me again. As we stepped off the train at Valencia, I was fully focused on what lay ahead for the rest of the day. Unbelievably, the stomach issues I'd endured for the weeks before were gone. Mental and physical health going hand in hand, maybe.

The Estacion del Norte (North Station) in Valencia is situated in the city centre and is beautiful, the façade looking like it probably did when it opened in 1852, and the insides have a unique feel. Wooden panels and marble floors, to keep the hall cool in the heat of the summer, it's far superior to the train stations of modern-day Europe.

You have to transfer to a different station to catch the AVE (the high-speed train) to Madrid. Either a shuttle bus or a walk in the heat of the morning sun? It was already that hot that we decided to take the bus, which took all of one minute to get from one station to the other. Would have been quicker walking but we were saving our energy, as it was going to be a long day and night. The station was modern and soulless as predicted, but it had a McDonald's, which allowed a spot of breakfast before our 10.30am departure to Madrid Atocha. In Valencia there were more Spurs fans than Liverpool, but that was the last time we'd see that over the next 48 hours. They were all obviously excited to be here, and that was lovely to see. It's exactly how it should be.

The AVE sped through the dusty heartlands of Spain, exceeding speeds of 300kph, and if you're old like me, that's over 190mph. Within an hour and 35 minutes, the train slowed through the suburbs of Madrid and pulled in bang on time at the main station, Atocha. As the train emptied out and hordes of fans descended on to the platform, there were more Reds on board than we originally thought. Even in the station you could feel the mid-day heat. It was going to be hot, and as the travelator took fans from the platform to the concourse, the first chorus of 'Allez, Allez, Allez' burst out.

We were heading to the main square, Puerta del Sol, to meet up with Mongoose and Mike, who had spent the previous evening in Madrid, having quite some time from the looks of it. While me and Zil struggled to find any sort of life in Alicante, they were living it up big time.

They'd recovered enough to meet us in the square and we could head off to our respective evening's accommodation. When I say accommodation, I use the term somewhat loosely. Where I was resting my head tonight wasn't exactly what I expected, but beggars can't be choosers. Mike, along with his lad Josh, had booked an Airbnb apartment near Opera, ten minutes' walk away. He said when he booked that he thought it slept three or four. He hadn't worked out where the third or fourth person would sleep, and he obviously omitted to tell me that until I could work it out myself. It was an apartment above a nightclub. That could either be alright, or it could be hell, depending on what happens later tonight.

As I walked in the door there was a double bed in front of me with a single wardrobe next to it. Beyond the bed was a set of shutters providing shade as the sunlight was fighting to get in the open floor-to-ceiling window. It was baking hot, and the room had no air conditioning. It was going to be a noisy gaff, even at the quietest of times, but there was no way that window was getting closed. There was a door in the corner to my right, and I thought maybe it was another room with a bed, but no, it housed a toilet and shower. That was it, not even a bath in which I could get me head down. The three-foot-wide space at the bottom of the bed was where I'd be getting my head down. It was free, and beggars can't be choosers. As the others sniggered, I lashed my bag at the bottom of the bed, and we were ready to go out. I don't know what Our Ian was laughing at. He was on a promise of a different place to kip, but he still didn't know where it was. For once in my life, I wished I was kipping with Mongoose and Zil.

It was hitting 1pm now and there was to be no sightseeing; while Madrid is an amazing city, it wasn't going to be seen today. We were heading to the fan zone, where we'd be meeting a load of others and seeing what the boys from 'Boss Nights' could deliver today. They had a lot to live up to after Kyiv's amazing day in Shevchenko Park; remember, the one we missed due to the horseradish vodka. Today we'd be off to see Jamie Webster, John Power and a cast of thousands.

The fan zone was based in the Goya area, in what was described as a square (more like an oblong), in the Plaza Felipe II. We jumped the metro, which was free all day with a travel card provided to all fans with your match ticket, and within six minutes we were on the platform at Goya. The platforms were packed, the metro had offloaded so many Reds that it was slow going getting above ground and towards the fan zone. 'Si Señor' (this year's song) rippled through the snaking red tide, getting louder with every step. Not everyone here had a ticket, that's for sure. Mike and Josh certainly didn't have tickets, and it was clear there wasn't a cat in hell's chance of getting them today. But those without had come to have a ball, many resigned to not going the game, but all having a great time, and loads with kids in tow as well. From the cool bowels of the metro, we headed out into the red-hot streets of Goya. Not only was it hot in terms of the temperature but the atmosphere was red-hot. As we entered the back of the square it was clear there were thousands here, tens of thousands. I thought we'd arrived handy, but it didn't seem to be the case. We were at the back of the square, and you could just about see the stage. There were thousands of people between us and the stage, so we were never going to meet anyone here. Or were we?

Meeting people was actually easier this time around than we could have imagined. With us staying out of the middle of the crowd, it helped, and with mobile phones and better access to the internet than in Kyiv last year, too. My cousin Brian was the first to meet us, and seeing him in such a place made a real change, as over the last few years we'd only met at funerals, so this was a treat. He'd been in touch through the weeks before. He was taking his kids, Callum and Codi, along for the ride. He knew there was no chance of a ticket but wanted to give them a wonderful experience. His plans had changed on several occasions in the weeks previous, from driving in a camper van, to driving a car, and ultimately flying from Birmingham to Faro (yeah, I know it's in Portugal), driving to Seville (yeah, I know it's not Madrid), driving on to Caceres (western Spain) for a night, and then on to Madrid to stay a couple of nights. All for a match he couldn't see, but an adventure that they'd all remember for a lifetime. It was great to be part of their adventure.

Our gang of four had become a gang of seven, so it was becoming an occasion. Meeting your family and mates in a far foreign land, there's nothing better. It was great to see Brian and the kids. I hadn't seen Brian and his brother Paul for years, until my dad's funeral a few years earlier, then unfortunately at their dad's funeral, that's my

Uncle Jimmy, who you'll read more about elsewhere in the book. I'd crammed my 50th birthday in between two such sad events, where we all had a ball in Liverpool with our respective better halves and the wider family.

There was no way of getting anywhere near the stage from here as we were so far back, and getting served a drink was a nightmare. One of Our Ian's mates, Si Mason, was in an adjacent street outside Brindis Bar, which turned out to be a little haven only a couple of hundred yards away from the Scouse chaos. We headed to the bar, it was a great home for people to come and go. We had a place that was identifiable and out of the heat. Even in the shade, though, it was over 34°C, so god knows what it was like in the centre of the Plaza Felipe II. With upturned wooden casks that you could sit your beer on, and a toilet that you could actually get to, this was the place to be.

Funny, the man who found the bar and gave us a home for the afternoon to drink to our hearts' content doesn't even drink. There's an amazing back story as to why, but he's been sober for over 16 years now, and he has published his amazing life story, *Too High, Too Far, Too Soon*, and is the founding member of The Hightown Pirates, a fabulous band of ex-addicts who've produced some of the best music I've heard in years. He's also a massive Red. Si had flown in from Marrakesh, where he'd been holidaying with his missus, and it was him who'd sorted Our Ian a place to stay for the night.

After being Facebook friends for a while I'd only met Si for the first time recently at the Barcelona semi-final, and then the last home game. Besides Zil constantly trying to get him to have a pint to celebrate after the win against Barça, and me constantly telling Si that it's amazing he's not dead, I think we actually got on pretty well. Even though he doesn't drink, he has the fortitude to be around those who do. Zil and Mongoose had caught up with us now after having a few quiet ones near their hotel, and the news about my bed for the night went down well with them, and no, I couldn't stay with them now! I'd made my choice to stay with Mike, my 'real mate', as Mongoose put it.

Si was ticketless like Mike and Josh, as was Tony Acko and his boys, Anthony and Harry, who caught up with us. Tony had been trawling the streets as he has loads of contacts. We'd all been looking for him, but there was absolutely nothing doing. They had one ticket between the three of them, so there was a tough decision coming his way and not one any of us would want to make: which child would he choose, or would he just go in himself? Well, it was never the second option was it. Ultimately, he'd choose his eldest son, Anthony, and stay outside the ground with Harry, his youngest. Heart-breaking, as they'd been all over Europe, but at least one of them would get to see the final. They'd gone all the way to Kyiv in 2018, but didn't see the big shiny thing get lifted. When they left us, they were still on the fruitless search, and it says it all when people like Tony can't source a ticket.

Liverpool and Spurs were always going to sell their full allocation of tickets, and with a massive demand the secondary market was always going to be inflated. Tickets coming from the UEFA family allocation sent prices spiralling to at least ten times their value. With 100,000 fans from England (and beyond) in Madrid, odd spare tickets were never appearing. Tickets for a showpiece final in one of Europe's most vibrant cities were on everyone's bucket list, whether they were a fan or not. That's what's annoying about modern football, money buys you anything; if you have it, you can go. The normal fan can't afford to spend the price of a family holiday on a ticket and two days away.

My phone pinged, and it was a message from my mate 'Dave from Dubai', that's his full name now, changed it by deed poll. I met Dave many years ago in the Dubai supporters' club. I was regularly working out there and we used to catch up on every trip to Dubai. I'll never forget the night we met, it was 2009 and Liverpool drew 4-4 with Arsenal, the night that Andrey Arshavin scored all four for Arsenal. Despite that, it was some night in Dubai. Even though it had been years since we last saw each other, he was here in Madrid, so if he could find us it would be great to meet up. With the help of Google Maps, it was easy enough, and the years rolled away as we saw each other for the first time in eight years. Dave had his little lad with him. When I say little, he was huge. Last time I'd seen him in Dubai he was off to university in the UK and now here he was, looking like Grizzly Adams. He was a mountain of a man, dwarfing his dad, with a huge beard. The catch-up was brief as Dave was heading off to the ground to get in early. He had tickets from a contact in Dubai, who had a 'contact at the Albanian FA'. I know what you're thinking. He had some doubts, but comparing his tickets to ours they looked genuine enough, so he was off up the ground. I shouted, 'See you in Dubai, Dave, shall I bring all the lads with me to stay at yours?' The people I've met following our team are brilliant, and he's one of the best.

You could hear the cheers from the square travelling on the warm afternoon breeze and they floated over the riot police, who stood in wait. They waited all afternoon, as they had nothing to do. You knew they wouldn't blink at having to get involved, but they had no reason to, absolutely no reason. Every 20 minutes I'd get someone to mind my pint and I'd walk across to the side of the square to watch the events through a wire fence. My timing was often perfect, with Jamie Webster belting out 'Allez, Allez, Allez' and the Virgil, 'he's our centre-half' song. It was Liverpool's fan culture at its best. A look to my left and I could see the thousands bedecked in red and white having an absolute ball. I didn't need to be in the middle of the crowd, this was enough for me. The Boss lads had come a long way from the bars at Sound and District on the streets of Liverpool, well done lads.

By 5pm it was time to start thinking about heading to the ground, as the last thing you want is to have a ticket in pocket and through no fault of your own not be able to get in. The last hurdle of the day was getting into the inner sanctum, inside UEFA's ring of steel, policed by the Spanish robocops, and they don't care what fair is. The Spanish police don't do reasonable, no questions asked, and you're easily met with a raised baton, and lucky to avoid a crack from one. To give us plenty of time, we started moving. We were saying our goodbyes to our ticketless brothers. We left Josh, Mike and Si to search for a bar to watch the match in. Rumours were already circulating that bars across Madrid were closing early or not even showing the match, and there was no public showing for the thousands without tickets. We'd catch them after the match, wherever they may be. Our Ian, Mongoose, Zil and I started queuing up to get into Goya metro station. We weren't alone, half the square had the same idea. At least they weren't overfilling the platforms, and a short wait kept us all safe.

We were heading to the end of metro line No.2 and Las Rosas metro station. With the train rammed and the temperatures inside exceeding those outside, it was a relief to arrive at our destination and head back into the afternoon sun. It was baking hot, and without a cold beer in your hand it was difficult to cope. I didn't have a clue how the players were going to cope. The gung-ho approach that got both teams through the semi-finals wouldn't be played out here, and anyone expecting a classic was always going to be disappointed. Finals rarely become classics as there's far too much at stake for that. There was a lot at stake for Jürgen and the Reds, Jürgen with a reputation as a serial choker and loser of major finals, and after the Basel and Kyiv defeats there was huge pressure to get over the line. He had to deliver, especially after losing out to Man City in the league by a single point. Spurs, on the other hand, had nothing to lose, arriving at a Champions League Final way before their time or anyone's expectation of them, and via a run where it was unbelievable that they even got through the group stage, never mind a semi-final (that was nearly as great as ours with Barcelona).

As we exited the metro station it was a sea of red all around us, so we just had to follow the sea down the hill towards the ground, or so we thought, as we still couldn't see it yet. We headed down a road hosting several banks, supermarkets, bars and restaurants. There was no call for us to find a bar or a restaurant, as this wasn't a time to sit and chill out, our aim was to be inside the ground as soon as possible. We did visit a supermarket to replenish the stocks of Mahou (the local brew), getting some cold cans to get us to the stadium. Mongoose, the thirstiest of all, came back from the supermarket with enough cans to get us to the ground. We weren't planning on hanging around outside. As the red throng moved down the hill, we took a right turn 90 degrees and there it was, the first sight of the Wanda Metropolitano; it looked magnificent.

We walked past hundreds of coaches, lined up after having dropped their cargo of fans, and we crossed the baked grassland. Between us and the stadium was a dual carriageway that was only being used for police vehicles; later, the teams accessed the stadium this way. There was a carnival atmosphere, and the babbling Reds were only talking about one thing, winning old big ears for a sixth time. The obligatory photos with the stadium backdrop were taken, and we were off to the first ticket check, manned by the local police and stewards. Within minutes, and with a cursory frisk, we were through and into the inner ring of steel. We could relax now and get a drink and

Faith of our Fathers – Rome 1977. Front and centre my dad Bob Salmon. Uncle Dave left and Uncle Len right

Drinking with Dortmund. With (left to right) Our Ian, Aki, Tommy and Mike

*There she goes – Basel 2016.
Before it all went wrong*

*Who remembers the first time?
Sadio Mané patiently waits for
Charlie*

Charlie loving Munich (honestly) with his dad and Tommy

Wunderbar – Munich 2018. Sharing a pint or two with Arthur

Olympic Stadium Kiev 2018. With (left to right) Mongoose, Phil, Tony Field, Zil and Gaz

Madrid 2019 – Feeling better by the hour. With (left to right) – Our Ian, Zil and Mongoose

We climbed the hill our own way! Anfield a beautiful sight, #JFT97

Tapas for everyone! Museo de Jamón, Madrid 2020. With (left to right) – Mongoose, Charlie and Zil

Allez les rouges – Friday night in Paris 2022. With (left to right) – Harry, Aki, Zil, Mongoose and Charlie

Anfield South 2024. With (left to right) – Our Charlie, Our Dan, Our Josh and Our Kev

The greatest moment. Me and Charlie, Carabao Cup Final, Wembley 2024

Thank you Jürgen. Nine not so normal years!

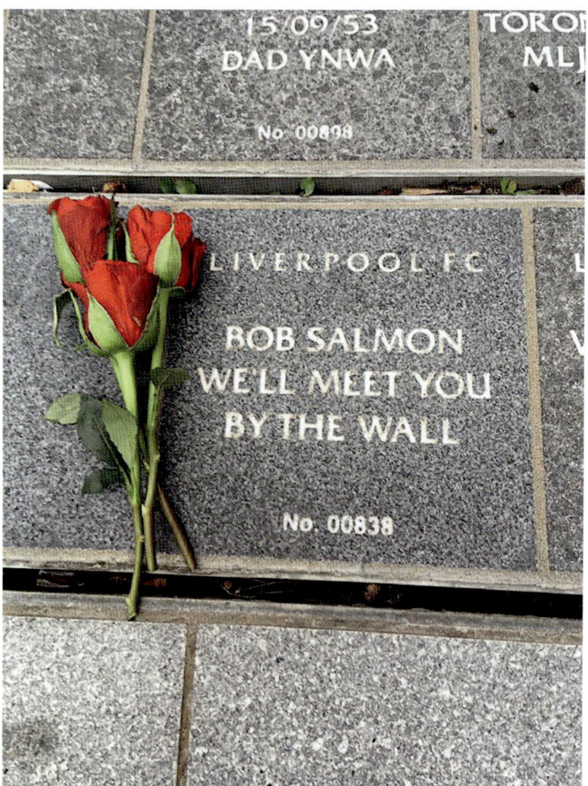

Bob Salmon. 'We'll meet you by the wall'

a bite to eat. I opted for a hot dog and gave a 'yes' to the question 'want onions?' It was the wrong choice. Whatever they served up to me was something that never resembled an onion in its life and made sure I had indigestion all night long and needed to drink copious amounts of water throughout the 90 minutes.

It was baking hot, and we sat down in the shade of the huge stadium to watch the world go by. This meant watching a game of cat and mouse between fans who'd managed to get past ticket check number one and the police manning ticket check number two. Even though fans had got past the first check, the second was much more stringent and fake tickets were identified, their holders marched back out and deposited unceremoniously outside the first checkpoint. These weren't blaggers, but people who'd spent a fortune on what they believed to be genuine tickets. They must have been gutted.

At 7.45pm, some 75 minutes before kick-off, we decided it was time to head inside and avoid getting caught up in any issues the more desperate people got. We were in different parts of the ground due to the nature of the ticket distribution, so we chose a point to meet afterwards. Our Ian was close to me and Zil, but Mongoose was in a different tier and had to enter through different turnstiles. The next time we met we'd be European champions, there was nothing more certain. We approached the second check ready for the full frisk under the fierce eyes of the riot police, and clean as a whistle the tickets were scanned, the lights went green and we were allowed through. A relief, even though the tickets were all from the club, but there had been numerous stories of people whose tickets hadn't scanned properly being dumped outside and their ticket taken off them.

We were in and quickly found our seats, which were fabulous, 12 rows from the front and just to the right-hand side of the goal, that's as you look on the TV. That's important, and it's something I've done ever since I was a youngster, finding myself in the crowd and pointing it out to anyone who's interested, or not. Thanks to a fella wearing an old yellow away shirt behind me, I know exactly where I am every time I watch the replay, which is often. Our Ian joined us. No one was sitting down tonight, so he might as well be with me and Zil to enjoy the night. It's been a rarity that I've been lucky enough to share these trips with Our Ian or Our Kev, but tonight was different.

The stadium was already pretty full, Spurs fans in early, and the Liverpool end in magnificent voice. The atmosphere was building. We hadn't left our atmosphere in the square, which had been the case at Basel in 2016, all sung out by the time we got to the match. Not tonight though, and the songs boomed out and the flags waved. The fan groups had done an amazing job and got UEFA to agree for us to have our flags with us, so the red end was the Kop on tour, a sight to behold. I was standing with loads of young match-going lads and girls who I recognised off Twitter, and older fellas from back in the day. Even the Imagine Dragons couldn't kill the atmosphere, and unlike our end in Kyiv, which exploded to Dua Lipa the previous year, our end was motionless, and we sung over their songs.

And then the Reds were there, walking out alongside the blue tracksuit tops of Spurs, covering their all-white kit, and the stadium rose to welcome the players. The boys in red made their way towards us and acknowledged us and our support. You could see the steely determination and focus on their faces. There would be no mistakes from these boys this time round. From Kyiv to Madrid, they'd grown in stature, and they were here to do a job.

As the game kicked off it was greeted by a guttural roar from our end and the Reds were on the attack immediately. With only 20 seconds on the clock, Mané played the ball towards the centre of the penalty area and right into Moussa Sissoko's arm. Only he knew what he was pointing at, but the ref was doing the pointing that counted, straight at the penalty spot. After the prerequisite VAR check, the penalty was confirmed, and within two minutes Salah had smashed the penalty past Hugo Lloris in the Spurs goal. What a start.

Then nothing happened for the rest of the half, besides two efforts by our marauding full-backs, Robertson and Trent. Liverpool did little, and Spurs did even less, not surprisingly, as it was that hot. The only other highlights of my half were two bottles of water at €5 a bottle. If you needed it, you needed it, as those onions had done for me.

At half-time my phone pinged. It was Dave from Dubai with a picture from a restaurant in Madrid, six of them waiting for their tea (dinner if you're not Scouse). His tickets hadn't worked, they were, according to UEFA, 'phenomenal' fakes. UEFA and the police were interested in their source as they were that good. The police and

UEFA officials offered them a choice of leaving or going down the station to file a report, so they chose to leave. Dave said, 'Shit happens,' and if the score stayed the same, he'd be a happy man all the same. Gutted but happy. Me? I'd have hunted the seller down and, well you can fill in the rest. Dave was one of many to be had off that night in Madrid.

The second half continued like the first, with my need for water, followed by the need for the toilet. The fellas standing by me must have wondered what was going on. I was a nervous wreck; I couldn't handle the slim lead, and one of those nights where they possibly paid the price for not getting the second goal. It was a night where if you didn't get into top gear and they equalised, you probably wouldn't be able to raise your game. It had been an unbelievably long season, and we were all exhausted. Not these boys, though, these boys were magnificent, and they were controlling the game until 75 minutes when Spurs decided to turn up and have a go.

Alisson, a bystander for most of the night, earned his money with two saves in a minute, then a great stop from a Christian Eriksen free kick. We were willing the Reds on to victory and, entering the last ten minutes, we were starting to sweat. The key moment came. On the 87th minute, boom! The big Divvy himself slots the real winner. The ball popped out from the corner and, as it pinged around on the edge of the box, I could see Origi out the corner of my eye, waiting in space. Somehow the ball came to Matip, who slipped it to Origi, and as soon as he took his first touch there was only one place it was going. I was right in line with Origi as he arrowed the ball into the side of the goal, scoring past Lloris's outstretched left glove.

Cue absolute scenes in our end. I probably don't have the words to adequately describe it, you need to watch it for yourself, as Origi runs arms outstretched towards the corner. Us? We were falling over and hugging anyone within arm's length, and some even further away. There was huge relief, great joy and the nerves disappeared. There was no choking tonight. That's not wholly true, I was choking, choking back the tears. As the whistle blew the tears came and I thought immediately of my dad. These are the moments you want to share with those you love, and I know I'm not the only one to think this. My thoughts went back to the man who gave me the passion and showed me the way. This one's for us, Dad. It was wonderful to share it with Our Ian, the immediacy of the victory, right there, right then, not outside the ground when you've calmed down. And Zil, for over 30 years I've been sharing moments like this with him, and it was as good as ever.

My phone pinged. It was Dave from Dubai again, with the simple message 'Yeeehhhh … 6'.

Nowadays it takes an eternity to lift the trophy. The lads don't just climb the steps, get the big silver thing and show it to the fans. Now everything must be a show. At least it gave us time to get our breath back and take it all in. The players broke ranks from the centre circle and celebrated with the red end of the stadium. Right in front of us Bobby was dancing to his own song as the end roared 'Si Señor'. It had been sung with ever-growing vigour on the way to the final and now it boomed out. Bobby wasn't the hero of the night, but it was a fitting end to the journey.

One by one the players got their gold medals hung around their necks. Last in line, but certainly not least, was the man who'd reinvented himself and driven his lads on to glory, Jordan Henderson. If ever a man deserved to lift the trophy, it was him. Derided by many of our own fans over the years, he'd converted them and now was his moment. He stepped forwards, shook hands, got the cup, walked over to his team-mates and faced them. Then he did the 'Hendo shuffle' in front of his lads, and swiftly turned around and lifted the cup to the sky. The stadium lit up with fireworks. You could feel the raw emotion of the lift, years of angst from the men in red washed away in seconds.

And the tears came again, for me, for my dad, for Charlie, for Lenny and Jimmy and those who'd gone before, and for all those at home celebrating in our magnificent city or wherever they may be. I was one of the lucky ones, I don't have to remember where I was, but in years to come, no matter where you were, you'll remember this moment forever. I still remember 1977, 1978, 1981, 1984, 2005, and now 2019. These are the best of times, the best nights of your footballing life, so drink it in, as we're the lucky ones and 'we see things they'll never see'.

Within seconds the Reds were down in front of us, and they stayed and partied for what seemed like an eternity. I was staying too. It wasn't a quick look at the cup for me,

I wanted to take a long lingering look, milking it in with the boys in red singing 'You'll Never Walk Alone'. And they were singing it to us. All the things that song means to each and every one of us were alive in that moment.

With the wonders of modern technology, I was able to share these moments with Charlie at home in the Isle of Man, at his mate's house, and they were all going nuts. We got to share 'a moment' that will stay with me forever. Only a brief moment as my phone battery was critically low, but what a moment. He could see the cup right in front of me, as close as I was going to get to sharing it. Little did he know that the Wanda would be a place of dreams for him in the future, and sooner than we could have imagined. It was ten minutes to midnight as we finally edged towards the exit, but I kept looking over my shoulder to see the lads celebrating. We were some of the last out.

The stewards quietly walked us up the steps and gently guided us out, with one last visit to the toilet. The taste of onions (or whatever it was) still lingering for me, we walked into the warm breeze that enveloped the stadium. By midnight we were heading back up the hill to Las Rosas metro station. We needed that supermarket to be open, we were dying of thirst once again and water wouldn't cut it now. As we got nearer the metro station the supermarkets were open. They weren't daft, there was a euro or two to be made tonight, so there was no way they were shutting early. Our only problem was whether the metro would close too early, which is not unknown in Europe, but we'd keep our fingers crossed. As Mongoose,

Our Ian and Zil headed into the supermarket, I sat down on the kerb outside, like I did in 2005 outside the Atatürk, and I rang home. In the warmth of a wonderful Turkish night, I'd rung my dad and talked through what I'd seen, but that wasn't an option anymore and tonight I felt it, but I had a great stand-in. I rang Nikki and told her all about it and I knew why I loved her so much, as she wanted to share this moment with me because of what it means to me. She'd been out to see The Feeling in the Isle of Man, but I'd bailed out on the night as I had something better to do and she went with her mate. She'd had a great time and got in the house just in time to see the end of the match. By the time the lads got back with the cold cans of Mahou it was bedtime for her, but not for me. I was ready to celebrate all night long.

The cold cans helped make the long journey back to Puerto del Sol bearable at least. Mike had messaged to say that he and Josh were still there, so we'd be meeting up with them as soon as possible. By the time we got to Sol, it was fast approaching 2am, the crowds were thinning out and things were closing. The local lads were doing a bomb selling supermarket cans for twice the price they bought them at. You weren't getting into bars now as they were all done serving. They must have run out of ale, and from the state of Mike and Josh, who were smashed, it was easy to see how. We'd had the chance to sober up for four hours while watching the match, but they hadn't had the same luxury. They were still standing up, not straight, more like the shape of a letter S. Our Ian decided it was time to find out where he was staying. He had an address and Google Maps and he was off with a cheery 'I'll see you in the morning'.

It wasn't long before the munchies were calling. We were all starving. Even though I could still taste those damn onions, I was hungry. Those stomach issues from the weeks before the final were a long-distance memory. All of a sudden, I had a stomach that could cope with anything. There was only a pizza shop open, and even though it looked ropey, it was the only choice, so pizza it was. As we were in the queue a fella came in and he was the spitting image of our hero Divock Origi. This fella was fully kitted out in the Liverpool strip, all bar his bright white training shoes. It could have been the man himself. He told us he knew Divock (think he was his cousin, but I was drunk) to which we were about to say, 'Yeah right,' but he whipped his phone out and showed us pictures with his mate Divock, and he was standing on the pitch with the cup. All in the pizza shop were amazed as he walked off into the night with his pizza, to the tune of 'Saturday night and I like the way you move, Divock Origi'.

Puerto del Sol was closed for the night by the police now, and Mongoose was moaning about not celebrating, and rightly so, but we were done for, it was time for bed. The emotion of the day had caught up and it was going to be a long way home. While it would have been amazing to celebrate in a tapas bar all night long, it wasn't going to happen. We said our goodbyes as we headed back to the apartment, and before long Mike and Josh had crashed out in the bed. I prepared my towel to be as comfortable as possible for the night, plumped up my bag for a pillow and proceeded to sleep.

Sleep? No chance, not on a marble floor, where every angular part of my body grated on the surface. There was no real sleep. By 6am I was in bed with Tweedle Dee and Tweedle Dum. What a sight it was. They were going to be fine, they weren't going home until Monday, but my night on the floor was going to be followed by a Sunday night on the floor in an airport. By 10am the sun was shining through the shutters again and the streets of central Madrid were warming up, so there was no sleep in any of us. By 11am I was getting ready to head out on my travels again. I braved a morning visit to the toilet and, following a day on the ale, that can go one of two ways. Luckily for me it was the better outcome.

A cheery goodbye from me and a grunt from the lads and I was gone, out to do a bit of sightseeing before meeting the other lads at Atocha. I walked through the square at Opera and straight into the Plaza de Oriente in front of the Royal Palace of Madrid, where I found a huge European Cup, a perfect photo opportunity. I couldn't find it in Kyiv, so this made up for it. Just as I arrived to see the 50-foot replica, and under the perfect blue sky in front of the stunning white palace, the speakers burst into life and played, yeah you guessed it, 'You'll Never Walk Alone'. I walked around singing it to myself, with a faltering voice as I fought with the emotion. 'This one's for you, Dad.'

As I walked back, the Mastercard sponsor tours were in full flow, all their guests looking like they'd had a full night's kip and a lovely breakfast too. Looking at me, the only thing fresh about me were my undies and T-shirt, and with my life in my backpack, singing a song from the 60s to myself with tears in my eyes, what must they have thought? They were the lucky ones, seeing a real football fan. They may not have realised it, but this is what they love about the game. They pay to see people like me and my compadres, massed behind that goal last night, cheering their team on. They pay to see the show, and we are the show, never let UEFA forget it.

Mongoose and Zil were resting in a bar across the road from Atocha train station, sitting in the sun, having breakfast and a beer. Thankfully, they told me the exit to use, and I didn't have to cross the busy road. We met like conquering heroes, this was *the* moment, the moment when it all sank in, and you could take in exactly what happened the previous evening. We were the champions of Europe for a sixth time. We toasted the Reds with cold bottles of Mahou, had a bit of breakfast and relaxed in the mid-day sunshine. It was time for the long journey home.

We dodged the traffic to get to the train station and find Our Ian, hoping he'd found his place to stay last night. No news was good news, so hopefully he was fine. He was waiting for us, and it was time to say goodbye to Mongoose, who was heading back to Torremolinos, via Malaga, for a few days on the ale in the sun. We were on the 2.10pm train back to Valencia, then on to Alicante. After the obligatory airport-style security checks, our timing was perfect, and as the train drew away from the station we were on the long trek home.

The first train to Valencia was fast as you like, but the second crawled back to Alicante, and with no buffet car, stale croissants from the station shop were the only sustenance we had until the airport. The two-hour journey felt twice as long. The phone started pinging with messages from home, with sights from the homecoming parade, the phone showing us wonderful sights from The Strand in Liverpool, full of red. It was beautiful. It reminded me of trundling through Greece after our win in Istanbul. In those days before smartphones, it was a text message that described what everyone else was seeing, but now it was in front of our eyes within seconds of it happening. Once again you can't win, go to the match and you don't get to see the cup come back home, but what would you rather have? That's right, both!

By the time we got off the train at Alicante we were running on empty. Our Ian was fine, though, in 30 minutes he'd be by a pool with a G&T in his hand, with his wife. If he knows what's good for him, he won't be saying anything about the last 36 hours. The secret of a happy mixed marriage is knowing when to keep quiet. By the time Zil and I had even got on the airport bus he'd have had his drink in his hand. By the time we got home, he'd have had a great night's sleep and snoozed by the pool for most of Monday. But I'm not complaining, as this is what we do and hopefully you've enjoyed the journey with us.

Alicante was only a stop as we flew eastwards. I know Gatwick is due north, but we flew east to Venice in Italy. Confused? It was only €19 with an airline called

Volotea. You've never heard of them? Neither had we, but a €19 flight, and Venice to Gatwick only costing us a further €52, it was cheap as chips compared to flights from Alicante to Gatwick (over £300 for that leg alone). McDonald's for tapas! Cheeseburger and fries, that is, and a pint of San Miguel, and we were set for Venice.

We arrived in Venice, the city of lovers, but all I had for company was Zil, so there would be no loving and no bed for the night. Arriving in Venice at midnight and flying to Gatwick at 6.50am, it was pointless getting a room. Getting your head down in departures would be okay, a few seats together curled up, you'd be fine. If only they hadn't closed departures for the night, we'd have been fine. We had to make do with a marble plinth next to a waterfall feature. How many trips to the toilet that accounted for I don't remember, and until 4.30am it was an uncomfortable night. As soon as they opened departures, we were in there like a shot. I was right on to the chairs, squeezing my 6ft 1in frame on to two seats, avoiding cutting myself in two with the dividing arm. Before I knew it, I was waking up surrounded by people ready to board the London-bound plane. Bemused Italians were looking at us and trying to figure out what we were doing in Venice. The sun was coming up over the city on the other side of the lagoon. In the distance you could make out the Campanile in St Mark's Square. It was pretty cool.

Don't ask me what the EasyJet flight was like from Venice to Gatwick. All I remember is the cabin crew being released for duty and seeing Venice blinking in the morning sun and the snow-capped mountains as we climbed to our cruising altitude. Then there's nothing until I was jolted awake as the plane hit the runway at Gatwick, and a welcome to Gatwick in Italian and English by the cabin crew. Not quite home yet, but the journey was coming to an end. We took the train from Gatwick to Victoria, where Zil and I parted company, him to Euston and the train north to Liverpool, and me to Luton to fly back to the Isle of Man at 2pm on another blurred flight with EasyJet.

As soon as I was in my seat, my head was dropping, you know that feeling when your head weighs that much you can't keep it up and your eyelids are so heavy that nothing is keeping them open. 'Welcome to the Isle of Man, where the time is …' 1999! Tranquillity awaited and I was back on home soil, but still not quite finished yet, though. Nikki and the kids were on the beach in the seaside town of Port Erin and said it would be great if I could go and meet them. We could all travel home together, as everybody wanted to see the man who'd won the European Cup less than 48 hours before. I jumped on the bus for the ten-minute ride to Port Erin and caught up with them. It was a lovely way to end the trip, in the arms of those you love. To top it off we took the steam train home to Douglas. Who else could have had that journey, the one that ends with a steam train. After 80 hours, five planes, five trains, three buses and a steam train, and I'd won the European Cup, well done me. Now it was time for a well-earned shower, decent meal and bed. And pack the Imodium away for next time.

As always, the journey is made better by the people you take it with. I couldn't ask for better travelling companions, and Madrid will always have a special place in my heart. Most importantly it was the start of a longer journey to make me better, bring me back to life. I'd taken the first step, and what followed was up to me. Thanks for listening boys, I'm forever grateful.

We Climbed the Hill in Our Own Way

THERE'S A banner held aloft on the Kop that proclaims: 'We climbed the hill in our own way' (inspired by the Pink Floyd song 'Fearless', which sampled 'You'll Never Walk Alone', I believe), and that's exactly what we've done, and we're still climbing. The fight for justice has been long and unending and has tested many of us along the way. We've lost many good people on the way who didn't live to see the truth come out. The fight against the Establishment and the lies and smears has taken its toll on the families, survivors and those present on the day.

I was at Hillsborough on 15 April 1989. My first book detailed my story on that day, but this is about what came next.

I don't see myself as a survivor, I was a bystander, one who looked on, one who didn't get involved, but one whose life is inextricably linked to the events of that fateful day. Chants of 'Justice for the 97' carry more weight for me and many others. This is our disaster, and we still live it. This isn't a slight on the people who pronounce their support, but do they really understand it? Ask many Liverpool fans whether they truly know what happened on that day, have they read the Hillsborough Independent Report? (If you haven't, I recommend you do). Have you seen the dramas? The documentaries? Do you honestly know what happened to us? How we felt? How we still feel?

That wasn't supposed to be how this chapter commenced, but as I started writing I recognised that it's something I need to say. Not on Twitter for trolls to get hold of and say that Liverpool fans don't get Hillsborough, it's not that at all, but do you get it? Have you ever listened to people who were there on that day. I mean listened? Many can't listen, it's too hard, but please give the time to listen to the survivors. *The Anfield Wrap* did superb podcasts with amazing guys such as Peter Carney, Richie Greaves and Damian Kavanagh. Check them out, three survivors of the pens who eloquently tell it like it was and how it still feels.

Many people, including Liverpool fans, said, 'What's the point? You'll never win,' 'Stop going on about it, it's pointless.' Fans of other clubs were more vicious, from a tribalistic perspective, I get that. It winds us up, but mocking the dead when it could just as easily be you or yours?

Since 2009 when a single shout of 'Justice for the 96' was joined by the masses in Anfield at the 20th Hillsborough memorial service, resulting in a deafening and defiant demand for justice, my life has been driven by Hillsborough. As Andy Burnham stood representing Prime Minister Gordon Brown, he couldn't have known what would happen next, and neither could we. That single shout for justice stirred the Kop, then the four stands rose to their feet chanting in unison, a seminal moment in the fight for justice. A campaign that had been fought expecting truth and justice from the Establishment had floundered and was seemingly going nowhere. The Hillsborough Justice Campaign (HJC), run from a shop behind the Kop, kept the hope and the fight alive. From stickers to support, a place to go or just a place to be, it was where we still believed our voice could be heard, but until a government minister was shocked to his core, we were pushing water uphill.

Andy Burnham was as good as his word and went back to Gordon Brown. Unlike Jack Straw and Tony Blair before him, he took decisive action. For Jack Straw, a lawyer by trade, not to identify serious miscarriages of justice will forever be a stain on him, and Tony Blair writing 'what's the point' across a note about a new inquiry, I have no words. The Government established the Hillsborough Independent Panel, tasked with reviewing all the documentation from the archives and truly investigating the causes and reaction to the disaster at Leppings Lane. I remember hoping beyond hope that they'd give us something, and come that momentous day we'd be unburdened; this had been a long time coming.

I want to give you a timeline of the fight for justice. Please take your time, read it slowly, feel the anger, feel the pain. Would you still have been fighting for over 30 years? Would you have given up?

15 April 1989 – You know what happens, but what comes next?

August 1989 – Lord Justice Taylor's official report into the disaster emphatically blames police mismanagement of the event and criticises South Yorkshire Police for blaming Liverpool fans instead of accepting responsibility. Peter Wright, Chief Constable of South Yorkshire accepts the findings, although ominously he suggests 'a very different picture would emerge at the inquests'. [Remember that.]

August 1990 – The Crown Prosecution Service (CPS) decides that there's insufficient evidence to justify criminal proceedings against anybody from any organisation for any offences arising out of the deaths.

October 1990 – South Yorkshire Police admits that it was negligent and failed in its duty of care to the people attending the match, when settling civil claims brought by the bereaved families and injured supporters. [Remember that.]

November 1990 – The first inquest opens in Sheffield, overseen by the local coroner, Dr Stefan Popper. South Yorkshire Police renews its claim that drunken supporters who arrived late and ticketless were to blame. Popper refuses to hear evidence from after 3.15pm on 15 April, saying the 95 supporters who'd died (Anthony Bland was still alive at this point) had all died or had sustained the injuries that caused their death by this time. This crucially means that the response to the disaster by the emergency services was out of scope.

March 1991 – Inquest jury returns a majority verdict of 'accidental death'.

October 1991 – South Yorkshire Police's Chief Superintendent David Duckenfield retires on medical grounds with depression and post-traumatic stress disorder.

January 1992 – Disciplinary action against Superintendent Bernard Murray, the police control box commander on 15 April 1989, is dropped.

November 1993 – An application, placed by six representative families, for a judicial review to quash the inquest verdict is rejected by Lord Justice McCowan in the divisional court. It's ruled that the inquest was properly conducted.

December 1996 – ITV broadcasts the Jimmy McGovern docudrama *Hillsborough*. The drama highlights the effect on the families, their complaints of injustice and allegations of a police cover-up, later to be proved true.

[For me, this drama was the closest thing to being there on the day. McGovern worked closely with the families to show what happened in the years afterwards.]

May 1997 – Hillsborough Justice Concert is held at Anfield to raise funds to support the families and features The Beautiful South, Manic Street Preachers, Lightning Seeds, Stereophonics, Cast and Space.

June 1997 – A new Labour Government fulfilling an election campaign promise orders the scrutiny of new evidence by Lord Justice Smith. It finds that South Yorkshire Police changed the accounts of 164 officers before sending them to the original Taylor inquiry. Home Secretary Jack Straw, according to a civil service note, didn't believe there was sufficient evidence for a new inquiry and said that an assertion had to come from an independent source, such as a judge, in order to be acceptable. Prime Minister Tony Blair had written across the note about setting up a new inquiry 'Why? What's the point?'

[These were our 'friends' in Whitehall, they had all the evidence available and did nothing. They should be ashamed.]

1997 – The HJC is formed, the first organisation to embrace survivors, everyday fans and the bereaved. Crucially the HJC recognises the long-term mental health impact that Hillsborough has had on many individuals, using funds from the shop and events to provide specialist counselling and keep the disaster in the public eye.

[Who could ever forget the yellow 'Justice for the 96' and 'Don't buy The Sun' stickers that appeared wherever Liverpool went.]

February 1998 – Lord Justice Stuart-Smith rejects any grounds for prosecutions or quashing the inquest verdicts. Jack Straw accepts that conclusion.

[The same Stuart-Smith who joked on his first day in Liverpool about Liverpudlians being 'late as usual'.

The families who met him do not speak kindly of the man.]

July 2000 – David Duckenfield and Bernard Murray face a private prosecution for gross negligence brought by the Hillsborough Family Support Group. Duckenfield admits to lying in his statements. Murray is acquitted and the jury is unable to reach a verdict on Duckenfield.

January 2007 – The Truth mosaic on the Kop. Live on TV, the third round FA Cup tie means the Kop has an opportunity to tell the world that they want: The Truth. For six minutes the mosaic remains aloft as the cards are held high while the fans shout 'Justice for the 96'.

[A new generation of activists is born, and the campaign strengthens.]

April 2009 – Andy Burnham's (representing the Government at the Hillsborough memorial service) speech is interrupted with shouts of 'Justice for the 96'.

12 September 2012 – The Hillsborough Independent Panel delivers its report, having reviewed over 450,000 documents. The police failings are highlighted and the campaign to blame fans is further exposed. The Conservative Home Secretary, Theresa May, accepts the report findings and orders a new criminal inquiry into the disaster. Operation Resolve is established, and the Independent Police Complaints Commission launches an investigation into alleged malpractice by the police in the case made afterwards.

12 September 2012 – Prime Minister David Cameron stands in front of Parliament and says he is 'profoundly sorry' for the failures that caused the Hillsborough disaster and the subsequent attempts to shift blame for the tragedy. He goes on to say that the findings in the report are 'deeply distressing'. He says, 'With the weight of the new evidence in the report it's right for me today as Prime Minister to make a proper apology to the families of the 96… on behalf of the Government, and indeed of our country, I am profoundly sorry that this double injustice has been left uncorrected for so long'.

December 2012 – The first inquest verdicts are quashed by the Lord Chief Justice and two other judges who find that the inquest wasn't properly conducted.

March 2014 – The new inquests begin in Warrington; they'll become the longest ever heard by a jury in British legal history.

26 April 2016 – A momentous day! The inquest jury delivers its verdict. It concludes that the 96 people who died were 'unlawfully killed', therefore overturning the verdict of 'accidental death' at the original inquest.

It confirms that no behaviour on the part of Liverpool fans contributed to the dangerous situation at the Leppings Lane turnstiles. This at last comprehensively exonerates the supporters who were blamed, in the immediate aftermath, for causing the disaster. The inquest finds that defects in the construction and layout of the stadium contributed to the disaster and adds that 'errors and omissions' by the police operation on the day contributed to the cause of the disaster. It states that 'errors and omissions' in the stadium's layout and design, and its lack of a valid safety certificate, contributed to the tragedy, as did Sheffield Wednesday's preparation for the match. On the question of whether Sheffield Wednesday's actions on the day of the game were a contributory factor, the jury couldn't say for sure but said they may have been. Errors and omissions by South Yorkshire Metropolitan Ambulance Service are also said to have contributed to the disaster.

There were 14 questions answered by the Hillsborough Inquest and there was a clean sweep of answers in our favour, the most notable questions that needed answering as survivors and fans was as follows:

Question 7. Behaviour of the supporters

Was there any behaviour on the part of football supporters which caused or contributed to the dangerous situation at the Leppings Lane turnstiles?

Answer – no

If your answer is 'no', please answer the following: Was there any behaviour on the part of football supporters which may have caused or contributed to the dangerous situation at the Leppings Lane turnstiles?

Answer – no

[The things we had been saying for over 25 years, our truth, was now proven to be the truth! The bile thrown our way, that we killed our own and it was our fault, was proved in court to be untrue.]

June 2017 – Following Operation Resolve, the CPS charges David Duckenfield with manslaughter by gross negligence. The charge relates to 95 of the people who died at Hillsborough. No charge can be brought in relation to the death of the 96th victim, Tony Bland, due to legal guidance in place in 1989, which stated that 'an accused could not be held responsible for the death of anyone who died more than a year and a day after they suffered their injuries'. Tony died some four years later in 1993. Graham Mackrell, the Sheffield Wednesday club secretary, and safety officer at the time of the disaster, is charged with two counts of breaching his duties under safety legislation.

January 2019 – Duckenfield's trial starts at Preston Crown Court. Now aged 75 he stands trial alongside Mackrell, both men pleading not guilty to the charges. The prosecution states: 'Duckenfield's criminal responsibility for the deaths flows from his gross failure to discharge his personal responsibility as match commander.' Duckenfield's defence says he's being 'singled out unfairly'. The judge refers to Duckenfield as 'poor chap', and he's allowed to not sit in the dock and to use the court's canteen, unlike other accused people.

April 2019 – The jury returns after eight days' deliberation and fails to reach a verdict on Duckenfield's charge. Mackrell is found guilty by a majority of 10-2, for breaching his legal duty to take reasonable care at work for people's safety, in relation to the allocation of turnstiles for the match. Mackrell is fined £6,500 following his conviction. The CPS seeks a retrial for Duckenfield.

7 October 2019 – Duckenfield's retrial starts at Preston Crown Court.

8 November 2019 – Duckenfield is found not guilty of gross negligence.

26 May 2021 – Three people (an ex-solicitor and two retired policemen) accused of altering statements and perverting the course of justice are acquitted as a judge throws the case out on a technicality, saying it should never have been brought. The CPS once again comes under scrutiny.

4 June 2021 – Two police forces agree to pay damages to more than 600 people over a cover-up that followed the Hillsborough disaster. The South Yorkshire and West Midlands forces agreed the settlement in April 2021 following a civil claim. Due to the ongoing trial, it couldn't be announced until the trial was over. South Yorkshire Police offers an 'unreserved apology' and acknowledges that 'serious errors and mistakes were made' by its officers, 'both on 15 April 1989 and during the

> subsequent investigations. Those actions on the day of the disaster tragically led to lives being lost and many being injured [while] the force's subsequent failings also caused huge distress, suffering and pain, both to the victims and their families.'

> **27 July 2021** – Andrew Devine dies and is officially declared the 97th victim of the Hillsborough disaster by the Liverpool Coroner, who rules that Andrew ultimately died as a result of the injuries sustained at Hillsborough on 15 April 1989.

Over the last three decades there have been four trials, two sets of inquests, a public inquiry and several other investigations and reviews, and just the one man convicted of a health and safety offence. Ladies and gentlemen, I give you British justice. They've shafted the families and the survivors one last time. There's nothing left.

Still with me? Are you angry? Are you confused as to why it took over 30 years and only one man has been convicted of an offence in relation to the disaster? And that man was fined the princely sum of £6,500, just over £67 for every life lost. The price of a life. Angry yet? The case has cost over £65 million to try, yet only one conviction. You can judge for yourself about whether there have been failings of the prosecutors and the judiciary.

The fight was never just about David Duckenfield, the focus wasn't on one man, but that was his defence in his trial: 'It was unfair to single him out,' or 'He wasn't the only one who should be in the dock.' Not much of a defence, is it? Why weren't the others alongside him? The focus should have been on all those who failed in their duty of care to supporters attending a football match. So much wrong from so many, the FA got away scot-free, Sheffield Wednesday, who changed the company so they couldn't be prosecuted, the South Yorkshire Ambulance Service for their response, the South Yorkshire Fire Brigade, and last but certainly not least, South Yorkshire Police, not just David Duckenfield, but loads of them.

Duckenfield's defence in court was that he was being singled out, and others should be in the dock with him or instead of him. They should be alongside him. Too fucking right they should be. The lies and smears that followed compounded the man's mistake, his thoughtless and ill-considered attempt to address his force's institutional failings. Are you angry? Well, I am and have been for years. Angry at what happened, of course, but angry at British justice, which has allowed this monstrous debacle to blight the lives of 97 families and thousands of supporters who were involved or witnessed the horrendous events of 15 April 1989.

Let me quote David Duckenfield when he gave evidence and admitted that he lied, at the Warrington inquests.

> Barrister: 'You have accepted a large number of failures have you not?'
>
> David Duckenfield: 'I have, sir.'
>
> Barrister: 'You have accepted that some of them in particular were grave failures. Serious failures?'
>
> David Duckenfield: 'I have, sir.'

> Barrister: 'The most serious failure was that of failing to ensure the closing of the central tunnel prior to giving the order of the exit gates to be opened, would you agree with that?'
>
> David Duckenfield: 'Yes, sir.'
>
> David Duckenfield: 'I was in a situation that I was totally untrained for, totally unprecedented. And I make no excuses, I was the man who did it.'

After years of lying, he finally admitted he did it, it wasn't the fans who forced the gate, it was him who ordered it open. He could have saved many years of heartache. The lies have just added to the grief.

We end up in a situation where a man admits his failings at a public inquest, which proves what happened and exonerates the fans, yet a court allows his defence counsel to blame others once again for their client's failings. A court that allows the facts of the inquest to be inadmissible, but allows the defence to peddle the lies of many years that have already been discounted and proved to be untrue. They escape without censure by a judge. A court that allows the defendant to not sit in a dock, to eat in the staff canteen and to be escorted to court on a daily basis. A man who'd already had legal aid in excess of £7.5 million to defend his case, before he admitted his failures, and then receives a further £2 million-plus for the final two trials, nearly £10 million in total to defend himself. Finally, there's the CPS, who can't get his colleagues in the dock alongside him, those who his defence say should be there.

Then when the three men who were acquitted on a technicality have their barristers talk about the myth of the Hillsborough cover-up, saying that there was no evidence, and finally that 'old men' shouldn't be in court. There were many who never got to live long enough to be old men, never mind be in court having to face up to their actions (or lack of). One barrister even spouted the years of repeated lies once again on BBC Radio without challenge, when those lies have been proven to be false for years. The media are fully complicit in the cover-up and are allowing people to rewrite history once again. The media who drove the narrative that has lasted for over 30 years, the story that we broke the gates down, we were ticketless, and I won't even mention what that rag said. We cannot allow them to regurgitate the lies, we cannot allow that to happen, since the sheep of Britain believe everything they read. That's why it's up to all of us to educate ourselves and know what happened at Hillsborough, then educate others, and never allow it to happen again.

How does it feel? Well, you can see the anger, but there have been so many feelings along the way. Tears of frustration, tears of belief, tears of relief, how many tears do you want?

I remember 12 September 2012 well. I was sitting at my desk in work watching the news come through on the internet, trying to make it look like I was working. I was half listening on a work teleconference that I was totally disengaged with. There were more important things happening in front of my eyes than the mumbling in my ears. The screen was showing me that after 23 years we'd finally got somewhere. We'd told you they'd lied and now we had the proof, we weren't to blame, we were telling the truth. And the tears rolled gently down my face. Nobody noticed as I headed out the door on to the promenade to get some fresh air.

I knew the truth on 15 April 1989, and I wrote about it in 2009. My truth was *the* truth, it was validated in the panel's report and now people are still trying to say 'it didn't happen like that'. This is the most-witnessed tragedy in British history, yet no one saw anything, except us, and they hate us talking about it. But it's not only about us now, is it? Start looking into the Grenfell fire and the Post Office scandal and the signs are there, no accountability, no need to tell the truth, and manipulating the media to make it all go away.

* * *

Was it any wonder that Hillsborough caught up with me over 30 years later? I sought out the help I needed, and as I sat in the chair in front of a huge bear of a man, with the gentlest nature, I was ready to unburden myself. I was ready to delve inside and take out what was holding me back. There was a lot going on. I had several things to deal with but one by one we whittled it down to what happened over 30 years ago in Sheffield and my dad's death, which, truth be told, I still hadn't dealt with properly. After a couple of sessions, it was clear that Hillsborough was a huge detractor in my life and needed resolving.

I had full trust in my therapist, Adrian, who was there to guide me. I had all the answers, he said. I was ready to work hard at getting to the answers to let me move on, measure myself and the impact the issue was having on me. I was asked whether I was a danger to myself or others. Honestly, I never felt I was, but on those dark days I could always relate to why someone wouldn't be able to find a way out. I never felt that bad, as I always had Nikki, and she could always sense where I was and help me find a way. I was sitting in this chair for her, for Charlie, and for Izzy, but ultimately for me.

The chair was a comforting place to be. Adrian helped me find my path and ultimately return to good mental health. There are things you can affect and things you can't, things you can do for yourself and things where you need professional help. I looked forward to my weekly sessions and, luckily, I'd done the hard work by the time Covid arrived, swiftly followed by redundancy, which hit me in 2020. But thanks to Adrian, I was ready for anything.

Although there were loads of great chats and welcoming cups of coffee, I ultimately needed clinical intervention. EMDR (eye movement desensitisation and reprocessing) has been found to positively treat traumatic memories, and for me it worked. In simple terms, the process is to find the traumatic memory, visualise it, enter a trance state and then, using a light bar (where you're watching the light travelling back and forth across the bar), the memory, or associated feelings to the memory, dissipate and lead to a return to good mental health. The problem with Hillsborough was that I didn't have only one traumatic memory, not one traumatic picture that

I could think of, but due to Adrian's skill an image that I'd buried for over 30 years came into view, and that was the image we worked with. I've battled with whether I should describe that image to you, but I feel that it's not appropriate, I feel that it's not right to share. All I can say is that I understand why I'd buried it for all those years. But it was tucked away in my subconscious, and that was causing me the issues, it needed releasing.

With Adrian's skill, that's exactly what we did. With the use of the light bar and the trance-like state, the colour faded from the image, as did the attached emotions. To such a point that today I can recall the image in black and white, but the emotions are no longer tied to it and it ultimately no longer has the same effect upon me. It took four or five sessions, but it was really helpful. I'd recommend it to anyone. I'm forever in Adrian's debt.

Hillsborough doesn't go away; it's there every day and it creeps up and bites you when you least expect it. You don't only think of it on the anniversary and put it back in the box until next year, at least I don't, it doesn't work like that. I was sitting in a cottage in the Isle of Man enjoying a week away with the family and it hit me again. I was watching *Forrest Gump* for the umpteenth time with Nikki and the kids, who weren't massively impressed, to be fair. The smart TV had frozen, and I had a quick look at Twitter, and a tweet stopped me in my tracks. From Liverpool FC and headed 'a statement from the family of Andrew Devine'.

This could only mean one thing if you knew who Andrew Devine was, and I did. I knew of Andrew ever since 1989, but many people didn't, until Liverpool won the Champions League in Madrid. At the end of the homecoming parade, James Milner made sure the bus stopped at the Devine family home in the south of Liverpool to show off the cup to the family, and in particular Andrew. Why such a special visit? Andrew was at Hillsborough, and he was so badly injured that it resulted in him needing 24-hour care for the next 32 years. He was still part of a loving family who looked after him for all that time, and he still even got to go to Anfield. He wasn't forgotten. He was out of the spotlight, as his family wanted. Now he was gone, and may he rest in peace. Now the shout is 'Justice for the 97'.

Unofficially, there are more than 97 victims of the disaster, as you won't see unlawfully killed written on their death certificate, but there's a direct correlation between Hillsborough and their death. The many family members who have passed away early because of the impact of the disaster and the nature of the aftermath. Many people who haven't yet found the way forward, and Hillsborough has eaten them up and they couldn't cope. The true numbers are much higher than 97, the human cost is incalculable.

All I ask is that we're educated, that we educate others and we tell our children about Hillsborough and to always stand up for the truth. Shout it from the rooftops and keep 'banging on about it'. You might not get everything you want or hope for, but you get more than if you just accept it. If it wasn't for 'banging on about it' we may still believe that we were the ones to blame, that it was our fault. It wasn't and we have 'The Truth', and for that I'm grateful.

People still ask me, 'Did that actually happen?' They're amazed at what happened and how it was covered up, and they're right. There's a need to keep educating, let people walk in our shoes.

Read *Hillsborough Voices* by Kevin Sampson, documenting first-hand accounts of the fans at Hillsborough on 15 April, or the definitive account in *Hillsborough – The Truth* by Professor Phil Scraton, who forensically deconstructs the myths and mistruths. Read David Conn of *The Guardian*, who has been the strongest voice in mainstream journalism for many years. For dramas watch the magnificent *Hillsborough* by Jimmy McGovern from 1996, as true today as when it was written. It changed the perception of many people about what happened on the day. It's the closest thing I've ever seen to being there. But a special mention for the drama that charts not only the events of 15 April but the battle that has lasted over 30 years. Do not miss watching the outstanding *Anne*, skilfully crafted by Kevin Sampson, and superbly acted by the amazing Maxine Peake and Steven Walters.

Whatever you do, I urge you to ask the question, why? Why did Hillsborough happen? Why did the fight for justice go on for so long? Most importantly, though, why did the truth mean nothing to the British judicial system?

I'll be 'banging on about it' until the day I die, and my lad will take over from me, that's for sure. One thing's for sure: I'm still climbing that hill with everyone else.

Justice for the 97!

Tapas for Everyone!

EVER SINCE he went his first match, Charlie has been on at me about going to an away match with me, not just any away match but a European away match. When I saw his little face as I left him behind as I went on my jaunts to Paris, Munich and Madrid, I knew I had to make it happen at some point. We watch every match on TV and share the joy and the pain of what's happening miles away from home, and sometimes we'll be on the Kop, hugging, as the Reds score another fabulous goal.

Charlie's a good lad and appreciative of everything that comes his way. He doesn't complain much, and he has been resigned to not being able to follow the Reds into Europe, because 'that's only for dads'. The Audi Cup escapades had given him the taste, though, and the memories only made him want more of it. Was 2020 going to be his year?

The Champions League draw for 2019/20 pitted Liverpool against Napoli, Red Bull Salzburg, and Genk in the group stages. There wasn't a cat in hell's chance of getting tickets for Genk and Salzburg – poor ticket allocations and places no one had been before, so everyone wanted to go there. I'd vowed never to go to Napoli, it's not my scene, looking over your shoulder every minute you're there, it's just not for me. As Liverpool made hard work of the group stages, all they needed to do was avoid defeat against a decent Salzburg side to qualify for the last 16, but they'd pushed us hard at Anfield and hadn't been beaten at home in Europe for a long time. Avoid defeat Liverpool did, and as Mo Salah slotted from an acute angle to make it 2-0, my mind was made up. Next up, wherever it was, we were going. Charlie was getting his wish.

The draw gave Liverpool a swift return to the Wanda Metropolitano, the home of Atlético Madrid (or Atleti as everyone seems to call them nowadays, we always called them Athletico). The first leg was in Madrid, sound! Surely it would be easier to get to Madrid this time round, straight in and out and no messing, and loads cheaper than the Champions League Final.

Within minutes of the draw taking place, I was searching for flights. Notice I was searching, not booking. You have to wait to see when the games are going to be played. UEFA in their wisdom (and TV rights) split the round of 16 games over a two-week period, and the game would be on either a Tuesday or a Wednesday on either week. I was searching for flights to Madrid on 18 or 19 February, or 25 or 26 February, take your pick. One week was the school half-term, but the other week was in school time, another potential fly in the ointment. As soon as the dates are officially announced the flight website prices start moving upwards, and rapidly, so you need to be more creative. From the island we can fly to Gatwick, Liverpool or Manchester, but from there where do we fly to? Direct to Madrid? Or the coast? Alicante, Valencia, Barcelona? All on EasyJet's route map. I searched Skyscanner, Expedia and EasyJet's own site. I had a million and one options, the cheapest not always the best. Flying at 6am on matchday was never going to be an option. Charlie didn't do the not sleeping enough thing well, so potentially getting up at 4am and to bed well past midnight was not on.

After what seemed like an age, the first-leg date dropped and it was Tuesday, 18 February, half-term week. I was looking at flights either side of that day, planning on two nights in Madrid. Expedia had flights straight in and out of Madrid from Gatwick for only £90 each. I went through the whole booking procedure, credit card details as prompted and hit the submit button. As the little wheel spun around on the screen, I got on the EasyJet app on my phone, like a true travel professional. Within minutes I'd booked the Isle of Man to Gatwick non-refundable flights, good flights out and back to connect with the chosen Spanish flights. Due to the high volumes of booking on the Expedia site, the wheel was still spinning. It warns you that whatever you do don't do anything to your browser as you'll lose your booking. Don't touch it, DON'T TOUCH IT!

I should have touched it, as the wheel stopped spinning after 40 minutes, the screen proclaiming that all seats were sold out and my booking hadn't been made. I checked my credit card statement online and they'd taken the booking fee, but not the full payment. Funny, when I went straight to the airline website, there were flights available from other airports, but the price had already doubled. Now, though, because I'd been clever booking my EasyJet flights, I was tied into Gatwick. Finding anything flying out of Gatwick to Madrid that tied in with our EasyJet flights was impossible. I started looking at the Spanish coast, thinking we could get a fast train into Madrid, and that would be much cheaper than last time. Alicante, Valencia and Malaga all had flights available, but getting back from Madrid the following day was impossible, so it would have to be Barcelona. I booked the flights to Barcelona, and the return flight gave us some leeway, in case of delays, ensuring we could get back to the island. Not needing additional nights in hotels either side saves you about £160, worth the messing around.

Tickets? I can't do anything about tickets; what will be will be. The club wouldn't announce the criteria until a few weeks before the game, and if we got less than 4,000 I wouldn't qualify on my own merits. A return to Madrid so quickly and the proximity to Valentine's Day, yes, it's a thing (see Porto), and there was probably a good chance of getting sorted somewhere down the line.

* * *

Do you know, when you've done something special for someone? That moment for me came at 7.30am on Christmas Day morning. We'd done the usual thing of opening stockings full of little presents (including a guidebook to Madrid for Charlie, and he didn't realise) and then we built up to the big one. In previous years it had been things such as PlayStations, doll's houses and bikes, but this year we'd gone all out on experiences. Our kids love doing stuff, they value experience over material things. The doll's house, the bikes, all used sparingly, but the trips away, the making of memories that last forever, they're constantly talked about, and every moment is lovingly remembered.

I forgot Charlie's Christmas present was already a surprise trip to Wolves at home over the Christmas period, including a one-night stay in Grandma's hotel (her house), bed and breakfast and a guaranteed portion of Grandma's homemade chips. What more could a lad want? Adding in a trip to Madrid as a Christmas present, he was a lucky boy this year. Charlie opened the Christmas envelope, a trip to watch Wolves at home. He feigned the disbelief, I think. He'd come to expect a trip to watch Liverpool play. What came next, though, was pure magic.

One more envelope to open and he found an A4 sheet of paper documenting the itinerary for a dad-and-lad trip to … Madrid! He didn't quite know what to say. He read it a few times before it sank in, then he threw his arms around me with the biggest hug ever. I told him not to forget his mum, as it was from both of us. We're making memories for our kids whether we're both with them or not. Taking loads of pictures on the journey leaves no one out of the experience. Please don't think we left out Izzy either, but that's for another book. You can't do fabulous things for only one child, that's not fair.

I had to point out to him one critical line: 'Tickets are NOT GUARANTEED'. We were going on an adventure, but I couldn't promise him something I couldn't deliver, could I? Charlie had always said he wouldn't mind just being there, being with the lads, being present. I had six weeks to sort out tickets. I've been locked out at a big away game, but putting in the hard miles to get somewhere this far away would be a lot worse. He still didn't believe that we wouldn't get tickets, but he had more confidence than his dad. It's tough nowadays, everyone wants to see the Mighty Reds, the champions of Europe. I didn't see much of Charlie for the rest of the day as his eyes crawled all over the Madrid guidebook and train and plane schedules.

With the flights on and off the island and to Spain and back booked, I now needed to get to Madrid. Let's have a look at the train. Jesus, how much? The prices were astronomical. Given there are so many trains a day, I thought it would be cheaper. I thought I was paying a Champions League premium last time, but this time it's a normal Tuesday morning. Looking at connections it was obvious that the train from Madrid to Barcelona the morning after the game would be cutting it fine. Charlie was looking at train sites and working out the cheapest (and generally least effective) ways to get to Madrid. He had us going via Zaragoza and fare splitting, but it didn't quite work out. I liked his way of thinking, though. Trains or flights weren't cheap either way, and I ended up looking at one way on the train and flying back. Even months ahead there were no early savers, and it was coming out at €150 one way on the train, so the plane had better be cheap, and it was relatively so at £110 for both of us, flying with Iberia.

Due to the ineffectiveness of Expedia's website, I was now massively out of pocket and Charlie's Christmas present was going to be his only present for the next ten years, including his 21st birthday. A cheap little trip to watch the Reds had spiralled out of control, but it could be priceless.

I called on everyone I know, asking to be in their thoughts if any tickets popped up. If they do, I'm your man. Promises of 'if we're lucky in ballots, we'll sort you' came, but they needed to be lucky first, sometimes you can't control what happens. What happened next was beyond my control. However, it was wonderful. A winner in a corporate ballot gave me a shout and, true to his word, the ticket had my name on it, well Charlie's name. I thought at least if I get him sorted first, he can go in with one of the lads. It wouldn't be the same without his dad, especially on a dad-and-lad trip, but he'd be in the Wanda watching the Reds. A wave of relief shot over me, and I started to relax. Surely, I could pick up a single ticket one way or another.

I didn't qualify on the sale. Most of the games I'd been to over the past four years were all on other people's cards, and they got the credit. I couldn't build my own history to qualify for future games. It all came down to the last lot of tickets and, as the clock clicked around to 11am on sale day, we were all logged in ready to go, five of us looking for tickets. Boom! Seven minutes in the queue, surely this was it. The seating plan appeared, I chose tickets and they disappeared. Frantic WhatsApp messages meant my phone was pinging and the rest of the office was intrigued as to what was going on at my desk, as I was loudly swearing at the screen. It looked like I was going to be pounding the streets of Madrid begging for a spare. Then the message came through, just one word: 'Sorted'. A wave of relief shot over me, and I pinged a message to Charlie at school that we were both sorted. One word back from Charlie: 'Cool.' We're going to Madrid.

* * *

Mid-February is not a great time for travelling, virtually four years to the day since my Augsburg travel plans were thrown into chaos by storms. 2020 saw storms Ciara and Dennis (back to back) battering the island. Once Ciara had blown itself out, I thought we were safe, until Dennis rolled in and battered the whole of Britain. With flights cancelled all weekend, and with a yellow weather warning until 6am on Monday morning (our departure day), this was going to be touch and go. Excitement had been building for weeks, and with tickets in hand now, god help us if the weather was to ruin things. Having a plan B is difficult, maybe even impossible, when living on an island, and with no boat for the previous four out of five days and planes cancelled left right and centre, we were at the mercy of the elements.

Waking up at 6am on Monday morning all I could hear was the wind barrelling up the road and smashing into the house, but apparently it was due to blow itself out soon. With the outbound flight leaving Gatwick at 8am it was going to be tight. Then at 7am the wind dropped, the storm had blown itself out. No wonder, it had been blowing a hoolie (gale if you're not Manx) for 24 hours. All was good now and we'd be on our way. The EasyJet app confirmed that our plane was already Isle of Man-bound and flying over London, so Madrid here we come. Charlie hadn't worried about whether we were in trouble or not, that was all on my shoulders and he couldn't understand why I was a little stressed over the weekend.

All our boarding passes were loaded on to my phone and we'd be through security in no time. You know what's coming, don't you. The modern phone thingy didn't work properly and none of the eight boarding passes were in the wallet on the phone or the EasyJet app. Bollocks, suddenly I was stressed out. I didn't have any of the emails as I'd completed the bookings in work. The words 'you can go and sort a paper boarding ticket out' were music to my ears, but the security queue snaking out the door wasn't a sight I wanted to see. Fingers crossed it would go down by the time we returned with our tickets. No such luck, the queue was even further out the door. Seemingly all of today's flights were leaving together and only one security scanner was working, resulting in longer than normal queues. As the time ticked down towards the scheduled departure, the shout 'anyone for Gatwick' was met by half the queue shouting 'yeah'. With a stroke of luck, we were in the bit of the queue nearest to the scanners and we dipped under the barriers to the head of the queue.

It was bound to happen, as the gate was closing imminently – we were chosen for a random test of our liquids. Nothing to report from a tube of Colgate, E45 and a pack of Imodium. A dash to the gate, down the stairs and on to the plane, no waiting. Let the adventure truly begin, up and away above the clouds with coffees in hand and a pack of Cadburys Fingers and Pretzels for sustenance. Next stop, Gatwick, the gateway to Europe. We were off to see two of the greatest European cities in the next 24 hours.

Approaching Gatwick, the plane dropped through the clouds and the remnants of Storm Dennis pushed the plane up and down and side to side, not exactly the world's scariest rollercoaster but enough for me to gently remind Charlie, as he went the colour of the clouds, that a sick bag was available. With a bump we were on the ground and ready to go, ready for four hours in Gatwick. I can't think of many things much worse than sitting round in an airport bored for four hours, can you?

Down to the Red Lion, a Wetherspoons with a name that screams Brits abroad, along with warm Watney's Red Barrel. That remark is one for the oldies, so you youngsters will have to Google it. The Red Lion seemingly takes over more floorspace every time I go through Gatwick. A couple of drinks and something to eat will pass a few hours. Add in some great company in the shape of the Isle of Man crowd – Terry, Nick, Graham, and Sam (from my Kyiv adventure) – who were going straight to Madrid. They'd be hitting Puerto de Sol as we were hitting Las Ramblas. Tapas for everyone! These guys (and girl) have been good company on quite a few trips across the Irish Sea to home matches and I usually catch them on our foreign sojourns too. BBQ chicken panini and chips were demolished, and all washed down with cherry cokes (got to keep him awake somehow) and Coronas (for me). Two hours later and the Isle of Man contingent was heading for their gates and their afternoon flight to Madrid. We'd only be an hour behind them. As we bid our fond farewells, we knew we'd see them again.

Our flight was called, bang on time, so we'd be in Barcelona as planned at 7pm and walking down Las Ramblas by 8pm. I might have been a bit optimistic, though. As we touched down in Barcelona, we were right on time, but we needed the longest coach ride in the world to take us to the terminal, with traffic jams on the apron and a heavy-footed driver who kept finding his brake pedal, throwing us forward at every opportunity.

We were taking the metro to our hotel at Place de Sants, one stop away from the main station, Sants Estació, where we'd be leaving to Madrid in just over 12 hours' time. Low-cost carriers generally end up at the worst terminal the airport has to offer, and it was miles to walk to the metro, the length of two whole terminals. We were already sweating by the time we tried to work out which ticket was best for only one night in Barcelona. It was far too difficult to understand. The lady in the information bureau did her best to help us, but 'non comprender senorita'. The one bit of English she had for us was left ringing in our ears: 'Watch pickpockets.' As soon as we sat on the metro there was a warning about pickpockets over the Tannoy, and signs saying beware of pickpockets. I think Barcelona has a problem with pickpockets! It doesn't feel unsafe, but you don't trust anyone who comes within ten yards of you, and with match tickets on my person I was being extra careful. Anyone within my line of vision was a potential robber. It's funny Barcelona has this massive problem yet Madrid seemingly not. Not trusting your fellow human beings is a sad state of affairs, isn't it.

After 20 minutes of keeping our eyes peeled for the robbers, we were at Place de Sants station and deciding which exit to use. Who knows? Just take your best guess and you'll still come out of the wrong exit. As we mastered the exit barrier (push it, you divvy) under the watchful eye of a policeman and his lazing muzzled Alsatian, we headed into the Barcelona night. Google Maps showed our evening's accommodation, Smartrooms Barcelona, was a seven-minute walk around the corner. It was chosen for its great location, as it's only a ten-minute walk in the morning to the main station and our train to Madrid. The Sants area was still vibrant even at this time of the evening, an enclave of artists and the well-heeled, with a bohemian vibe down the back streets, which were festooned with the flag of Catalonia.

Seven minutes later we were outside Smartrooms, which looked fine, and check-in was easy enough. Charlie didn't even try to speak Spanish, even though he's studying it now. No matter how much I pushed him he was having none of it. I reverted to the traditional use of sign language and slow English, and our hospitable host smiled and checked us in. He reliably informed us that Las Ramblas wasn't, as I thought, just a short walk away, but the metro would get us there quickly. The room was great, like a lime-green version of a Premier

Inn's predominantly purple rooms. It had everything you needed for a place to get your head down. There was time for a quick toilet break.

'I don't need one, Dad,' said Charlie. He's 13, so said he can be trusted for such basic decisions.

'Not even a just in case?'

'No, Dad, I don't need one.'

It was also going to get colder in the February night, and he wasn't taking his coat.

'I don't need it.'

'You can do without the wee, but you need your coat.' Listen to your dad.

Within ten minutes we'd checked in, rung home and were back out heading to Las Ramblas for tapas. That was Charlie's dream, that was what he'd been promised, and that's what we were doing. Not once did I believe that it would happen like that. I was thinking we'd end up in McDonald's after a little walk, taking in the sights and sounds of one of the most famous streets in the world.

We were heading to Place de Catalunya, at the top of Las Ramblas, where it would be certain to have anything we needed, even at this hour of night. It was gone 9.30pm as the train approached Place de Catalunya and Charlie started asking whether they had toilets in the metro station. Even Charlie has visited enough metro stations to know the answer was likely to be no. He knew he'd made a mistake not going for the pre-emptive wee and he was now hanging on, his need immediate. Lesson learned, always listen to your dad!

We rose out of the ground at Catalunya with a spring in our step. We were on a mission, as he was bursting. Last time I was on this exact spot in 2009 I saw Chris Kamara waiting for an open-top bus to take him around Barcelona. I didn't scout out the toilets, and we were on a flyer here. You can't just piss in the streets here, it's not like Germany. Thank god for KFC. The smiling face of Colonel Sanders would guarantee a place to go, but this one was being cleaned, so no chance. The anticipation of going had already excited Charlie's bladder and he was ready to empty.

There were banks and shops everywhere but where do you go for a burst? Tapas was promised and would deliver the opportunity for a wee. Txapela (not a spelling mistake, honest), a Basque tapas bar in Catalonia and, due to desperation, this is where we were eating whether it was any good or not. Charlie shot off in search of the toilets as I pulled up a seat. It looked okay, until you sat down and saw the menu, complete with pictures of food I didn't recognise. I thought what the hell is that? Or that? Or that? You could see the food on offer from the pictures on the paper menu, which also doubled up as a tablecloth, class. Besides Spanish omelette and patatas bravas I didn't recognise anything, and to top it off it was all in Spanish. I've done tapas a lot, but this was on another level. Another level of 'I haven't got a clue'.

As I was contemplating heading back to KFC, the waiter smiled and said, 'We have English menu too.' As if it was that obvious that I was … not from here (I nearly wrote English, god forbid), of course it was. By the time he brought the menu over Charlie was back and the colour had returned to his face, and he was starving. I thought, one look at these pictures, and we'll be off (to KFC). Nothing of the sort, he was on Las Ramblas, and he was ready and willing to try what was on offer, within reason of course. The English menu confirmed what I expected from the pictures, that we wouldn't be eating half of this stuff, rows of uncooked meats and fish. Even though I had the traveller's friend with me, Imodium, there was no way I was looking forward to a day at the match with the wildies, so let's choose carefully. Charlie chose all manner of stuff that was spicy, even though he doesn't like spicy, and there was no influencing him any other way.

Tapas dishes were chosen and within ten minutes a veritable feast started to arrive, little by little. It's a brilliant way of eating, as food is brought to you in stages, so nothing goes cold and the portions are neither too big nor too small. You can always order more as well if you didn't order enough first time round. Calamari, patatas bravas with and without the spicy sauce (two lots of roasties), croquettes with ham, breaded chicken with goats cheese, a spicy sausage called sagardoa, and pulled pork slider, each neatly positioned on top of a small piece of crusty baguette. It doesn't sound a lot but add in the bread and we were stuffed by the end of it. It was tasty, each little dish had a salad side and an accompanying dollop of flavoured mayonnaise, much better than KFC. It was now past 10.30pm and there was still room for dessert.

'Are you sure, mate? On top of the coke and everything?'

He was sure, and five minutes later he was demolishing his ice cream, as I gently swallowed my creme de Catalunya (creme brulé to the English). The ice cream finished Charlie off. He'd gone from being bright and bubbly to now being out on his feet, in a food coma. Oh god, what have I done?

We headed out on to Las Ramblas to walk off the food before he crashed out for the night. Las Ramblas was closing down, the cafés had decided it was time to go indoors, and we wanted our beds now, as there was a big day ahead tomorrow. Not far down Las Ramblas was a metro station, so we took the opportunity to head home. Charlie wasn't feeling his best now; the ice cream had done him in. With an almighty burp his symptoms eased a touch and what I half expected was avoided. He did need another wee, though, and as we headed out of the metro at Place de Sants, the seven-minute walk needed to be a trot. But he didn't have a trot in him, he was knackered and I had to cajole him to get to the hotel. Given a choice, he'd have just laid down and gone to sleep. Only 20 yards from our hotel I heard those dreaded words, 'Dad, I've stepped in something.' Yeah, you guessed it, the last thing you want on your shoes in a confined hotel room, dog shit! It stunk, so there was no way his Nikes were coming in the room with that on them. I made him take his shoes off outside and we made our way to the room to see what I could gather up to clean his shoes.

Besides Andrex wipes for your own arse, another one of the traveller's friends, there was nothing. I headed to reception and asked if he had any cleaning materials to help with my problem. Limited Spanish might help you check in, but getting stuff to clean dog shit off your shoes? There wasn't a lot of hope. The best I could get was a wooden stirrer (for stirring sugar into tea), a handful of tissues, a bottle of water and a plastic bag out of the bin in the room. With only one pair of trainers with him, this was non-negotiable, and if you were standing downwind of the shoes, you'd get a waft of what the dog had to eat over the last few days. I stood in the gutter outside the hotel and gingerly scraped away at the faeces. I caught the eye of a couple of local youths, who started to take an unhealthy interest in me, alone in the street at midnight. One sauntered over and flicked his cigarette to one side as he cockily stood over me, crouched in the gutter gipping. He laughed and said something in Spanish to his mate, who had also edged closer. Not a clue what he said but he was becoming more threatening as he realised I didn't speak Spanish. I rammed the training shoe under his nose and shouted, 'Shit, dog, merde [I know it's not Spanish], dog shit.' Luckily, he was downwind, and he got a proper waft of it. His eyes watered, he spun on his heels quickly and disappeared into the night. Saved by the shit!

Job done, shoes sprayed with Lynx and carefully placed in a bag, and it was time for bed. Charlie was well away from sleeping, though, and as is his way, he ran through his day in minute detail. He'd had a wonderful day and his dad had certainly pulled this one out the bag. We were on a fabulous adventure and the best was still to come.

The Magic Wanda

THE IPHONE alarm pinged into life at 7.30am and the anticipated nightmare of getting a tired 13-year-old out of bed didn't materialise. Excitement outweighed tiredness, and he jumped out of bed. Would he be paying for it come kick-off time tonight? After a day of travel and beers in the sun (for dad) by 9 o'clock tonight it might take its toll on dad or lad.

Up and out and within ten minutes we were at the door of Sants Estació, our gateway to Madrid. The station, in a city full of magnificent architecture (think Gaudí and the Segrada Familia) is disappointing, it's a horrible concrete box. Unlike the grand train stations of Italy and Portugal, Sants is a functional working train station with none of the grandeur. With the watery Mediterranean sun rising over the city, it was hopefully a sign of things to come. Madrid's forecast was for 17°C and sunshine, even though it was reportedly cool on Monday. Charlie was more interested in coffee and pastries for breakfast than whether he needed shorts on or not. All sorted, we headed to the platforms for the 9am service to the Spanish capital.

With an initial ticket check we were directed to a series of security scanners. Getting a train in Spain, especially at the big stations, is like getting a plane, and a high level of security applies. Luggage is scanned and backpacks are checked before you get anywhere near the platform, so whatever you do in Spain, don't rock up five minutes before departure, or you'll miss it.

Bang on time the train to Madrid pulled in and we found our coach and seats with great ease. Fast trains in Europe are generally reservation only and you actually get a seat, unlike the UK, where you may have to stand, or sit on the floor all the way to London from Liverpool. In Europe you pay for a seat and reservation, and you get the seat you pay for. The train, El Ave, is Spain's version of the Japanese bullet train, and is one of the fastest trains in the world. El Ave would speed us to Madrid, some 300 miles in 2 hours and 45 minutes. Fast and smooth, the journey flew by, and our feet touched the floor in Madrid at 11.45am.

As we stepped off the train it was freezing. We were expecting warm sunshine, but we were hugely disappointed. No shorts day here, although I'm sure it wouldn't stop some of the Scouse lads. It was time to put our coats on. Surely it would warm up soon. We were promised 17°C. Our advanced guard was already in Madrid. Mongoose had arrived the night before and done a recce of all the watering holes and places to go. It always helps when someone else knows the territory, it saves you loads of dead-end walks. Zil had flown in on a day trip from John Lennon Airport early that morning. We were meeting them at Puerto de Sol, the centre of Madrid and close to our evening's accommodation. Just a couple of minutes on the metro, easily navigated following last year's trip to Madrid, and we were at Sol. Local knowledge and knowing the metro makes your day easier and more enjoyable.

Our accommodation was a hostal (not hostel), and, while basic, it was more than adequate. You don't need a swimming pool or a spa on these trips. It was central and clean, with two toilets and a kitchen, so what more could you want? We dropped the bags and headed back out on to the streets to take the leisurely ten-minute walk down to Plaza Mayor, where most people would be congregating for the afternoon. We had no plan. I'd asked Charlie whether he fancied a trip to the Bernabéu, home of Real Madrid, but he wasn't bothered. He wanted to sample life as a Red abroad.

The Plaza was starting to come to life and, as we entered, who were the first people we saw? Yeah, the Isle of Man crowd, Graham, Nick, Terry and Sam, who'd been joined by Tristan and his young fella James, on his first European trip too. Tristan, thankfully, had helped secure Charlie's ticket. You meet all sorts of great people on these trips, often the same people time and again. Meeting people isn't as easy as you think, as you make all these grand plans, but they never go according to plan, as you turn left instead of right and end up somewhere else that's fabulous and you don't move on.

I'd made loose plans (via Facebook) to meet someone I hadn't seen for 34 years. Adele, who I'd last seen in 1986

(I think), but I wasn't sure whether it would happen or not. Then as we headed to the other end of the square, I heard a shout of 'Keith'. There you go, after 34 years we met again and it felt like yesterday, and it was all our yesterdays as we quickly started to catch up. It was a good job that her husband John got on with the lads well enough and wasn't bothered that and Adele and I were somewhere back in the 1980s. They'd commandeered a table in a little café for themselves. The sun appeared, this was the place to be. With bottles of Mahou ordered, and a coke for Charlie, along with churros to nibble on, we were set for a while. Two hours later and five bottles of Mahou each, it was time to say goodbye. Charlie had his pictures with the banners in the square and it was time to go.

We walked out of the Plaza and straight into the Mercado de San Miguel, a stylish covered gastronomic market (that's what it says on Google Maps). It was stylish and there was a different crowd in here than in the square, many more locals, and while pricy, there was tapas as far as the eye could see. Alongside little pizzas were rows of empanadas with numerous fillings, and they sold Mahou on draught. There was a brilliant atmosphere in here, a real taste of Madrid. After half an hour it was time to move on and try to find some other people, back towards Sol and through the backstreets around Plaza Mayor, where there was a row of tapas bars. As I've learned since, each was specialising in individual tapas. I need to come back here for a weekend with Nikki at some point. The idea is, you have a drink, a little tapas, and you move on, for a drink and some different tapas, and repeat until you're wasted.

We found ourselves back up at Sol, but avoided the Irish bars, which we do as much as possible on away days, only using them as a last resort. We hit the back streets to find a bar that Mongoose was in the night before with his cousin. We may find them in there again. No such luck, and after a pint in there we moved on to a place on the corner, which was a cross between a delicatessen and a bar, seemingly only populated by men. Now (after research) I know this to be a branch of Museo de Jamón (Museum of Ham) at Calle de Victoria, a five-minute walk from Sol metro station. It seems that the way to use it is to order a beer, peruse which cooked meats you want to buy, sip on your beer, purchase your meat, finish your beer, then take your meat home to the wife and family. When I say meat, these were too numerous to mention, but they were things such as chorizo (several types of) and cured hams, which are carved off the bone. M&S sell them at Christmas. There's a big silver bar to stand at and put your beer on, and it was standing only as there were no seats. It wasn't a place to hang around. The shop was a riot of colour, with rows of hams brightly decorated in red, green and blue stockings, hanging from the ceiling. I asked whether the colours meant anything, and I gathered from the staff's response that it was to make it look pretty, no difference in the meat. Charlie was living his best life, another coke in hand and a free sample of all the meats on offer, which he was chomping through. All I'd bought him to eat all day was a mini-pizza in the Mercado. He was troughing around Madrid for free otherwise. If you're ever in Madrid, get down to Museo de Jamón.

It was 6pm local time, so time to start moving closer to the ground. Having Charlie with me meant I didn't want to leave it too late. Spain is a notoriously bad place to get into grounds, previous experiences in Barcelona, Real Madrid and Valencia told me that. The travel advice provided by Liverpool prior to departure advised that our fans would be escorted to the ground from Canillejas metro station. For the Champions League Final, we went to Las Rosas metro station, and it was a 15-minute walk down the hill, but now they were sending us in the opposite direction. We were at the 'wrong' end of the ground this time. A quick check of Google Maps showed that there wasn't a lot there, no squares to congregate in, only a few bars. It wasn't a place to be kettled by the local police.

As we stepped out the metro we could tell this wasn't going to be the place to be, as riot police were already milling around and there was hardly anyone here. We went to the first bar outside the station and ordered a beer and patatas bravas. We were starving by now and these were beautiful with a beer. If truth be told, it's a packet of Aunt Bessie's roasties tipped on to a plate with some sauce that blows your tastebuds off. At least it made you drink more. Charlie was in his element.

As more fans arrived, we took it as our cue to leave, and with Google Maps in hand, Mongoose led us through the back streets of the suburb of Canillejas towards the Wanda Metropolitano. As we walked through the tenements in the tidy little suburb, we found a tiny bar with an Atlético flag flying outside, Bar Café Vega. Was it a bar? Was it a café? Well tonight it was definitely a bar, and full of Atlético fans. Full meant about 20 of them, as it was that small, but we could see it was okay, so we sauntered in and perched ourselves by the window. You could see the bright lights of the Wanda Metropolitano not too far away in the distance. Mahous ordered and the lady behind the bar pushed a plate of chorizo sandwiches towards us. Charlie was in like a shot. Sitting there in his Liverpool shirt there were nods of approval from the locals, and the landlady took a shine to him, bringing him more tapas and some curried meat. What meat? Who knows, but he and Mongoose demolished it, and with a cheery 'gracias' we were on our way to the ground. Can't have been more than half a mile away now, just like walking over Stanley Park from Goodison to Anfield.

It was getting busier now as it was only an hour to kick-off. The streets were full of cars trying to bump their way into spaces too small for them. It's a European thing where you don't need a space bigger than your car, just one you can make big enough for your car. It's why cars have bumpers. Time for one more drink, just a can or two from the supermarket we were passing to help us on our way. As we were waiting for Mongoose to get the cans, a big bear of a man came storming towards me and Charlie. I stood in front of Charlie, thinking, *Here we go. Where's the way out?* I didn't need to, as he raised a huge smile and pushed his mate towards me and muttered something in Spanish. The lad said to me, 'You are from Liverpool, yes?' I said, 'Yeah,' and he proceeded to interview me on behalf of his mate, who couldn't speak a word of English. The lad interpreting happened to be a Liverpool fan from Madrid, and they were mates. He wanted to know what we thought of Atlético, how did we think they'd do, what the score would be, all those normal questions.

Lovely fellas they were, and after every question the big fella gave me a big bear hug. Before we left, he wanted us to do one thing, he wanted me, and especially Charlie, to shout something for him: 'Sergio Ramos, hijo de puta.' He said slowly, 'Sergio Ramos … hijo … de *puta*,' with the real emphasis on the 'puta'. As Charlie shouted it loudly for a third time, the man burst out laughing at him as he was shouting all over this little corner of Madrid. His mate then told us it translated as 'Sergio Ramos, son of a bitch'. Well, I've translated it using Google and it can be that, or it can be much worse. Because everyone was laughing, Charlie was made up. Don't tell his mum.

With that we were off, leaving the big man laughing. The fun of meeting the locals, that happens all the time in Liverpool too. Often you'll see Liverpudlians looking after stray foreigners, making sure they get where they need to be. I remember getting an Argentine lad, whose only words were 'Messi' and 'Maradona' back to town via Sandhills after the soccerbus had gone. No way he could manage 'a single to central please, lad'. I even paid his fare. I'd like to think what goes around comes around.

Fifty yards down the road and we were accosted by more locals, much drunker than the last set, but every bit as nice. As we were walking towards the ground and in his broken English, a fella was telling me how excited they were to be seeing Liverpool, and how excited he was to visit Anfield. Charlie was hanging on his every word and said, 'He's a nice fella, isn't he dad.' My job was done. He had all the learning he needed from this trip already – go to a place, respect its culture and its people, talk to them and generally you get a great response.

We swung around the corner and what a sight, in front of us was the wonder of the Wanda, it was magic. Beyond the huge car parks was the Wanda Metropolitano lighting up the sky in all its glory. With a dad-and-lad picture to commemorate the moment, we were quickly on our way to the turnstiles. It was strangely quiet, except for Liverpool fans, all the Atlético fans were in already. Later, when we saw video of the coach welcome, which saw thousands welcoming their team, it was obvious they'd been in for ages. The expected nightmare at the turnstiles didn't happen. We were in with loads of time to spare, also having time to bump into Adele and John again, I've not seen her for 34 years and now she's stalking me!

Into the ground and, besides the man-to-man marking on the toilets, everything was good. They were searching for pyro, allegedly, and everyone going into the toilets was being searched by stewards and police. As we headed towards our seats, though, we were bang in the middle of a fight that was about to kick off. An Irish lad was being abused by a Scouse lad. I'm not up for the Scouse vs Wools shout, this is what happened. Whatever had gone on, the Scouse lad wouldn't let it lie, and he was the drunkest of the two, and the Irish lad was happy to walk away. I tried to make the peace as the last thing you want is the riot police wading in because of a beef with two lads, and after a tense five minutes they went their separate ways. The last thing I wanted was my lad stuck in the middle of Spanish police waving truncheons. A one-on-one wasn't worth half the block getting it.

We found seats right at the back nearest to the divide with the Atlético fans on the other side, as it was 'just sit where you like' (designated seating doesn't count for much away in Europe), and that was all that was left. The noise was booming, and as the Champions League music played, the Atlético fans ramped up the volume, with our end giving it a good go back at them. It was a great sight, with the fervent Atlético fans in full voice. Liverpool are the biggest name in Europe, and no matter how popular we were with the fans outside, they were proper going for us inside.

Within minutes Liverpool were 1-0 down, Saúl appearing from nowhere to convert a second ball from a corner. Surely he was offside. We calmly waited for a VAR call, as that's what you do now, and it took a while, but the goal was confirmed. The corner came after the ref and linesman joined together to give a throw-in to them that should have been ours, the first of many poor decisions from a referee who had a shocker. Last time he refereed us was at PSG the previous year and, guess what, he had a shocker there too, letting Neymar referee the game for him. He fell for the Atlético histrionics, the diving to try to get Mané sent off (meaning he was withdrawn at half-time), the fervent crowd and the constant berating from Diego Simeone in the Atlético technical zone. Simeone fed the crowd all night long. No complaints with that, as it's exactly what Jürgen does at Anfield.

The truth is, Liverpool didn't perform, and we didn't get behind them. Everyone was off colour on a big night, and keeping it to 1-0 in the end wasn't the worst result. It was one of those nights where the clock ticks down faster than you could ever believe, and we could have played all night long and not scored. As the final whistle went, the ground erupted as if they'd won the Champions League Final. That's how big we are now, we're a major scalp. It took me back to the 80s when, if we got beat anywhere, the ground would erupt. It's the biggest compliment you can get. There was still 90 minutes to go in the tie and we'd seen enough of Atlético to know they didn't carry any great threat up front and when we got one, we'd get two, I was certain of that.

We waited to leave the ground, a common thing in Europe as they clear the home fans from the surrounding areas and get you back to the city centre, anything between 30 to 90 minutes, in my experience. I turned to Charlie and said, 'Don't be too disappointed, mate.' He said, 'I'm not, I've had a great time, and those nice men we met before will be pleased, won't they.' I said, 'That's right, mate, and that's what it's all about.' Love winning but be gracious in defeat if you don't deserve to win, and we didn't.

There was no going anywhere, not even the toilets, with a string of riot police and stewards across every exit denying any movement. No point arguing and there was an air of resignation in our sector, a poor performance and the obligatory lock-in. It was gone 11.30pm by the time we exited the stadium. We said goodbye to Zil as he headed back to the airport for his flight back to John Lennon and we took the opportunity of going to the stadium's own metro station. We were on a train within five minutes. It might have been rammed but we were on the way back to the city centre. It has been known in Spain, Barcelona specifically, for them to hold you back that long that you miss the last train, so this was good, and 40 minutes later we were heading up into the night sky at Sol.

Fans had already started drifting back to their accommodation or late-night bars. We walked up to our hostal, and Mongoose said, 'Fancy a nightcap?' We were in Madrid and Charlie going into the bar at half past midnight wasn't even questioned. They must have known he was coming, as a plate of jamón was placed in front of him. Get him a coke and he was in his element. El Matador was the bar, and it was brilliant, complete with a constant supply of tapas and beer in a bohemian environment, not like going to Frosts on County Road. Charlie was living his best life, just one more drink and he was still buzzing, probably all the coke he drank during the day, so I made him drink water. We had to be up in six hours so he'd need sleep, don't ever underestimate the journey home. He wasn't happy with the change of drink but within minutes he was yawning, and it was time to head for our beds at 1.30am.

My concerns from Barcelona yesterday morning were unfounded, and my boy had come of age. Forget the result, we'd had the most wonderful day out and that's what counts, dad-and-lad days, one to tell his kids about in the future. In Liverpool he'd be a legend in school, but in the Isle of Man most of the kids wouldn't get it. Charlie is living his dream for himself, he doesn't do it to impress others. My gift to my son, my job is done.

* * *

The iPhone alarm burst into life at 6.40am and signalled the start of the journey home. I vaguely remembered Mongoose leaving at 6am to get the first metro to the airport for his flight back to Manchester via Frankfurt. To my amazement, Charlie didn't take long to wake up and by 7am he was up and ready to go. We headed into the morning air that was cold and still. The city was just starting to go to bed, never mind wake up. The nightclub stragglers were still weaving their way around the back streets of Sol and there was a mix of places closing for the night and opening for the day.

The metro was waking up and the early morning commute was underway, with standing room only on the metro towards the airport. Coffees in hand, this was going to be a long day, but Charlie was bullish. I speak from experience, though. It sounds good when you book it but flying back from Madrid to Barcelona then on to Gatwick and finally on to the Isle of Man meant it was going to be a gruelling day.

Madrid airport is huge. Look at it on a map and it seems bigger than many towns and cities, and by the time we got checked in and through security it was only an hour until our 9.30am flight to Barcelona. The Mahou from the day before was starting to affect me and it was time to 'drop the kids off at the pool'. In a huge airport to find the toilets only had four cubicles and they were all in use was a disgrace. More shops than bogs, that can't be right, can it? After a heavy day before, the toilets were needed and there was no way I wanted to leave this one on a plane. After what seemed like an eternity, I lightened the load as our flight was called to the gate.

Charlie was oblivious to where I'd been as he had a croissant and coffee in hand, so he was more than happy. We were officially on our way home. Some 12 hours later we were back home after a day of nodding off on planes, the whole day spent either flying or in airports, three lots of security checks and jostling to get on planes. I almost forgot the lady sitting in front of me, who was coughing her head off all the way back from Barcelona to Gatwick. She was coming down with something bad, I was sure of it.

* * *

Boom! Then the world changed, the coronavirus, Covid-19, just Covid, call it what you want, but it rocked the world. The week after we returned home, I remembered that lady on the plane from Barcelona to Gatwick. I remembered her every morning and every night as I was coughing up my lungs, and news of the respiratory virus that was taking over the world was now coming closer to home. My doctor wasn't too concerned as I hadn't been to Italy, the European epicentre at the time. I'd only been to Madrid, which was on the verge of becoming a Covid hotspot with thousands of deaths.

News also came through that my Uncle Dave, the last of the three musketeers who went to Rome in '77 had passed away, suddenly, at home, surrounded by those he loved after a four-year battle against all sorts of things. The last match link to my dad was now gone and all their stories were now ours to pass on, and there were loads of them. It was now down to me to pass them on, and I did just that as I regaled the tales of their match-going days to an overflowing room at Thornton Crematorium. To laughter I described the man he was and the glory of Rome with his fellow Reds, my dad and Uncle Lenny. They put the miles in and trod the paths we were to follow. In the footsteps of our fathers, they showed us the way. As luck would have it, obviously planned by Dave himself, his funeral was the afternoon of the return leg against Atlético, and it was written in the stars that a fitting goodbye would include a stirring 'You'll Never Walk Alone', in both the crematorium and at Anfield, inspiring the Reds to victory.

It looked like it would with a magnificent performance from the men in red. After Bobby slotted the second in extra time, the volume ramped up and it was to be another glorious night, thanks to Dave's divine intervention. Then it all went wrong, a bad goalkeeping mistake killed the tie, and the crowd couldn't lift itself and the team. It wasn't to be, but we'll come again, we're the champions of Europe and the glory they've given us and the trips and the stories, it will all come again.

Football wasn't that important anymore. Covid took over the world and closed it down. Would trips to Madrid ever happen again? At least, whatever happens, Charlie has the memory of a lifetime, as do I. By April 2020 and with thousands of deaths recorded, a third of the world was in lockdown in their houses. It was madness, we'd never seen anything like it.

We do have our memories and fabulous they are, so here's to making more when the time is right.

The Glorious Last Chapter

This is the ending we all wanted; I can think of no better ending to my journey. Ever since John Arne Riise ruined the ending of my last book, I've been waiting for the moment to finish it on a high note.

I KNOW what you're all thinking: hold on, there's more to come. I know there is, obviously there's more to come, but you need to think of this as 'The Glorious Last Chapter' because that is what it was, sort of.

I've lost count of how many people asked me what it felt like for Liverpool to be champions of England again after 30 years. I was lost for words, but obviously, being a book, I need to find some words for you to read, otherwise it's not going to work, is it?

Thirty years of waiting for the league title is finally over, where did all those years go? Thirty years on and my life is unrecognisable to the life I believed I would have. I was expecting a terraced house in Walton, or if I did well for myself, a house with a garden in Maghull or

Crosby (the posher suburbs of north Liverpool). Somehow, I've ended up in the middle of the Irish Sea and I've seen and done many things beyond my wildest dreams. The terraced house in Walton 'vision' had two kids and a lovely wife in it, and the kids were Reds, just like me. I have the two kids and the lovely wife; I have a son who's mad on Liverpool, and a daughter who loves nothing more than shopping with her mum. I'm cool with that.

My life has always gone hand in glove with the achievements of the Mighty Reds, though. I've gone from being a man who'd travel everywhere in England, following the Reds, to being a bit-part player where I feed on scraps of games at home and abroad (they're some scraps, eh?). My passion is greater than ever, but that passion had been laced with fear and desperation over the last few years. The fear that I wouldn't ever see Liverpool win the league again, it's mad, but I actually started thinking like that. I was only 54! Fear drives the desperation. If you told me in May 1990 that it would be 30 years before we'd win the league again, I'd have asked you, 'What have you been smoking?'

Liverpool were serial league winners in my youth and early adulthood, but of all the league titles, 1990, the last one, is the one I can't remember, I just can't. Even using Google I find it hard to recognise the season, and it certainly didn't feel glorious to me. I remember the maddest, minutest details of my journeys with the Reds, but not that year; 1990 was the year I walked around in a daze, the year after Hillsborough. I was barely sleeping and was living life on autopilot, and that included following

Liverpool. I still followed them to every game, home and away that season. A head-clearing three-week trip around Europe with Our Kev and Zil had helped get me through the long hot summer of 1989, but then I must have hit a wall. The only games I remember are the 9-0 thrashing of Crystal Palace, and a tearful goodbye to Aldo, a tense return to Hillsborough to play Sheffield Wednesday (a horrible day), lifting the trophy after beating QPR at home, then, lastly, a day in the sunshine celebrating with a massive win against Coventry on the final day. That's it, that's everything. There's no glorious trophy charge. It was relief after losing the title the previous year to Arsenal, which to me didn't matter, none of it mattered, I was still consumed by Hillsborough throughout 1990.

Roll forward to 2019 and we missed out by one point and by 12mm, that's all it took for the ball to be classed as not crossing the line against Man City. We were destined not to win it, maybe never win it again. After Rafa released the reins too late to win it in 2009, Stevie's slip in 2014 when Brendan Rodgers had us believing, and after Jürgen's boys defied everything and everyone in 2019, it just wasn't to be. As 2019 turned into 2020, the Reds were magnificent, the games rolled by and everyone started to believe, but I couldn't let myself, not fully. I'd been hurt too often. On the couch at home, more like stalking around the living room or kitchen as merely sitting on the couch, became unbearable. My blood pressure was through the roof, I was terrified during every game until the final whistle blew, terrified to look at Twitter or BBC Sport if the game wasn't on TV. I never had those feelings in the ground, I was strangely calmer. At least there I could play my part and cheer them on to glory. I remember the league-winning moments, Norwich at home, coming from behind to win at Villa, dismantling City at home, smashing Leicester 4-0 away on Boxing Day, Salah's last-minute goal against United to finish them off, and then coming from behind to beat West Ham. I didn't need Chelsea to beat City, we were champions from Boxing Day onwards.

But Chelsea did beat City the night after we dismantled Crystal Palace at an empty Anfield, with four of the best goals to be seen in any one game. I was half watching the Chelsea game, and when Chelsea took the lead I started taking a real interest. I wasn't in the camp of wanting us to win it at the Etihad against City the following week, I wanted it over and done with so I could soothe my tortured soul. At half-time we were believing that tonight was the night. Even Charlie took his eyes off his PlayStation to keep me updated from upstairs. He was excited, it was lovely to see. The second half put me back in my box again as City in their rhubarb and custard-inspired away kit battered Chelsea, equalising through a stunning De Bruyne free kick. City then hit the post shortly afterwards, Raheem Sterling of all people. There was no way Chelsea were holding out against that attack.

Then came the newly introduced post-Covid water break, which had become a tactical break, and a change in tactics worked wonders. Frank Lampard changed the shape and Chelsea got out of their own half for a rare foray. City messed it up defensively and Fernandinho deliberately handled it on the line. It's a penalty, and a sending off. The referee didn't actually see it, which is amazing as I could see it in the Isle of Man, and for once the newly introduced VAR nailed it. It took an eternity, though, when in reality it was clear as day. They knew the enormity of the decision, sending Fernandinho off, awarding a penalty and it was likely to end the agony for millions of us. As Willian calmly rolled the ball into the net, the celebrations started.

Then all the nonsense came: 'Chelsea hand Liverpool the title'. No one handed Liverpool the title, they'd earned it all season with every last ounce of energy the players and the supporters had. No one gave us anything, we were immense. Stick an asterisk next to this 2020 – Liverpool were immense*. There you go, I'm saving everyone the bother.

My phone lit up like a Christmas tree, Twitter and Facebook exploded and Sky Sports went into an hour-long celebration programme. We were 'back on our perch'. I wonder what that Scottish fella who knocked us off it was thinking now. The Reds are coming up the hill boys, the weight has gone, and Jürgen and his boys can kick on now. This was going to be a great hour, then bang, claps of thunder boomed over the house, flashes of lightning lit up the sky and the telly went off. Wow, the boys upstairs were having a party, my dad along with my uncles Lenny, Jimmy and Dave were having a party with Shanks, along with the thousands of Reds who've left us far too early. This was for us, but it was for them too. I remembered my dad not living to see them win it one last time, that's what hurt the most in 2014, it was his last chance, and he knew it. This one was for him, and as that thought came, so did the tears. As in Madrid less than 12 months before, our thoughts were for those we'd love to share it with but couldn't. What I wouldn't give for one more phone call to my old fella to say, 'There you go, mate, that's for you and the boys.' We follow in the footsteps of our fathers, and I'll never forget they're some big shoes to fill. The footsteps we take follow those men in red who trod a wonderful path.

I might not be able to share it with him, but I had my own family. Charlie bounced into the room and dived into my arms, knocking me on to the couch, floods of tears from him too, pure elation driving his tears. In 2019 he was at home while I was in Madrid, so this was our first one, our first celebration of winning together. Up to now we'd only seen an Audi Cup and Charity Shield defeats together, so this was for us. Nikki gave me a massive hug and kiss, she knew what this meant, she shared the euphoria, and Izzy joined in, not knowing the enormity of what two teams in London who we didn't like had just conspired to do. Ringo, the dog, was confused as to why he was no longer the centre of attention, so we put him to bed to avoid the thunder. With the fiercest thunderstorm I've ever seen in the Isle of Man still raging, the neighbours were out videoing nature's finest. I'm told that hearing me shouting 'get in there' was louder than any clap of thunder.

I tried something we hadn't even done in lockdown, I tried getting all the lads on a video call, with varying degrees of success, due to technical capabilities and varying states of drunkenness. It sort of worked, as the ones you want to share it with were all there together for a few wonderful moments. We planned to celebrate in style when our borders opened (we were still unable to leave the island properly until 2021, though). I had grand plans to have a week on the lash in Liverpool, which unfortunately never materialised.

By midnight the house was quiet. Charlie had finally gone to bed, but the storm was still raging outside, and I could hear Ringo whimpering in the kitchen, scared of the thunder. There was no sleep in me anyway, and Sky had come back on. I went and got Ringo and sat him on the couch next to me as we watched the celebrations together. I was telling him how this was only the start of great things, and we watched the video of the players celebrating. He was snoring in no time and no longer afraid of the thunder. Send a glass eye to sleep, me! My work was done, and at 2am I thought it was probably time for bed. I hadn't even had a drink to celebrate.

You'll read loads of books that will no doubt chart the relentless march to our first Premier League title, so I'll save you that here, but Covid-19 had seen the season suspended with Liverpool leading by 25 points and only recording one defeat, on a poor day out at Watford. The league would have been well done and dusted by the end of March, but we had to wait until the end of June instead, with life outside and inside stadiums still nowhere near normal. During Covid we faced the talk and possibility that the league would be declared null and void. With much of the season played and the amount of money involved, the Premier League was always going to return. They could have just given the Reds the title, can you imagine that? The null and void shouts were led by the usual suspects, the fans who've been goading us for years about not winning the Premier League. It was the only thing they had left to hold over us. Outside of the bitterest elements, many football fans believed that Liverpool deserved the title, and it had only been a matter of time before we were declared champions. From being null and void supporters, they turned their attention to having an asterisk against the title win. Crack on lads, have as many asterisks as you want, it would always stand out as the year in which we were far superior to anyone else.

Remember this is Twitter world, it's *not* the real world. A mate who's a Spurs fan, as soon as we won, sent me a celebratory message on Twitter congratulating Liverpool. He sent it privately because of the nature of Twitter and its public face. Messages flooded in from fans of Arsenal, Wolves, West Brom, Brighton, Luton, the two Manchester clubs, United and City, and even Everton (through gritted teeth obviously), but all decent people, decent football fans, they all knew Liverpool deserved it. Back in the day I hated United, and Ferguson especially, as he always had it over us. He'd knocked us off our perch, hadn't he, and he revelled in it, but I had a real respect for him and them. You had to admit it, they always found a way to win, played to the last seconds of injury time, won games at the death, and we all shouted, 'You jammy bastards.' Now that's what everyone was shouting at us – Leicester at home, Tottenham at home, Villa away, games where we always found a way to win. That's what great teams do, and Liverpool are a great team, there's no doubt. Ignore the noise from people with their agendas. We're a great team and will go down in history.

And do you know what? When Leeds and West Brom got promoted and Luton stayed up, I was one of the first who said, 'Well done, mate, made up for you,' to my mates, because that's what it's all about. I've sat next to a lad in work who's a Leeds fan, and seeing the agony over the years has been no fun. If you can't be pleased for someone with a passion for their club, for me you're doing something wrong.

I try to keep away from the seedier side of Twitter. The constant baiting, endless Hillsborough and Heysel shouts have replaced the 'you've never won the Premier League' shouts. Posts generally come from anonymous accounts with a handful of followers who've only just started posting, strangely. The wind-up isn't funny but people bite. The toxicity of Twitter means it's not always fun, but then you meet some wonderful people through it. Liverpudlians became unbearable and who could blame us. After years of abuse we were always going to rub it in, and why not, what goes around comes around. LFC Twitter will ruin you if you mock Hillsborough or use Heysel as a tool for your own agenda. Ask the idiots who've lost their jobs through their atrocious posts on social media. I have no sympathy for them, as using a social media platform comes with responsibility, and abuse it at your peril. I always think before I post. I don't always check the spelling, unfortunately, damn predictive text, but I consider what I'm writing and how I'm writing it. Not everyone on all sides is as considerate.

I was resigned a long time ago to not seeing Liverpool lift the Premier League trophy. I'd planned to not be in my seat as Jordan Henderson lifted that trophy above his head. I'd be in Liverpool with a ticket, but I was giving my ticket to Charlie so he could see his first league win and have that wonderful memory. I've seen enough trophies lifted over the years, and trophy parades. Charlie's seen neither, he's missed out on his moments, but when the time came to party, as Jürgen promised us, I'd make sure he was there and we could watch the Reds on the top of the bus driving through my wonderful city amid red smoke and confetti. It was the least I could do. Last year I was still making my way home through the Spanish countryside as the Reds were driving up The Strand, and Charlie missed the homecoming parade.

I'd had a wonderful couple of days. The Reds had won the league at last and the day before I'd been told I was being made redundant after 20 years of working for the bank. Might sound crazy but it's a wonderful opportunity, a payoff, a great chance to go out and do some amazing stuff for myself, and the Isle of Man is a place where you can do it. Most of all a chance to finish this bloody book. I walked around with a silly smile on my face and started looking at what my new life would look like. You can rest assured that following Liverpool was in there, a new-found flexibility driven by fixture lists, especially in Europe, and Charlie could be having a few unauthorised school absences here and there.

The weeks went by in a blur of activity for me professionally, and the football came and went. I was fuming when City beat us in a depressing fashion and then we lost our perfect home record for the season, to Burnley of all people. The pressure was off, the intensity dropped and it cost us, then the same against Arsenal, where they scored from two mistakes from Virgil and Alisson, so the record points total was gone. I fumed, and Klopp fumed, Twitter fumed. Then I realised I'd become a terrible loser. After years of being used to it, now it wasn't acceptable. As Graeme Souness said on Sky, you can't explain the drop-off, they're trying their hardest, but it just doesn't happen, it was just the way it was. It didn't matter, none of it mattered other than the fact we were champions of England for a 19th time, well and truly back on our perch. We'd wrapped the title up earlier than anyone had ever done before. Records don't matter that much.

By the time the Chelsea game came around I wanted us to go out on a high, and they were chasing a top-four finish, like we used to. There should be no handing them anything, especially after the official Chelsea Twitter account posted the Gerrard slip video before the game. They cost us the league in 2014, let's return the favour. This was the night that we'd finally lift the Premier League trophy, it would all be done, there would be pictures to prove we were the champions, and we'd buzz all summer, unless you'd rather think about transfers! Remember how toxic Twitter is, well today for the main part it was beautiful, with fabulous content from the club and fan groups.

One piece stood out for me, brought tears and encapsulates what it's all about. 'Proud to be a Red', a beautiful piece from Dave Kirby and the Schofield boys. 'These memories last forever son, be proud to be a Red,' the piece proclaimed, and that sums up my life, from grandads to dads, from dads to sons, my life, these memories will last forever, I'm proud to be a Red! The ones who've gone before are always with us, the ones who follow us will be taught the way to follow our team, the team in red, the mighty Liverpool FC. My thoughts turned to my uncles, Len, Jimmy and Dave, all gone but never forgotten, but most of all to my dad, what I wouldn't give tonight to just have those words. Those words from his mouth that would have been something like 'what was all that bloody nonsense about?'

All that 'nonsense' was the modern version of a trophy presentation, 30 minutes after a match, none of the old handshakes and a trot around the pitch. Without fans, though, the trot around the pitch was hollow. These boys deserved a show, and maybe I'm old, but it was a bit crap, I thought. Twitter had been moaning about them playing Coldplay when they picked the cup up. If you could actually hear it, you were a better man than me. Confetti and fireworks covered the Anfield pitch as the injured Jordan Henderson gingerly walked up the Kop steps to the podium, took the trophy from King Kenny, did his little shuffle in front of his boys, then lifted the trophy to the skies. No tears, not tonight, I sat there like an idiot smiling away to myself, and Charlie was overwhelmed as he watched Gini's Instagram live stream. The modern way to watch or be a part of what you're celebrating, watch it through a lens. And years of disappointment were gone. Within days people would be talking of transfers and money, but give it a rest, eh, we've just won the league. Sit back, milk it in and be unbearable. But many in the modern world were already complaining about FSG not spending money. For crying out loud, look what we've done over the last five years. Really? If you loved us, you'd take it all in and be happy, for a while at least. I suppose this is the world where stories need to be made to support the ravenous appetite of social media, creating stories for clicks.

I had an 'interaction' with a 'fan' on Twitter, the day Dejan Lovren departed for Zenit St Petersburg. He'd created a montage of all Lovren's errors, and when I called him out on it, he said it was 'for entertainment', and that if I wasn't entertained, loads were. That's what we're dealing with now. He wrote articles, a 'senior writer', for a fan site with 110,000 followers. If this is entertainment, I want no part of it, it was character assassination of a lad who played his heart out for us. He might not have been good enough at times, but he was appreciated by the ones who matter, his manager and his team-mates. I wish him luck, alongside Adam Lallana, who departed for Brighton, devastated that his time was over, leaving his mates and what he'd achieved behind. They deserve their medals; they've been great professionals who've supported the club to get to where it is now, and they deserve great thanks. We make legends out of people for no apparent reason and villains out of others who don't deserve the tag. Just appreciate the men who wear the red shirt with pride.

I'll remember 2020 for the rest of my life, sharing it with my lad, getting to see his first league win. This is the glorious end, the glorious last chapter, there's nothing topping this now.

Up the Mighty Reds!

'This is the glorious end, the glorious last chapter, there is nothing topping this now.' Jürgen Klopp just read that line and shouted, 'Hold my beer!' What comes next is glorious, you'll see.

These Are the Days

'THESE ARE the days, these are the moments, these are the times that you will remember.' Prophetic words from Ian McNabb. Maybe I should dedicate this book to him. We're living in glorious times, take a deep breath, breathe in, and reminisce. Things are happening so fast that you need to look back and take stock. I've been following the men in Red for over 50 years and, believe me, these are unique times.

I know I said the previous chapter was 'The Glorious Last Chapter', but this one is guaranteed to usurp it. The last chapter was tinged with sadness for me. After 30 years we finally won the Premier League, but the moment was lost. There was no celebrating at the back of the Kop or at the Pier Head for me as, due to Covid restrictions, I was locked in on the island for my own safety. It was all a bit flat. As the Reds lifted the Premier League trophy in a near-empty Anfield, we were all longing to celebrate with Jürgen and the boys in person.

By the time we could all get back into the ground, the moment for celebration had been lost. There was no week on the lash following the title-winning moment and no meeting with friends who I'd dreamed of sharing the glorious moment with. By the time we got to meet again it was time to start over again. Following the league-winning season we endured a nightmare campaign beset with injuries to key players. Virgil and nearly every other centre-back on our books were injured (ending the season with Nat Phillips and Rhys Williams, who amazed us all), but a seemingly threadbare squad managed to somehow drag itself gloriously over the line into fourth place, and a coveted Champions League spot. Elite sport means winning by inches or glorious unbelievable moments of great skill. There was a pivotal moment that we'll replay forever.

It's the 95th minute against West Brom at The Hawthorns and Fat Sam is drinking his mug of gravy nervously as Trent, with the last corner of the game, looks to pick out a red shirt in the centre of the goalmouth. He can't pick out a red shirt, but he can pick out the black shirt of Alisson Becker, who'd arrived in the box at the last second. Ali met the ball with his head as sweetly as any centre-forward ever has. You won't see a finer header. In the 95th minute, with a Champions League place at stake, it was the stuff of dreams! As with every Liverpool-supporting house in the country, we went mad, the dog ran away, and Nikki and the neighbours were wondering what was going on. The celebrations on the pitch were every bit as emotional as those across the country. Ali had done it, he'd rescued us. If you believe in God, which Ali clearly does, there was an element of divine intervention. He'd tragically lost his dad during Covid, and this goal was for him. The goal gave us the platform to beat Burnley, then Palace, and ultimately pip Leicester to fourth place. If we could get everyone fit, we'd go again.

And go again we did, by god did we go again!

August started with the news we all wanted to hear, Virgil was back and in decent shape. He looked like he could only run in straight lines, mind, but his presence is immense, and we immediately looked better. A fit Jöel Matip and a new mountain of a man in Ibrahima Konaté, and our nightmare year was behind us. A re-energised Ali buoyed by his fabulous header was back to his world-class best, and a strike force that now included master goal-poacher Diogo Jota complementing Mo, Bobby and Sadio, and we'd be more than okay. While many of the pundits ignored us as title contenders, laughably believing United would join Chelsea and City as the clubs with real title hopes, Jürgen said, 'Hold my beer.' What comes next is the stuff of dreams for us and nightmares for the red half of Manchester and our blue neighbours.

Covid measures had been removed by August, so we could join a full Anfield once again. With a full season between us and winning the league, we sang our songs and cheered the boys, but to really celebrate we needed to win something again, and that's exactly what we set out to do.

A glorious Champions League campaign in the 'group of death' saw us win every game, against the mighty Atlético Madrid, AC Milan and Porto (I know, we never make Porto look mighty). There was much pessimism in the media about the group, but we absolutely strolled through, our squad coming of age. In years gone by, the fall-off with our squad players could be quite dramatic, but now standards were being maintained, and we had a great Christmas, having progressed in all four competitions. We were in the last 16 of the Champions League and had progressed in the League Cup (I struggle to call it the Carabao).

Good progress, but a 'nightmare' January was supposedly ahead of us as we lost two of the best players in the world to the Africa Cup of Nations. Mo and Sadio would be pretty much gone for the whole month, and they signed off after a disappointing 2-2 draw at Chelsea, disappointing as we were 2-0 up and cruising, only to concede two quick goals, losing ground to Man City in the league. January, though, would be a defining month in the life of Liverpool Football Club. It could be the platform to the greatest year in our long and illustrious history. Here's hoping. Remember, as I'm writing this, I don't know how it all pans out, so let's see how we get on.

January was the month that Diogo Jota came of age in a red shirt, and a new legendary song boomed across the terraces: 'Oh, he wears the number 20' rippled across the large away following populating one end of the Emirates in north London for the League Cup semi-final, as Jota slotted two goals to finish off a supposedly fabulous Arsenal team. From the minute he scored the first there was only one winner, and Liverpool would be returning to north London at the end of February, only a few miles away under the Wembley arch.

It had been a while since we'd been to Wembley, not since 2016, and ticket demand was huge. Everyone wanted to go, tickets were like gold dust. I'd decided that, whatever happened, Charlie was going. He hadn't seen the Reds win a trophy in person yet. He'd been denied Madrid in 2019 due to age and tickets, denied the Premier League due to Covid and he was desperate to see them win one just for him, as was I. I've been lucky enough to see it all in my time following Liverpool, now it was his time. As I pressed submit to enter the ballot, all our fingers and toes were crossed, and we were successful! I fully expected spare tickets to pop up, especially with Covid still raging in England. Illness meant tickets would surely come up.

The boat was booked to Heysham in Lancashire for the Saturday morning, and we'd drive down to London on the Sunday morning. I was driving down with Charlie, Our Kev, and my nephew Daniel, who like Charlie hadn't seen a live trophy lift. It was going to be like old times with Our Kev. For years we'd travelled up and down the country following the Reds, but it had been over 20 years since we'd done a road trip. Another ticket was bound to come up, but in case it didn't, Our Kev purchased Charlie's ticket to sit next to him. My single would naturally be somewhere else, it made sense.

By the time we left the Isle of Man on the Saturday morning there was still no ticket, and it was looking unlikely that one would pop up. All my usual contacts were unable to help. I did say I didn't mind missing out, but I never thought it would happen. As we hit the M57 on the Sunday morning it was slowly dawning on me that my luck had run out. I suppose it had to at some point. After a five-and-a-half-hour journey, due to accidents and road congestion, we parked at Stanmore at the end of the Jubilee line, four stops from Wembley Park and the famous Wembley Way. My plan B was a pub a few stops down the line in West Hampstead, where all of us (me and friends) without tickets had chosen to meet. None of the pubs around Wembley, thanks to the police, were allowed to show the game on TV.

Due to our late arrival in London, after a quick McDonald's it was time to head to Wembley, and the lads would have to go straight into the ground. I went to the top of Wembley Way with them, so I could at least get a picture of me and Charlie. There was no point begging for spares here, I was resigned to going to the pub. With the pictures taken and with Charlie excited to see the Reds, it was time for me to go. I was off against the tide of excited fans arriving by tube train.

As the train headed into central London it was a horrible feeling. I was empty and had to fight the urge to cry. It's only football, eh! Ten minutes later, though, I was in the arms of my mates, Peter, Mike and Bryan, all in the same boat as me and we'd watch the match together. If I couldn't be in the ground, the Railway pub in West Hampstead was a good second choice. Loads of TV screens and rammed with people, mostly supporting Liverpool. It was worth the tube ride. As I was the idiot who'd volunteered to drive to Wembley and back, I had to make do with drinking J2O to ease my disappointment, while most of the others were on pints. They were getting merrier by the minute, while I felt like throwing up. A combination of the sickly sweet orange and passion fruit and what I was watching had me biting my lip for long periods of the tense match.

Liverpool were lucky to survive numerous Chelsea attacks and offside goals, and, in my opinion, were the luckier of the two teams to still be level 0-0 at the end of the tensest 90 minutes you'll ever watch. For a neutral I'm sure it made riveting viewing. The pub went quiet as the clock hit 90 minutes as one of the fellas on a table to our right took the knock, I think you call it a medical emergency these days. While it scared the life out of his mates, with the great care and kindness of some of the regulars he was well looked after as an ambulance was called. By the time the match reached its conclusion, and the inevitable penalty shoot-out, the ambulance still hadn't arrived. Even though he was regaining his faculties and any immediate danger was seemingly gone, I felt bad watching the Reds on telly only yards away. As the penalty shoot-out started, the ambulance finally arrived and the medics looked after him as the shoot-out passed the 5-5 stage, with no one missing in one of the greatest penalty shoot-outs you'll ever see. The way it was going, the paramedics would have more customers. At 5-5 all the players who wanted to take a penalty had done so, and now we were at sudden death. The score went from 5-5 to 6-6 and all the way up to 10-10, which meant only one thing. It was down to the goalkeepers!

Up first stepped the young lad in yellow for Liverpool, Caoimhín Kelleher. I know you're trying to pronounce his name in your head, it's like Kevin, but how we get Kevin out of those letters is beyond me like. But Kevin was boss. He'd played in all but one game of the cup run and deserved his place in the starting XI. He'd made several great saves to keep the Reds in the game. As he stepped up to the ball, I remembered that he started life as a striker in Ireland, and when you see him with the ball at his feet, he can play a bit. I thought he'd be sound, and he was, calmly slotting the ball beyond the Chelsea goalkeeper.

Eyebrows had been raised earlier, as with a couple of minutes left of extra time Thomas Tuchel decided to replace the Chelsea goalkeeper Mendy, who hadn't put a foot wrong all afternoon, with Kepa (you're not getting me to write his second name) for the penalties. The move had hardly reaped rewards as he hadn't got close to any of the Liverpool penalties. Kepa placed the ball on the spot, stepped back and skyed it into the mass ranks of Liverpool supporters behind the goal. Cue pandemonium as the sea of red at one half of Wembley exploded, and so did the pub, just as the lad who'd taken the knock was being gently passed through the window on a board by the paramedics. So much for Covid, it was hugs all round. Liverpool had done it, phase one of the quadruple done and dusted. Delight in West Hampstead, as the Reds lifted the cup and started the party. I was taking my leave and starting my journey back to Stanmore to meet the boys and hear all about it.

It was only a 50-yard walk to the tube station, and I could hear a train pulling in. Taking the stairs two at a time, within no time I was on the train and six stops later at Wembley. The early Chelsea leavers were getting on with their plastic flags, met by me and a silly grin on my face as wide as the Mersey. In no time at all I was back at Stanmore and waiting for the lads. I moved the car up the road closer to the tube station so we could get away as quickly as possible. They'd be here soon!

Nah they won't! It was a good hour until they found me waiting at the car. If you've been to Wembley lately, you'll know that when they win the cup it takes an eternity to actually get hold of the trophy. It takes even longer to celebrate in front of the fans, and to top it all off it takes ages to get away from the ground. While Wembley Way and the walk to Wembley Park and its 'stop and go' approach to crowd management means everyone is safe on the tube platforms, it's not the quickest. I'd messaged Kev, saying take your time, you don't win a trophy every year, cherish these moments, make the most of it. This would be the boys' first trophy in the flesh. In all honesty, I wasn't looking forward to the long drive home. Sober and driving home in the dark as others snore is not the way cup finals should end, but I'll take it.

As they finally walked round the corner they were still buzzing, amazingly lost for words, though, finding it impossible to describe what they'd witnessed, physically and emotionally drained. Charlie is never usually lost for words, this was a rarity. I'd just spoken to Nikki, and she wanted to hear all about it from her boy, not someone like me stuck in a pub watching it. I called her and lashed her on the speaker phone for Charlie to speak to, but he couldn't say anything. An historic day, it may never happen again. A mile from our parking spec was the entrance to the M1 and we were on it in no time at all. Besides a quick pit stop near Coventry, we made good time, with the two youngsters snoring in the back, the old men in the front reminiscing about the old days and how they compared to the current version of the Mighty Reds. These boys in red were going to give the teams of the past a run for their money, we were sure of that.

It was gone 1.30am by the time we dropped Our Kev and Daniel off and headed through the deserted streets of north Liverpool and back to my mum's house. Charlie woke up in time to go to bed. He dragged himself up the stairs and straight to bed, sure his dreams would be delightful that night. For me it was time for a cup of tea and some toast and catch up on the highlights and social media output from the day's triumph. After such a long drive there was no way I was sleeping anytime soon, I was wired. I might not have got into the ground, but I'd had everything else and that would have to do, and most of all I did it for my lad. Now he had his own history written and his own dreams, he was no longer trading off his old fella's escapades. He could go to school on Tuesday as a conquering hero. Monday was a day for travelling and the afternoon boat from Heysham to the Isle of Man. He'd learned enough this weekend.

* * *

With one trophy already in the bag it was time to see what else we could win. Still in the FA Cup, magnificent in Europe and fighting neck and neck with Man City in the league, a fight destined to go to the last day. There were adventures to be had between beating Chelsea at the end of February and the end of the season. Our eyes were firmly set on the Champions League Final to top off the season, and there were early shouts of 'they might win all four, you know'. Let's see, we'll take one game at a time, the Liverpool Way!

The next game in our sights was Nottingham Forest away in the FA Cup. This tie brought back loads of memories, some good and some not so good. As soon as you mention Liverpool vs Forest your mind automatically goes back to one moment in time, 15 April 1989 and the horrendous event on a sunny day at Hillsborough, and this game would be played out against the backdrop of those events. Several Forest fans endeavoured to galvanise many in their own fan base, they showed great empathy and understanding, and they built bridges and friendships that will stand forever. Unfortunately, a large minority of their followers should be ashamed of their actions on a crisp cold day in Nottingham.

Charlie had been banging on at me for ages about going to an away game, and Forest at the City Ground, with them flying after smashing Leicester City and Arsenal in the previous rounds, had the makings of a classic FA Cup quarter-final. I knew a lad who sorted me two tickets and, with the cheapest boat I could find, Charlie would be getting his dream away match.

He was made up when I broke the news to him. He wasn't even bothered that the boat home was at 2.15am on the Monday. I made him promise that he'd be at school on the Monday morning, no arguments. There were no arguments initially, but the moans would come, he's 15, for crying out loud. He did say he'd do anything to watch the Reds – sleep on airport floors, boats, cars, trains, whatever he needed to do to be there, he would. Here was his first real test. If you can do the 2.15am boat back to the Isle of Man in the middle of winter you deserve to watch the Reds.

I hadn't been to an away game in England for ages either, as it's difficult to get the tickets. We already owed the girls big time, in terms of money spent and time away. Life was revolving around the Mighty Reds, and goodwill was starting to wear thin. With a boat virtually all to ourselves, who in their right mind goes anywhere on a boat on a Saturday night, and a plate of chicken curry half and half in front of us, we were off. We were excited with what Sunday had to offer. The Irish Sea was surprisingly calm, and with the lights of Blackpool glistening in the distance – it was either Blackpool or Paris as you could see the big tower lit up in the distance – we were on our way to Heysham. After a dream crossing, we were docking and tying up alongside by 11.15pm. Even more amazingly, due to the handful of passengers, we were disembarked by 11.30pm and on our way to Liverpool. We'd be there by 1am, no bother.

Who closes main motorway junctions? The same people who create diversions that take you to the middle of nowhere, that's who. How do you lose the M6? It's impossible. We lost it and couldn't find it. After an hour of driving around back lanes and villages that didn't exist on my sat nav, we had to retrace our footsteps all the way back to Lancaster and start all over again. As we left Lancaster for a second time, heading out of the town centre on the A road towards Preston, it was nudging 1am and my front-seat passenger was asleep. My head was banging after concentrating so hard down those back lanes in the pitch dark, with corners, ditches and walls appearing out of nowhere. Hitting Liverpool by 2am was an excellent result. As always, my mum was up waiting for us, as she could never settle until we were safely home. It was a quick hello and good night as Charlie dragged his exhausted body up to the bedroom that he has now made his own. While he sleeps, he's protected by a bookcase full of books regaling the glorious years of Liverpool's past. They were all his grandad's, and he loves to pick them up and see what all the fuss was about.

The door to my room slowly opened at 8am and a vision in a dressing gown and a mask gently announced, 'I've just tested positive.' My mum only tested herself because we were coming, no other reason. She didn't feel unwell, it was out of a duty to her son and grandson. I must admit I'd rather have not known. We spent the morning avoiding each other and sanitising everything that moved. We were still in that Covid phase, the one where we were desperate not to catch it, so we avoided each other like the plague. Totally ignoring that this afternoon we'd be sharing public spaces with thousands, be it in pubs or the away end in Nottingham. Mixing with my mum wasn't going to harm us, was it? But still, better safe than sorry. As she waved us off on our travels there were no hugs this time round.

It must have been nearly 25 years since I'd last been to the City Ground, but I remembered the way. There was no sat nav in those days, you had to check the map before you started driving and note the roads and motorway junctions down or rely on someone in the passenger seat being sober enough to navigate. M6 down to the A500 at Stoke and turn left, through Stoke and Derby, and at the end of it would be Nottingham and the river Trent. That's pretty much how it played out. Some of the roads may be easier now; you go past the Bet 365 stadium in Stoke and you don't have to go through the suburbs of Derby, but you still end up at the Trent.

All those years faded away as we parked up at County Hall, on the banks of the Trent. We were a stone's throw from the City Ground and Trent Bridge cricket ground, standing side by side on the other side of the main road. Last time I was here there was a chase and fists were flying all around us, but those days are gone, aren't they?

I knew you could park in County Hall, but I forgot that there's only one exit for hundreds of cars. I knew I was going to pay the price later, but I put that to the back of my mind as we headed towards Trent Bridge. I struck up a chat with a couple of Forest fans, one of those normal chats: 'Your boys are doing great,' and 'Yeah, but what about your fellas, they're amazing,' with a parting shot, 'Enjoy your day, lads, but not too much, eh.' Maybe Nottingham had changed, maybe it was never as bad as we remembered, we were all normal fellas going to watch their team try to get to the FA Cup semi-final. Before the match the olive branches had been out between the more sensible Forest and Liverpool fans. We'd all suffered on that sunny day in April 1989, and there was a real recognition of the fact, and the vast majority of the ones who'd let us down today weren't even born in 1989.

Heading across the bridge towards Meadow Lane, the home of Notts County, and even with a police van patrolling close by, it started. With random shouts of 'wankers' floating on the air and even with no colours on show, we still stood out as 'not from round here'. 'Just walk on, Charlie.' There's no point getting involved with idiots, especially when you're on your own. Within 200 yards we were among friends in the Broken Wheelbarrow, a pub attached to Notts County's Meadow Lane ground. A warm welcome with food and drink attracted hundreds of Liverpool fans. The Broken Wheelbarrow was full of mates. Zil, Robbie and his lad Craig had made their way down by coach. Bono was in there with the Barrow Boys, and young Keifer, who I'd met outside Wembley for the first time a few weeks earlier. He was at pains to point out he wasn't stalking me. We were now a nice little group and excited to be back at a real football ground in the FA Cup and aiming for Wembley. It was like the good old days. Charlie was beyond himself with excitement, and I must admit I wasn't far behind him.

Kick-off approached, it was time to leave and, as directed by the police, we headed across the Trent using a different bridge than the one we initially came across. This path would take us directly to our end of the ground and away from most of the home supporters. As we were walking across the bridge it was like the old days, having a good old natter with Zil and Robbie, and our two boys were ahead of us having a natter of their own. To think

Craig used to come with us at six years of age and here he was, as a fully grown man, looking after my lad. Where had all the years gone? The feeling of excitement was still the same even after all these years.

I must admit I wasn't ready for what we found in the ground, and it took me back, approximately 30 years. The online behaviours of the decent Forest fans and those we'd met walking from the car were certainly not matched by the inhabitants of the Brian Clough Stand to our right. The atmosphere was febrile, there was a real energy in the City Ground and some of that energy wasn't great. Our tickets were good, between the corner flag and the edge of the penalty box, six rows back. That meant we were directly in the target area for the abuse coming from the Forest fans on the opposite side of the corner flag. It wasn't only one or two, it was whole blocks closest to the fan divide, and in the tier above us. There were thousands of people seemingly more focused on us than anything else, with a variety of hand signals that we'd seen a million times before. It seemed that you had to be clad in 'Stone Island' clothing, and if in the top tier of the Brian Clough Stand, as you entered through the tunnel into the seating area you had to run to the front and gesticulate towards us, 'flicking the Vs', 'go swivel' or the 'wanker' signs, or even all three, cheered by all those around them. We stood slightly bemused and laughing at them, which infuriated them. The teams weren't even out yet and the place was bouncing.

As the teams came out the noise levels blew the roof off, it was fabulous, and the focus went on to the pitch for the time being. The game wasn't the magnificent cup tie we'd hoped for. Liverpool took control and, while at times it was tense and there were a few scares, Forest certainly didn't have anywhere near the effect that they'd had against Arsenal and Leicester in the previous rounds. With the sting taken out of the game it was only a matter of time before Liverpool stepped it up a gear. After the hour mark we saw four substitutes, with Henderson and Thiago pulling the strings and more movement up top with Díaz and Minamino. Liverpool wanted to win this in the 90 minutes. With 12 minutes remaining a teasing cross from Tsimikas found the toe of Jota and the ball found the back of the net. The Liverpool end erupted. With the customary nervous wait as VAR drew its lines, along came the Hillsborough shouts. They'd done so well up to then to avoid that, but 'always the victim' cascaded from our right-hand side and above us from the home fans. When people say it's not about Hillsborough, don't believe them, because that's exactly what it's about.

Besides a big penalty shout and a glaring Forest miss that had our hearts in our mouths, the final whistle blew and the Reds were off to Wembley. Liverpool were still in every competition, and as we cheered the lads off the pitch the Jota song rang out from the away end. We were supremely confident.

I wasn't that confident about getting out of Nottingham safely, mind you, as the police let us all out together, which was a mistake. The car park outside the away end saw several skirmishes and antagonism from the home support. Charlie and I had to head away from the main body of Liverpool supporters and through the home fans towards the cricket ground and past the Trent End to the safety of the car. The 'Stone Island boys' were looking for trouble, that's for sure, and I had to remind Charlie a couple of times that this was not the time to talk. If he could temper his excitement for a couple of minutes until we got to the car it would be great.

I nervously surveyed the crowd and listened to the chants of how 'the cheating Scousers' had won the game. To be fair, you'd hear exactly the same outside Anfield if we'd lost 1-0. Within sight of County Hall and the safety of the car we crossed the road by Trent Bridge and to our right under the bridge there was a roar and shouts of 'come on'. Under the bridge by the banks of the river it was going off and the police were on their toes. As always, everyone starts rubber-necking and some want to get involved, but I guided Charlie by the arm towards the car. No need to look here, we were obviously on our own and no need to draw attention to ourselves.

As we jumped into the car, trying to get away as quickly as possible, we paid the price for parking at the back of the car park with only one exit. I weaved my way through the car park, following the red taillights of cars that seemed to be making good progress, only to grind to a halt time and again as everyone was bunking in at the head of the queue. I looked nervously at the clock; what time was that boat again? It was sailing at 2.15am, we'd be sound, but it was a good three-hour drive from Nottingham and we weren't moving an inch.

The game hadn't finished until nearly 8pm, and by the time we were on the road out of Nottingham it was nearly 9.30pm, so it was going to be a dash for the ferry. Thankfully the roads were good and the M6 was nice and quiet, so we were at the sea terminal at Heysham by 1am. Charlie jumped in the back and tried to get some kip. It took him that long to get in his sleeping bag that by the time the cars started to board he'd only had about 20 minutes, but he was in a dead sleep and none too happy to be woken up.

The ferry was rammed, which for this sailing was unusual. The previous day's boats had been cancelled, so everyone was on here. We headed to the bar (closed for drinking) with a pillow and a sleeping bag and bedded down for the night. Unsurprisingly, it wasn't comfortable on a hard carpeted floor, and they kept the lights on all night as the ship tossed in the Irish Sea. You have to close your eyes and pray to god you get to the other side as quickly as possible.

As the Tannoy announced our arrival into Douglas, Charlie was moaning about his lack of sleep and not being able to go to school. Honestly, with all the best intentions, he was going, but the boy needed his sleep. As we disembarked, he was done for. His stories of being a conquering hero, having stormed Nottingham Castle and come home with the victory, would have to wait until Tuesday. Before his head hit his pillow at home, he was already asking about the semi-final and whether we could get tickets. 'We'll see, mate, I'll do my best.'

By Any Means …

THE GAMES were coming thick and fast, and we had to get across the Irish Sea by any means possible now. With the amount of money we'd spent on the Isle of Man boats we could have owned one by now. It was turning out to be a year of fantastic memories for me and Charlie. The following story probably deserves a chapter of its own, but it's only a semi-final so I'll be brief. There's so much more to come in this fabulous season.

I didn't fancy the boat and a drive again, not after the League Cup Final, so I booked flights to Gatwick on the Friday night at 9pm and the Premier Inn outside the terminal for two nights at an acceptable rate. There are no good rates post-Covid. Tickets would be easier to come by for the semi-final, as loads of people would keep their powder dry for a potential final. We were still fighting in two cups, and it was looking like it would be an extremely expensive year. I was right about the tickets, they weren't a problem. A couple of lads I know who qualified were unable to go due to their holidays and work commitments. After dropping my line in the pool, I came up with an embarrassment of riches, which meant I could sort out my nephews, Dan and Josh, as well. City at Wembley would be a great day out. If you beat them you deserve to win the cup.

Post-Covid air travel hadn't been too good, cancellations everywhere, and if there was ever a plane that would be cancelled it would be the 9pm flight to Gatwick. I kept an eye on it all week. It had been arriving in the Isle of Man and departing, later than expected, but still departing. On the Friday afternoon I was watching the flight departures board thinking we should have got the 6pm one, but that was a lot more expensive. Little did I know that the expense was going to go through the roof. We left home at 6.30pm in the car to head to the airport. As we headed along the promenade and out of Douglas, I got Charlie to check the EasyJet app flight tracker to see where our plane was now. According to the app it was set to leave London on time, after coming in from some random airport in Europe, so all looked good. As we passed the sea terminal, any plan B would go out the window. Plan B was the boat to Heysham at 7.45pm and then drive to Wembley. As we headed to the airport there was no going back. If the plane didn't go, we'd be knackered. There was no plan C or D.

As we passed Mount Murray (a big hill really) at the highest point en route, it was shrouded in fog, not normally a good sign, but as we dropped down the other side the fog seemed to fade away. By the time we got to the airport everything looked alright. Thirty minutes later, though, with a bottle of Budweiser in my hand, I looked up and we were shrouded in fog. 'Where did that come from?' It wasn't looking good. I was in good company, with another dozen or so Reds, including Mike Holt of the fabulous *Going the Match* podcast (check him out, I had the honour of being his first guest). We were all in the same boat now, or should I say plane! The boat had sailed.

Everyone was frantically looking at the EasyJet app, which offered a glimmer of hope, as did the departure board. The rule is usually that if the plane lands it will also fly out, so our hopes were resting on it landing. The app was showing that the plane had left Gatwick and we tracked its route over Birmingham and on towards Liverpool. Our hopes were high. That was until the plane did a giant U-turn over Liverpool and headed back south. I've been on enough of those flights to know this only ends one way, the plane ends up back at Gatwick.

There was no plan B; we'd left that behind as we passed the sea terminal, so we were right in the shit now. That was the last flight out of the Isle of Man and there were now no morning flights to anywhere close to London that would help us get to the match on time. I desperately searched SkyScanner for options. The only one that gave any glimmer of hope was a 7am flight to Liverpool, but with no trains running and seats on coaches being rare as hen's teeth, we were stuck as to how to get from Liverpool airport to Wembley. Car hire was showing at £350 for only one day's hire and that was if they were open and ready to go that early in the morning.

I messaged my brothers in Liverpool, who were travelling together, but there was no room in the car, and while they both drive, they only had one car available, and it was full. Coaches, even if you had a seat, were leaving Liverpool by 8am and there was no chance of landing there until 7.30am at the earliest. It was looking a bit grim, but I took the plunge and booked the Liverpool flights anyway, as Mike and the lads around me checked out taxis for seven or eight to Wembley. It was all about getting there now. We were £200 lighter in the pocket and more costs to come, so it had better be worth it.

Our Ian messaged me and, out the blue, Charlie and I were sorted. Ian would pick us up at Liverpool, if we were on time. The lads had been able to persuade their better halves to manage without a car for the day. I told him that if we weren't there by 8.30am to go without us. Fingers crossed that with a 7am flight, which takes 25 minutes, and accounting for the usual messing around on disembarkation, we could hopefully be on the road by 8am and on our way to London. Memories of a five-and-a-half-hour journey in February at the front of my mind meant it could still be tight.

We were eventually called back through security and asked to leave the airport. We'd need to be back at the airport again before 6am in the morning. The clock had ticked past 9.30pm as we headed home. When we got there it was straight to bed for Charlie, but for me it was a long night of cancelling hotels and getting refunds on whatever I could. I'd lost that evening's Premier Inn cost but got the Saturday evening back, and EasyJet would refund the flights. I'd also lost the cost of return train tickets from Gatwick to Wembley. I had to think about how we'd get home from Liverpool, and I booked a boat for the Sunday evening. I was over £300 out of pocket by now. By 1am Mike had a taxi booked. Unfortunately, one person had to drop out, but the rest were booked on the 7am plane to Liverpool and in a £400 taxi one way to Wembley. Fingers crossed for us all.

The alarm burst into life at 5am and Charlie was up like a shot, dressed and ready to go. By 5.45am we were heading into the airport and meeting up with our bleary-eyed fellow travellers. The departure board told us the flight was on time and the weather was looking good. The previous evening's fog had lifted and left us looking at a beautiful morning. Here we go again.

A short taxi out to the runway and bang on 7am we were rumbling down the tarmac and on our way to Liverpool. Only 25 minutes later we were landing at John Lennon and heading out of arrivals by 7.45am, it couldn't have gone any smoother. Today was going to be a great day!

Our Ian was there to meet us and by 8am we were on our way to Wembley. See Charlie, here's a lesson for you: 'Never give up hope, mate, we'll always find a way.' Brave words, I know. I didn't think we would get there, so no wonder he had his reservations. By noon we were in Stanmore and heading to the tube station. So much for the expected nightmare journeys as tens of thousands headed down the M6 and the M1 from the north to Wembley. We headed for a pint at the Premier Inn, then met the lads in the McDonald's car park across the road. Don't say we don't do Wembley in style.

As you know by now it's generally never about the match, it's about how we get there and what goes on around the 90 minutes, but today the match was fabulous. I'd say it was one of the epic FA Cup semi-finals. Liverpool sent us into ecstasy in the first 45 minutes as they toyed with Man City, and by half-time we were unbelievably 3-0 up and it could have been many more, as Mané and Díaz ripped City to pieces. City didn't know what hit them and Wembley had never seen an end like ours in those 45 minutes. We were in Row 6 of the bottom tier and it was bouncing.

All the trials and tribulations from the Friday evening were forgotten about as the referee blew his whistle for half-time, but we didn't want it to end. The noise that greeted the whistle followed us into the bowels of the stadium where there was a full-on party underway. We were laying down a marker for the rest of the season as we chased City towards the title. Could this be a hammer blow that would affect their pursuit of the Champions League and Premier League?

The second half couldn't match the energy of the first, on or off the pitch. We were all exhausted. City got one back early on, but in all truth Liverpool cruised through the second half and should have extended their lead. City got another one back late on, making the last five minutes nervy, but they'd been well beaten by the better team. We bounced out the stadium and would be back here in a few weeks' time to face the winners of the second semi-final; as it turned out, it was Chelsea again. No cup final could match this day, though, as we bounced out of Wembley. We were invincible, the quadruple was well and truly on. Well placed in the league, in a second cup final and in the semi-finals of the Champions League. If City couldn't stop us, nobody could.

* * *

As we neared the end of April the games came thick and fast. We ripped United to bits (again), we pushed Everton a step closer to relegation (they ultimately avoided it) and we had one foot in the Champions League Final, having beaten Villarreal 2-0 at Anfield in the first leg of the semi-final. All the talk now was of the quadruple, with the focus on overhauling City in the league. There was no way we were losing a cup game, we were supreme in the knockout competitions. It was bubbling nicely, and City were the only team who could realistically stop us doing the quadruple. The team that Jürgen built were to be adored.

Grinding out a 1-0 win at Newcastle to keep us on track in the league was the forerunner to a night of drama in the lashing rain in Villarreal, where Liverpool booked their place in the Champions League Final (more of that soon). Normally, when you reached a Champions League Final all eyes would be on that game and that game alone, but not for these Reds. Liverpool still had an FA Cup Final and four league games to play, so the next month could be the greatest month in our history.

The following Saturday saw Liverpool take on Spurs at home and, sadly, it proved to be the defining moment in the season. While it can be argued that one result doesn't cost you the league, this one probably did. We started to see the signs that Liverpool were pretty much running on empty. On a frustrating night at Anfield, we were undone at the back as Son scored a tap-in. Even with a deflected Díaz shot that got us back level, we never looked like getting the winner. Spurs were good value for the point. While we went top again, a win the following day for City against Newcastle would see us chasing them down again. If we'd managed to win against Spurs the pressure would have been on City after their midweek failure in Madrid in the Champions League semi-final. It might have made them crack. As it was, Liverpool's result gave them confidence and they went and smashed Newcastle 5-0. It wasn't over, but we now needed City to lose games, and they didn't look like they would. They had a decent run-in and expectation gave way to hope and prayers. City only had the league to focus on, while we had two cup finals to prepare for. Jürgen's boys were made of strong stuff, though.

Three days later they showed it again, coming from behind to win away at Aston Villa. One down after only three minutes, the boys were doing it the hard way at Villa Park. Matip equalised quickly, giving us hope, and Sadio Mané proved his worth again, heading the winner midway through the second half. We believed again. The pressure was back on City, but we had to put our pursuit on the back burner again, as we had the FA Cup Final against Chelsea at Wembley on the Saturday. The games were coming thick and fast, and every one had been a cup final for months. Saturday was no different.

* * *

This time around it was my turn to go the cup final, and because Charlie had his turn in February, he was going to be staying at home and watching from the couch, annoying the life out of his mum as he screamed and shouted at the telly. That was until one of the lads on the Isle of Man came up trumps with a spare ticket. I don't know who was more pleased, Charlie or his mum? Actually, it was me, as we still hadn't seen the Reds win anything together.

I was taking no risks with the planes this time and booked the boat and took my car. I was driving to Wembley and having another alcohol-free cup final experience. As long as the Reds won, I didn't care. The Friday afternoon boat from the Isle of Man on a calm Irish Sea had us waving to the Liver birds by 6pm as we disembarked. One more sleep.

With Our Kev in the navigator's seat, regardless of the fact that the car and the driver knew the way to Anfield South, a 9am start saw us down in London by 1pm for the strangely timed kick-off at 4.45pm, all for the telly folk. No thought for the fans travelling from the north or any interest in what time we'd be back home. Many of my normal match-going crowd hadn't been lucky enough to get tickets this time round, but we'd try to meet whoever we could. Mongoose and Zil were holed up at JJ Moons on Wembley High Street. On our way we got side-tracked as the team was departing their hotel next to Wembley. Even though they were staying only 200 yards from the stadium, they needed the coach escort for obvious reasons. We thought they were leaving imminently but we ended up wasting an hour waiting around for them to leave, and even then we only caught a glimpse of the lads as they got on to the coaches. This was for Charlie, not for me.

As we were waiting, I saw Chris Kirkland and Neil Mellor with their families. I was dying to tell Neil Mellor where I'd watched his classic goal at the Kop end against Arsenal in November 2004. I was in the ESPN Sports Bar in Las Vegas with Nikki, drinking beer and eating chicken wings. As he smashed the ball in the net from 25 yards the Kop went wild and so did I. The plate of bones went up in the air, my pint went all over the floor and the sports bar crowd looked on bemused. Nikki just shook her head. I wanted to tell him, but I didn't because he was with his family and friends; he was only a fan today and I didn't want to ruin it. I'm glad I didn't, as I realised as I was doing my research when writing that it wasn't him who I watched score, it was Luis Garcia, and it was in February 2006 not November 2004. I wasn't even in Vegas when he scored, I was on the couch in the Isle of Man. If I ever see Luis Garcia, I'll tell him the story of the beer and chicken wings. Honestly, I try to tell the truth, but I need to get these stories down before I really am making them up.

As we cheered the team off, we headed up to Wembley High Street to meet the lads, but by the time we found the pub they were ready to leave. It was probably over 25 years since I was last on Wembley High Street. The memories of Spurs and half of London turning out to meet our special train in 1982 and then chaos with Man United fans running wild up and down the High Street in 1983 came back, and thoughts turned to my dad, who sheltered me from harm in those mad days. Now here I was, off to an FA Cup Final with Charlie, and I had no such concerns.

That was until we got to the turnstiles, where chaos ensued, and due to the events of Paris two weeks later, and the fact we won at Wembley, many forget about what happened at the turnstiles that afternoon. It may be too easy to say but it reminded me of Hillsborough, seriously it did. At our entrance we were met with a mass of people and there was little movement through any of the 16 turnstiles (I spent enough time counting them) through which we were to enter. It was an hour to kick-off. We'd be alright, though, or so I thought. There was no sign of stewards outside, no crowd control and no police to be seen. Inside the stadium you could see the escalator up to the concourse was only working intermittently. As always there was no communication, nobody was telling us anything, and people were fearful of not getting in for kick-off.

Due to the layout of the ground, the lack of movement was creating blockages behind us as people tried to get past us to the other turnstiles. There's not enough space outside when large crowds are there. Several people couldn't cope and took a step to one side, away from the throng, reminding me of my own actions in 1989. This was dangerous now. I was trying to keep my feet and keep Charlie in my grasp at the same time. There were lots of frightened kids in the queue. Stewards intermittently opened the turnstiles to allow small groups in, but there were far too many people outside now. Any initial delay like this means a crowd builds up, and it builds up quickly until you lose control. Keep that thought in mind, because in less than two weeks I'll be saying exactly the same thing.

A gap opened to our left-hand side, and I dragged Charlie through, some breathing space at least, and as if by magic the turnstile ahead of us started to let people into the stadium. Our national stadium, what a disgrace. The stewards inside had no clue what to do. Were they to search you? Check your ticket? Where should they direct you to? Once again, fans being let down by people who are supposed to protect you. We later found out that Wembley had sacked their security company only two days before the cup final and replaced them. Obviously they'd replaced them with people who hadn't been trained properly. I don't blame the individuals in the roles, I blame those who run the show, they're the ones who always get away with the criticism, leaving the person on minimum wage manning the door to get all the grief.

After 45 minutes we finally got in, sweating profusely after standing in the beating sun outside. It was a massive relief. The teams would be out soon, and I was worn out by the time we found our seats high up in the top tier. Within a minute, the opening bars of 'You'll Never Walk Alone' were played out by a brass band on the pitch. In no time the teams were entering the arena to a crescendo of noise. Liverpool were resplendent in all red and Chelsea in the most vivid yellow away kit. Why they didn't wear their normal blue, who knows.

There was no way we were losing, no way whatsoever. As you know by now, you're not getting a detailed match report. My report goes like this: 'Luis Díaz battered them all by himself.' He could have had six goals, he was on fire, but somehow the game ended 0-0 after 90 minutes for the second cup final in succession. We hit the post twice, Chelsea hit the post, and there were loads of near misses. For a neutral it was probably one of the most entertaining finals; even at 0-0, it was a great game. We lost Salah to injury and, as we went into extra time, Virgil went off as well. Never mind this game, everyone was thinking about the next three games, Southampton, Wolves and Real Madrid. Would injuries kill our season as we hit the crucial last two weeks? Extra time couldn't split the teams, as tiredness and nerves meant extra time finished goalless as well, and the final would be decided on penalties. A brilliant way to win a cup final, a terrible way to lose one. You keep your fingers crossed you're on the right side of the shoot-out.

The penalties were taken at the far end of the stadium in front of the Chelsea fans, and Chelsea went first. Liverpool got the advantage early on as Azpilicueta (I had to check the spelling for that a few times) missed Chelsea's second penalty. We were faultless for our first four penalties; this was going to be our day. Up stepped Sadio Mané to take the fifth and final penalty. If he slotted it, he'd won the FA Cup for Liverpool. What an end to an amazing year for Sadio. He had won the Africa Cup of Nations, scoring the winning penalty in the final's shoot-out, with nerves of steel after missing a penalty in the 90 minutes. With all the pressure of a nation on his shoulders, he'd scored. Now he had the hopes of a Scouse nation on his shoulders. There was something odd about his behaviour in the lead-up to the penalty, as he stood away from the rest of the team, seemingly agitated. As he strode up to collect the ball, he seemed calm again. All he needed to do was slot it past his Senegal team-mate Mendy and trophy number two was on its way to the banks of the Mersey.

Of his two penalties in the Africa Cup of Nations Final, unfortunately he replicated his first; yeah, the one that missed, and our hearts dropped, the advantage had gone. We were into sudden death now and penalty shoot-outs turn on moments like this. I pulled Charlie in tight as Mason Mount stepped up and fired his shot to Ali's left-hand side. In slow motion, we saw our keeper save it with a strong left hand. Our end went nuts, now we were in control again. Who was going to be our hero? I dare anyone to say they called it that the Greek Scouser, Kostas Tsimikas, would score the winner. He'd quickly attained cult status and was a popular member of the squad, and he was about to fire himself into Liverpool folklore.

Nobody, I swear nobody, knew whether he was any good at penalties, but my mind went back to Alan Kennedy and the European Cup Final, a left-back with a spot kick to win the cup. He must score. And he did! As Mendy went the wrong way, the ball nestled in the corner of the net and the Greek Scouser turned, fists clenched and headed towards our end. A sea of limbs and pyro, the Liverpool fans masked in a cloak of red smoke, a scene that we'll remember forever. Charlie and I hugged each other, our first trophy together, and it was a wonderful moment to share. As Dua Lipa's 'One Kiss' boomed over the Tannoy, the Reds were delirious and the players joined the party in front of us. I don't know where they got the energy for the dancing. Charlie bounced up and down with his lucky red and white chequered flag, this was one for the memory bank. The Liverpool end burst into song: 'I'm so glad that Jürgen is a Red'. Nothing could be truer. As Jordan climbed the steps with the lads, the 'Hendo shuffle' was ready to go again. As he lifted the cup and turned to face us, we roared our approval. Within minutes our heroes in red were dancing in front of us with the cup. Where would these boys get the energy to go again at Southampton on Tuesday night? I was sure they'd find it from somewhere.

As we bounded out of Wembley Stadium and on to Wembley Way, there was a sea of red, the blue of Chelsea long since gone. Who cared about the long drive home, with two cups down and two to go. The next two weeks stood between this Liverpool team and immortality. They were playing every game they could play in the season, and we still had a chance of winning all four competitions we'd entered. Roll on Southampton on Tuesday night, then Wolves on the final day of the season at Anfield, for which, as usual these days, I was without a ticket. It was going to be a stressful week of begging. By the time we got to the bottom of the tube station steps the energy was gone, the long drag home beckoned. Firstly Liverpool, then back on the boat on the Sunday night to the Isle of Man. Five days later we'd be back on the boat for the final game of the season, with the hope of watching the Reds win the league.

* * *

Watching the Southampton match was difficult. I'd binned Sky off earlier in the year due to the cost, and the pubs weren't allowing a youngster to watch beyond 9pm. We found a local restaurant that had the match on, and if we had 'a meal' we could stay after 9pm. By the time we got out the house and to the restaurant we'd already heard the first ten minutes' commentary on 5 Live, and we hadn't started well. The team was a real mix of youth and reserves. The TV stream was about two minutes behind and no sooner had we sat down than my phone pinged, a simple message 'FFS'. We were one down already and we hadn't even ordered our 'meal' (a plate of chips). The dream ending could be over right here and now. The team that played 120 minutes late into the night on Saturday and danced for a further 30 minutes were out on their feet. Could they find a way?

Of course they could, this team could always find a way. After Bobby had a goal disallowed for offside, we were level after 27 minutes and dominant. When you look back at the stats you'll see how dominant we were. Our second string had 24 shots and 73 per cent possession, the only surprise being that it took so long to get a second goal. The winner came from our unlikely cult hero, Jöel Matip. As his looping header went in down on the south coast, the Reds behind the goal celebrated wildly and my phone pinged. I didn't let on to Charlie that we'd scored but I knew what was coming, and two minutes later enjoyed it as he whooped with delight. A tense last 20 minutes came to an end (on my phone), and I relaxed as Charlie punched the air two minutes later. The dream was still on, it was down to the last game, at home to Wolves on Sunday, and one last trip across the Irish Sea. I didn't have a ticket, I was facing being locked out again, as tickets were going for mental money, and I wasn't playing that game. Let's see if something comes up, everything was crossed.

Begging on Facebook, begging on Twitter, begging via WhatsApp, begging face to face, somehow it had to work, otherwise I faced being locked out of what could be one of the biggest games in 30-odd years. Twitter begging worked. Friday afternoon, from one of Our Ian's Twitter followers, a quick retweet from Our Ian meant that a boss lad from Ireland dropped me a message and I was sorted. Face value, he didn't want me to miss out. When we got to eventually meet, I bought him that pint I'd promised, what a fella. I could finally relax. It sounds great saying, 'I'm not arsed, I'll watch it in the pub,' but it's crushing when you actually have to do it. Missing the Carabao Cup Final will stay with me forever.

As we boarded the boat for the trip to Liverpool we were among friends. There were many good Reds on the boat, and they all put the miles in watching Liverpool, by air and sea, and they are among the best people you'll meet. Most of them had never seen the Reds win the league in the flesh, so was this to be the time? In just over 24 hours we'd find out. If we won and City drew or lost, we'd be champions!

It was as simple, and as difficult, as that. City were playing Aston Villa, who in all honesty had nothing to play for, but were managed by Liverpool legend Steven Gerrard and had Philippe Coutinho in their ranks, who owed us one after his 'bad back'. We'd been dreaming of the headlines for weeks: Stevie G, who'd never won the title at Liverpool, would exorcise some of his own demons by doing it for the club he loves. Everyone would have one eye on the game in front of us at Anfield and one ear to their transistor radio, or modern equivalent. It's easier to keep up to date with scores these days with the likes of Twitter. Back in the 80s the most popular fella on any defining title day was the lad with the transistor radio glued to his ear. He'd be celebrated or abused in equal measure depending upon the information he was relaying from his earpiece. Today the wind-ups travel faster than the truth and a shout that someone has scored is taken up, often without any evidence.

The 3pm boat got us into Liverpool, and we were miraculously off by 6pm and within 90 minutes I'd dropped Charlie at my mum's, had some tea and was back out to catch the train back into town. I was off to *The Anfield Wrap*'s end-of-season do at Mountford Hall at Liverpool University. I was meeting up with Our Ian, Mike, who'd travelled up from Kent, and Peter, who'd travelled down from Scotland, a real expat reunion. A fabulous night full of Liverpool talk and a Liverpool singalong courtesy of Kieo (Kieran Molyneux), and what started off as a rather subdued evening by the end had us believing that anything was possible on Sunday. The fun went on long into the night at Pogue Mahone's in Liverpool city centre. Anything was possible.

Simple mathematics, that's all it was: we win, we get three points, and if City don't win, we win the league; if they win and we win, we lose the league by a single point, for the second time in three years. The talk before the match outside the Glenbuck was whether we could go again, could we give it one more huge effort after a great win at Southampton. The team news saw the Reds stronger than the Southampton game. Mo Salah was back, but on the bench, with one eye on the game in Paris the following weekend. A half-fit Salah could make the difference, though. We walked up to Anfield with hope in our hearts, but if we were honest we didn't expect Villa to get anything. Once we saw that their Argentine goalkeeper Martínez was out, and Everton's old second-string goalie was in, any confidence we had drained away.

I was up in the gods in the new Main Stand, and by the time I got to my seat, as the teams were coming out, I needed oxygen. There was little chance of me roaring the Reds on as I had to get my breath. And just as I was ready to roar, we were 1-0 down, another defensive lapse seeing Neto tap the ball in as we all waited for VAR to intervene. But there would be no intervention. The goal sent the Wolves fans wild in a corner of Anfield, and 40 miles down the round it sent the Etihad into raptures. It looked like the title was slipping away, but these Reds were made of tough stuff. They always found a way to win. Sadio Mané was often the man to find a way, and so it was to be again, as he raced clear and beat Sá in the Wolves goal with a powerful shot. The energy returned to the ground, but Wolves were a constant danger and could have scored another couple. Minutes before half-time the ground exploded as Villa took the lead at City. We only needed a winner now, as if we ended up level on points, they'd win the league on goal difference.

After half-time, though, there was only one winner in it as Liverpool pressed for the winner that could make them champions, but struggled for the breakthrough. After an hour of play a buzz went round the ground, surely not! Philippe Coutinho had scored a second for Villa to put them 2-0 up. The headlines were coming true, City now needed to score at least twice and realistically three times, as we were sure to score here. We roared the Reds on, we were 15 minutes away from glory. City needed to score three in 15 minutes, come on Villa!

Boom! The bubble burst. City scored three goals ... in just under six minutes, the irony being that one of Klopp's old Dortmund players, İlkay Gündoğan, got two of the goals to ruin it for his old boss. As for the goalkeeper, the less said the better; City would never have beaten Martínez three times in six minutes. The Villa nerves started when City got one back, and as they got a second everyone knew what was going to happen. Liverpool kept the dream alive with two goals in the last six minutes, through Mo and Robbo. Could Villa nick one? We hung on the shoulders of anyone who had people at home watching both games, desperate for some good news, and nothing happened. Nobody believed Villa could lift themselves again. They'd pushed City harder than any of us could have imagined, but City saw the game out and won the league to kill our quadruple dream. We'd been chasing City for months and had clawed back 13 points since January, but the only problem was we were 14 points behind. We'd pushed the most expensive team ever assembled and one of the best teams in the world as far as they could go, and they'd risen to the challenge. Take nothing away from Pep and his players, they were magnificent to hold us off.

I was gutted, not devastated, as there was never a point in the afternoon where we had it in our own hands. City had turned it around before we scored, we were never top of the table. I was so proud of the boys in red, down and out on the pitch, but they couldn't have done any more. This was not a time to cry. In six days these boys would be walking out in Paris looking to win us the Champions League. If this was the final act of the season, maybe it would have been devastating, but it wasn't, all thoughts now led to Paris. As we retired to the Glenbuck to mull over the afternoon's events, there was no mudslinging, no crying and certainly no time to be morose, we celebrated a great season by the boys in red. Then we sorted out our plans for Friday night in the Pigalle. Monday would see me and Charlie head off back across the Irish Sea to get a change of clothes, for him to spend a couple of days in school and me in work, and then go again. It had been a wild ride – one last push for the men in red.

From the Mersey to the Seine

IN FEBRUARY 2022 the world turned on its axis. Russia invaded Ukraine, taking the world by surprise, even though they'd been massing on the Ukraine border. They actually invaded. It wasn't a five-minute thing either, they were in it for the long haul, decimating Ukrainian cities and destroying the country's infrastructure, along with people's livelihoods, and the loss of many lives.

On the face of it, football seemed to be the least important thing to consider, but the 2022 Champions League Final was due to be held in St Petersburg, Russia on 28 May. Surely that couldn't happen now. More importantly, Ukraine, that beautiful country that we'd all been so enamoured with only four years earlier, would never be the same again.

UEFA held their breath. One of their major sponsors was the Russian firm Gazprom, and all their planning for years had been aimed at St Petersburg. Holding their breath wasn't enough, though, and they were forced to change the venue. With the Reds going deep into the tournament it was potentially going to affect us as UEFA announced a change of venue. The new venue would be the Stade de France in Paris.

Along with thousands of others I immediately checked out booking.com and sorted a room in Paris as soon as the announcement was made. A European Cup in Paris? I wanted to follow in my dad's footsteps. He watched Phil Thompson lift old big ears in the Parc des Princes in Paris in 1981, so now it was my turn to see the 'Hendo shuffle' in the same iconic city. If Charlie was lucky, he could see it alongside his dad. I had to make do with the telly in 1981.

Liverpool were looking good. They'd cruised through the group stage, winning all six matches in a so-called group of death. In the knockout stages we faced Inter Milan, Benfica and Villarreal. In the semi-final against Villarreal, Liverpool cruised to an emphatic 2-0 victory at Anfield, with me and Charlie on the back row of the Kop. I'd never seen such a dominant display in Europe, there seemed little danger in the return leg. At half-time in the return leg, in the middle of a Spanish rainstorm, it was touch and go about getting to the final, as we made such a meal of the first 45 minutes. They were fighting on all fronts at home, still in three competitions, and seemingly trying to conserve their energy. It nearly became their undoing but Jürgen worked his magic at half-time. Whatever he said worked as the Reds came back out with an improved second-half display against the Yellow Submarine, scoring three goals with no response to make the aggregate an emphatic 5-2 win.

Man City weren't going to stop us winning the Champions League, that would be down to Real Madrid.

On a crazy night in Madrid they delivered one of the great Champions League comebacks. I was desperately hoping it wouldn't be City in Paris, as two English teams wouldn't be the best day out in the French capital, and the last thing we wanted was City beating us in Paris and winning their first Champions League.

As City went 1-0 up on the night, and 2-0 up on aggregate, they played Real off the park and there looked to be only one winner. My Twitter stream was two minutes behind the live feeds, and the excitement of the WhatsApp group meant I knew what was coming. Madrid had scored two goals in a minute and my stream hadn't even seen the first goal. From what I was watching there was absolutely no chance of Real scoring, they were useless. Even when I knew they'd taken the game into extra time, I still couldn't believe what I was watching. Two late goals killed City, and with a third early in extra time Real Madrid booked their place in Paris to play the Mighty Reds. With echoes of 1981, it was written in the stars.

It was a good job we'd beaten Villarreal, as after the emphatic first leg win we'd booked our French travel and we were excited. Charlie knew that if we got there, he'd be going, no pressure Jürgen!

Flying to Paris was a non-starter, and flying anywhere within a train ride to Paris often meant you could get a flight, but no train or coach from the airport. Complicating matters, Charlie had exams and needed to be back on the island by Monday morning. I should have taken the hit and booked flights when I booked the room, but the room was refundable, the flights weren't, and I never like tempting fate. I wouldn't want to be blamed for Liverpool failing to get to the final.

Aki was a knight in shining armour. He said he was driving anyway, with his lad Harry, and allowed us to jump in on his ferry booking, Dover to Calais at 8.45am on the Friday morning (the day before the match) and back early afternoon the day after the game. Aki showed his kindness once again and said there was no problem dropping us off at Gatwick Airport on the way back from France. As long as we could get to Liverpool in time to be picked up by car on the Thursday night, we'd be sound.

Three days before we were due to leave, they moved the ferry from 8.45am to 4.40am on the Friday morning, giving us four hours' less time to make the ferry. Accounting for at least a five-hour drive, we'd have to leave Liverpool by 9pm, and our flights were only leaving the Isle of Man at 6pm (if on time). Post-Covid that was a huge if. I'd kept an eye on the flights in the days running up to our departure and that had made me nervous, even before the ferry change. Days of cancellations and delays, we were in the hands of the gods. There was no plan B, so fingers crossed. Preparations meant meeting the French Covid requirements to get into France, easy enough for me and Charlie sorting out our digital Covid passes. By Wednesday night, with Covid passes sorted, passport in the bag, euros sorted, T-shirts and a bucket hat from Hat Scarf or a Badge, we were all set to go. Charlie only needed to get through Thursday at school without spontaneously combusting, and he was off to see Liverpool play Real Madrid in Paris.

* * *

It's a long way from the Mersey to the Seine, the two mighty rivers miles apart, but inextricably linked to Liverpool. Tales of 1981 and drinking wine by the Seine are the stuff of legend. Now we're writing our own tales. Our flight was on time and by 6pm we were trundling up the runway, propellers at full pelt, pulling us skywards towards Liverpool, and onwards to Paris.

By 8pm we'd flown over the Mersey, landed at John Lennon, taken a bus to South Parkway, two trains to Aintree, visited the chippy and were on our way to my mum's to say hello and pick up the gear that Mick from Hat, Scarf or a Badge had kindly dropped off. By 9pm Aki and Harry were at the door, and we were ready for the long drive south. Everyone else was on their way now, except for Our Kev, who was on the coach the following evening from Liverpool.

While we had our Covid passes, I'm sure Aki was carrying it himself, as his throat was killing him and he was coughing like a horse. Our journey was sponsored by Strepsils and Soothers. If we were catching Covid from Aki, we wouldn't get it for a few days at least, so it was worth the risk. The car was well prepared with sleeping bags and pillows for the car journey and ferry. Sleep was going to be in short supply, but if we caught some while we could, it would mean everyone would be more awake in Paris. Combined with adrenaline, we'd be fine. Energy was required as we'd be in Paris by lunchtime Friday, and had all day and night to then navigate.

Thanks to Aki we were in Dover by 2.30am, a quick petrol stop a couple of miles from the docks and we were within sight of the coast, and our 4.40am boat. No chance of sneaking on to an earlier boat, so we took the chance to have a quick kip. The boys had done pretty well with their sleep. In the boredom of the traffic jam the pillows and sleeping bags had come out and they were off, waking only at the petrol station as the cold blast of air entered the car. The ferry holding area quickly filled up with the overnight coaches full of Reds. *God help Our Kev*, I thought. I did Paris by coach back in the 80s with about 20 council colleagues. We had a ball, but the journey back scarred me for life. For me there was no fun going all that way on a coach.

We started boarding the ferry at 4.15am and, while excitement was building, tiredness was catching up. Being one of the first on the ferry, we had prime choice of places to get some sleep. Securing some decent seating, we could stretch out, and we crashed out, our eyes were closed before the doors were. By 7am we were alongside in Calais. Next stop Paris, driver!

Before long it was obvious Aki needed to take a break, so we pulled into a rest area and had a 90-minute snooze. Aki assured me that would see him through to Paris, and it did. By 11.30am we were on the Peripherique (the Paris ring road), one of the craziest roads we'd ever seen, it was chaotic. We were tailgating two motorhomes adorned with Liverpool flags, your travel and accommodation all in one.

Aki had booked a good hotel at a decent price, just off the ring road, not far from Paris Orly airport, and the end of a metro line was only a mile away. He'd been driving on and off for 15 hours and covered over 500 miles. A nice warm shower was waiting for him, and well deserved.

We headed towards our hotel near to the Gare de l'Est in the centre of Paris. I gave Charlie the choice of a tram or a 20-minute walk to Villejuif Louis Aragon metro station, and he amazed me by choosing the walk. After 15 hours' travelling it was the right option. Rucksacks slung over our shoulders and passport and cash in my jeans pocket, it was good for me and Charlie to stretch our legs. The metro station was at the end of metro line No.7, and 45 minutes to Gare de l'Est.

The Hotel Little Regina was 100 yards from the front door of Gare de l'Est station and was an absolute bargain at £190 for two nights in the heart of Paris on Champions League Final weekend. We checked in and within minutes Mongoose and Zil were outside, shouting up. Seconds later they were checking out the gaff. With a nod of approval from Mongoose, our expert hotel booker, he was off to check out his 'shithole'. We promised to stay in touch. They'd find us later, as they knew I had to look after Charlie and couldn't stay on the ale all day.

Charlie and I grabbed a bite to eat at 'Le Burger King' next door to our hotel and then headed up to the stadium to have a look in the calm of the day before the big match. We walked to the Gare du Nord and jumped the first RER (the express train) on the D line, and five minutes later we were at Saint Denis station. RER B line would have taken us nearer to the ground at La Plaine Stade de France station – that's an important piece of information.

We walked along wide boulevards, through a world of office blocks and, after a leisurely ten-minute walk, we were gazing at the huge bowl that's the Stade de France.

The Stade de France is in Saint Denis (this is not Paris as you know it), and there were signs of what was to come. One of the bars opposite the stadium had Jamie Webster blasting out 'Allez, Allez, Allez' and the stadium was a hive of activity. I don't think we understand how much goes into staging an event of this magnitude, it's important to get things right (yeah, okay). We felt like the odd ones out as everyone else seemed to have an official UEFA lanyard around their necks.

We saw Melissa Reddy, now of Sky Sports, and went to say hello, reacquainting her with Charlie after he'd met her all those years ago on Liverpool's pre-season in Germany. She was taken aback that the little lad she'd met in Munich only a few years earlier was now a huge teenager. There was a nice atmosphere around the stadium with Liverpool fans mixing with those of Real Madrid. We decided to head into Saint Denis itself as UEFA had one of its fan zones in the middle of the town. There was no warning about its potential dangers. On the walk from the stadium, we were stopped on numerous occasions by locals asking if we wanted tickets. I pretended to be looking for tickets for friends who weren't with us, so they knew we had no money on us. Men in £5 Primark jumpers were asking for €2,000 for a ticket. They promised they'd meet us here tomorrow, over by the metro, because the police wouldn't allow them anywhere near the ground. They told us there would be lots of security. They'd all amazingly got their tickets from FIFA, odd that when it's a UEFA tournament. We walked on but many other fans were already snared, everyone was desperate to see the showpiece. If you didn't have a ticket by the time you got to Paris, you weren't getting one. There were no spares around. Many Liverpool fans knew that before they even headed to Paris, and they were resigned to seeing a beautiful city and enjoying the fan park.

The fan zone in Saint Denis was nothing to write home about, a big silver inflatable cup in the middle of the town square keeping us interested for all of five minutes. We did get talking to an American guy, a native of New York, now living in Paris, who was intrigued about the journey we'd taken for the match. His warning now rings true: 'You need to be careful out here.' With that as his parting shot it was time to go and meet the lads.

Our first stop was some culture, the Sacre Coeur Basilica at Montmartre. One of the truly iconic sights of Paris, and close to the bars and nightlife in the Pigalle. There was no tiredness now, the Salmon boys had a second wind, although by the time we'd hiked it up the hill to Sacre Coeur, some of that second wind had blown out. Instead of the long slog walking up the steps to the Basilica from the metro stations at Pigalle or Anvers, I thought, being clever, we'd go from the other side, from the metro station at Guy Môquet, thinking it would be a flatter walk, no hills. A big mistake as it turned out. The walk was longer, still steep and it was hotter now. When we eventually got to Montmartre it was very busy and we walked right on through. Past the artist enclave, where when quieter you can stay for hours and marvel at the Parisian artists at work, straight past the Basilica and straight on down the steps. Everyone staying in Paris was here, it seemed, and there were surprisingly few football fans among the throng of people. Paris is always full of tourists, and they all gravitate here on a Friday evening. It was time for a drink and to rest our weary legs. The second wind was now a slight breeze and we needed to take some time out, there was a long night ahead of us.

We found a bar out of the way of the tourist crowds where Charlie spotted two remaining seats outside on the pavement, next to a group of Scouse lads. Even close to one of the busiest tourist sights of Paris it sold relatively cheap beer, with a 'special offer' on Hoegaarden. No wonder it was cheap, it was like that horrible craft stuff, the colour of a bad urine sample, and the taste wasn't too dissimilar. Google says that it's a Belgian wheat beer, but I think I'm right with the urine sample, but in the heat of the late afternoon it was great to have something cold in your hand.

Soon enough it was time to move on. Mike and Josh were still south of the river on the Left Bank, Tommy was on the outskirts with Bryan, and Zil and Mongoose were nearer to Notre Dame than the Sacre Coeur. Zil and Mongoose would head up to the Pigalle to join us, and Aki and Harry would catch up with us as soon as possible. My job was to find an appropriate watering hole, with a table for at least six and maybe 12, good luck with that, it was getting busy now. With my local knowledge it shouldn't be too hard to find a decent bar. This was our stomping ground the night before PSG in 2018, and there were loads of great bars that I'd visited with Mongoose. Roll on four years and I was more sober than that night. It was still daylight and sunny as opposed to dark, miserable and wet. Nothing looks the same in daylight, does it? Amazing how when your senses are depleted it's easier to find great places to drink.

A row of bars lies a couple of hundred yards from the Moulin Rouge and were worth checking out. Surely we could find a good one there to start with at least, and meet everyone. I chose the wrong one, no atmosphere and terrible beer. No wonder we were the only ones in here. Another pint of piss, but thankfully the lads would be here before too long. As I nursed the dregs of my beer, Mongoose and Zil arrived and that was the signal to move on immediately, they wouldn't thank me for choosing this one.

There was already an expanding police presence by the Moulin Rouge, and we chose to walk a little further away to Place de Clichy and find a welcoming pavement café, Bar Le Carolus. Now we were sitting outside a restaurant in the sun ordering beer and perusing the menu. I was thinking about how long Charlie would be able to stay awake for. I didn't want tonight to ruin tomorrow; it had already been a long trip and the clock was nudging 7pm. But I had no worries with Charlie, he was going to last the distance, he was running on adrenaline. By 8pm with pizzas and beers (and cokes for the youngsters) we were set for the night.

The police used Le Carolus as their staging point, their vans parked up outside, and every half hour they'd change the guard in the Pigalle. Those being relieved would jump in their vans, eat their pack-up and catch a quick coffee. It was obvious they had little to do at present as the new inhabitants of the Pigalle were well behaved, and the police let them enjoy themselves. Unfortunately, some 24 hours later that wouldn't be the case from the police. As always in Europe, the daytime police and the riot squads behave in a different manner. For now, there was no provocation from either side and that was to continue throughout the Friday night. From what we saw, good-natured, raucous and fun.

Harry and Aki found us, quickly ordering pizzas, and we all caught up on what we'd been up to during the day. The laughs and stories started to flow, and the young boys were loving being part of the joys of a European Cup Final build-up. This was the first time I'd actually been in a host city the night before the final. I've always been on the way, arriving to meet lads who were hungover from the night before, and now I know why. The Friday night was brilliant!

By 10pm it was time to head back to the Pigalle and the real fun. We'd heard the noise getting louder by the minute, so we headed off to see what was going on. The songs were ringing around the boulevard and the smell of flares and smoke canisters were filling the air, the sights and sounds dragging the young lads in. This was a night to remember for the rest of their lives. As we headed into the James Hetfeelds pub on one corner (let's call it the quiet corner) 20 yards away outside Corcoran's Irish bar, the party was in full swing and the young lads were right in the middle of it, loving life. Harry was on Aki's shoulders but there was no way Charlie was getting on mine, as he'd grown this last year and was huge. 'I'll go to the bar then.' I bumped into a lad who I used to go to the match with in the 80s and early 90s and had a quick catch-up, which was nice. We fell out many years ago, why is no longer important, but it was nice to bury the past, it felt good.

In no time at all it was time to move on. The Pigalle had been great, but it wasn't time to overstay your welcome, there were more people coming into the area, the roads were starting to get blocked, the songs were getting louder and the crowd more boisterous. With all that, the police looked more nervous than when they were eating their tea earlier. We took the opportunity for a team photo outside the Moulin Rouge, one for the living room wall. That will always be a great memory of a brilliant night.

Unfortunately, what was to come in the next 24 hours would mean it would take some time to think fondly of Paris again anytime soon. Tonight, though, we were having a great time. As we walked against the crowds pouring out of Pigalle metro station, we were heading south to Les Halles, an area full of bars near to Notre Dame. Most of Paris must have had the same idea, it was rammed. This was as close as we were getting to the Seine. You could almost smell it. It was gone midnight now and the night was in full swing. Tomorrow we were going to be European champions for the seventh time, we were sure of it. Tomorrow's hangover would be worth it.

One of the abiding memories of Paris will always be a

bottle of tabasco sauce, or two to be precise. In his usual manner, Zil was up for entertaining the rest of us, and in front of him there was a yellow bottle of mustard, which he decided to squirt on the back of his hand, lick his hand and then his lips. The boys burst out laughing and he knew he had an audience. Out of the blue he picked up the bottle of tabasco sauce and necked it, washing the sauce down with his beer, the boys were roaring laughing, as were the rest of us. Then he went for it again, and again, picking up another bottle, and now he was necking two at the same time. The more he did it, the more we laughed, god help his guts in the morning. He drained the contents of the tabasco bottle, and the night was done. It was a night that the lads will remember forever.

Allez les Rouges

EUROPEAN CUP Final day – Saturday, 28 May.

It was going to be a long day, if my hangover was anything to go by! Drinking from mid-afternoon until far too late, after about two hours' kip wasn't the brightest idea. Awake from 5am with a booming headache, guzzling every last drop of water we had in the room had managed to keep the worst at bay. I genuinely feared for what the day would bring.

Our matchday kit was laid out and, once showered and refreshed, we were ready to hit the streets of Paris for some sustenance to see us through the early part of the day. Only 200 yards from the hotel was the Le Prévoyant café on the Boulevard de Magenta (sounds so Parisian). We were surrounded by Liverpool fans regaling their adventures of getting to Paris. Few of them had the pleasure of the Pigalle on Friday night. The sun was out, the day was warming up and we planned our day.

The main event at the Stade de France was at 9pm, and in the afternoon we planned on heading to the fan zone with Boss Nights at Place de la Nation. Due to start early afternoon, the culmination was to be a rousing rallying cry from the brilliant Jamie Webster; it was high on Charlie's wish list. Before that, though, we had a couple of hours to kill. The Champs Élysées was out, as the police had banned anyone wearing football colours, apparently. Complete madness, and it wasn't even their worst decision of the day.

A typical Parisian breakfast, petit-déjeuner for the cultured, arrived. A fresh croissant, a decent slice of fresh crusty baguette with butter and jam, accompanied by fresh orange juice and a steaming café au lait (milky coffee to us). This would make or break my guts, loosen, or bind them together, it was a 50/50 shout. Thankfully, breakfast immediately made me feel better. With the sun on your face while eating a great breakfast and the Reds in the European Cup Final, what more could you ask for? As we were eating breakfast Ted Morris of the Liverpool Disabled Supporters' Association went past. I'd been following Ted's adventures with his wife and girls around Europe for years on Twitter, and I made sure I went to say hello. He told me they were heading up to the ground. Little did we know what the day had in store for us and especially what Ted had to deal with, as he's in a wheelchair.

We called for the bill: 'Le bill, garçon, s'il vous plait,' along with the traditional hand signals. The waiter smiled politely and probably thought, *Just speak English.* In fact, I know he did, I could see it in his eyes, and the way he delivered the bill on a silver platter, like a discus thrower. It nearly took my fingers off. We video-called home, making the girls jealous, the boys sitting in the sun in Paris drinking coffee and having a great time. Why wouldn't you be jealous? As we regaled stories of our Friday night on the tiles in Paris the girls quickly lost interest – wrong audience.

Seeing this was Charlie's third visit to Paris he wasn't that bothered about seeing any sights. We'd seen it all before, and he was focused on seeing Jamie Webster and the match. I argued that the Eiffel Tower might be worth a visit as it would be a magnet for fans of both sides, so today would be different. I expected that it would be quite a good experience this early in the day, a natural meeting place for fans arriving in the city. There would be a wave of colour flooding around its base, with Liverpool and Real fans sharing the space.

The Eiffel Tower, I don't think you could ever get tired of seeing it. The green grass of the Champ de Mars beckons you towards the tower, and the 15-minute stroll towards it in the morning sun was everything a European Cup Final should be. The two sets of fans mingled well, the red of Liverpool and the white of Real Madrid in equal numbers, excitement flooding the walkways of the Champ de Mars. A real photo opportunity. Victorious, and the photo would be sitting on your mantelpiece or hung on the living room wall (if you have an understanding wife). If vanquished, you'd never see the picture again. We took our pictures, fully expecting the Reds to be victorious, and any day soon there would be a picture of dad and lad grinning from ear to ear, sitting on the mantelpiece at home.

Breakfast, the metro and the walk up to the Eiffel Tower had sapped our time by now and the fan park was already open and filling rapidly. The last photos were taken, and we were off to Bir Hakeim metro station (nearest to the tower). It looked as if we'd be ahead of everyone, as nobody in red seemed to be moving yet. How wrong we were, thousands were well ahead of us. If anything, we might have even been stragglers.

Place de la Nation holds a significant place in the history of Paris, and France. Situated in the east of Paris, a series of avenues lead to what in real terms is a giant roundabout. A central grassed area is dominated by a huge bronze sculpture 'The Triumph of the Republic', which sees Marianne (depicting the Republic), riding atop a chariot pulled by lions. This was the place where the guillotine was used the most during the French Revolution, and this is the place where many modern-day Parisian demonstrations start from. Later today the exodus to the stadium would start from here with thousands of Reds heading north to the Stade de France. Whoever chose the spot had chosen well, the number of people here, though, surely took the authorities by surprise. The success of Kyiv, then the massive success of Madrid, meant that whatever the guys from Boss Nights were doing today was going to be hugely popular. And so it turned out to be, with more than 50,000 supporters taking in the atmosphere on a hot Parisian afternoon.

Our Kev had messaged me saying his overnight coach had arrived and had parked up close to the fan zone. Even though we sort of knew what to expect when we got there, a sea of red obviously, as we climbed the escalators from the bowels of the metro and back into the bright sunshine we weren't prepared for the sight before us. The place was rammed, and what about Marianne? Surely it was a mistake not to fence her off, as fans filled the crevices and hung off any possible point, pyro filling the air. There was a red revolution in progress. There were people everywhere and the noise was immense, excitement in the air. It was the day when we would win the European Cup for the seventh time. You must believe, and this crowd did, and the narrow failure to win the Premier League hadn't affected our belief. You'll have noted me say this before, but 'this is what we're meant to do'. Liverpool FC is made for winning European trophies; we've won more than our fair share; whisper it, we've lost a few as well. Let's hope we're on the right side of history today.

Charlie's face was a picture as he struggled to take in the magnitude of the sight in front of him. It was like one of those pictures hanging in the Louvre depicting the French Revolution. There were bodies everywhere and the grass was covered in people enjoying the sun, and their purchases from the local supermarkets. The queues were so big to get in the fan zone that many people had given up and stayed outside, taking in the raucous atmosphere.

There was no point trying to get into the bars around the periphery, they were packed, but my eagle eyes could see people emerging from an alleyway with cans and bottles. This was an education for Charlie: if you move away from the masses, it makes life easier. There's always someone who wants to make money on a cup final day, no matter where you are in the world. A couple of streets away, and far from the maddening crowd, a small supermarket was doing a roaring trade. While stocked with all manner of goods, the only things it was selling were trays of beer, bottles of wine, soft drinks, packets of crisps and nuts – you need something to line your stomach, don't you! This was the greatest sales day of the shop owner's life. If the cost of the beer was anything to go by, he may have even been able to retire. Double your normal price, but still cheaper than all the Parisian bars, but all the drinks that were left were now warm. The trays of beer didn't stay in the cabinets long enough to get any hint of a chill. But beer is beer, and the lads were on the way, and if we didn't buy this now, there would be none left. So, €40 lighter in the pocket, we headed off with a bag full of cans and bottles. It took me back to Istanbul and the warm cans of Efes that we drank all afternoon. If the result is the same, I'll take that.

We headed back to the statue of Marianne and past the queues of people slowly entering the fan zone. Jamie Webster wasn't on for hours yet, there was no rush. In Madrid you just walked up to the huge square and filled it from the back, but here it seemed to be overly controlled to get in. People were hanging off Marianne, and flags covered her base. Nobody was doing anything wrong, but I was surprised the monument hadn't been fenced off to stop people climbing on it. Pyro was drifting across Place de la Nation as we found a clear piece of grass to claim in the name of the Salmon boys. Our Kev was on his way, Zil and Mongoose too. Amid all the mayhem we found a good spec near the statue, and with a picture to help people find us, within 20 minutes we were all back together. Our Kev looked remarkably fresh considering he'd been travelling all night on the coach, and surprisingly positive about the whole experience. It was lovely sharing this foreign field with Our Kev, as he has missed many of these days. We went all over England together in the 80s and 90s. By the time the great European trips returned he had young kids and responsibilities, and then no luck in the ticket ballots for Madrid and Kyiv. This is what I did with my mates, but unfortunately him and Our Ian never got to share enough of it. Now, though, I'd shared Madrid with Ian and Paris with Kev. One day it will be all three of us, I'm sure of it.

By 3.30pm we had a choice to make. Do we go into the fan park or give it a miss completely? It was now or never. My plan was that by 5pm we'd be making a move towards the ground, as this wasn't a time or a place to rock up late. I walked over to the fan park entrance on our right and, tiptoeing among the cans and prone bodies, I could see there was hardly anyone in the queue; it was time to go in. Zil and Mongoose weren't bothered, as you couldn't take beer in the fan zone, so I left my remaining cans with them. They could do as they wished with them; they'd meet us outside the Gare du Nord before heading to the ground.

For us, though, Jamie Webster was not to be missed, as it had been on Charlie's wish list, and I'd missed this in both Kyiv and Madrid. Today was for Charlie, he wanted to get in the mood with a Boss sing-song. We headed across to the entrance, a series of crowd control barriers in front of two police vans parked nose to nose with a six-foot gap between them, protected by a line of police.

None too friendly and none too helpful. They'd already had enough of the afternoon frivolity. I kept Charlie close. Even locals who lived within the cordoned-off area had a job getting through, and they were speaking fluent French, so speaking Scouse didn't help whatsoever. Keep your mouth shut, don't antagonise the police, and don't let them trip you up (yeah seriously). A simple misstep could mean the baton was ready to come out. I was relieved when we got through the opening and could freely walk towards the fan park and more security checks carried out by stewards. The actions of the police, unfortunately, were only a sign of things to come.

We were right at the back of the fan zone, by a huge video screen, and a long way in the distance was the stage. The crowds were huge (check it out on YouTube). At least at the back there were places to get something to eat, and toilets as well, which after an afternoon on the cans would come in useful. When I say toilets, there were more *pissoirs* than toilet cubicles. *Pissoirs*? It's a free-standing portable place to have a pee in the streets. Sometimes fences shield the person peeing and hides their modesty, sometimes not. These had no fences, but no one cared. *Pissoirs* were initially commissioned to expand options for well-hydrated (but lazy) Parisian men looking to empty their bladders, and they're still seen on the streets of Paris today, stopping issues with public urination. They're taking the piss! Today there were more than enough well-hydrated men who needed to use them. These particular *pissoirs* were plastic, circular, with four urinals, and you faced your fellow hydrated man, whistling and avoiding eye contact while you had a pee. They were much quicker than a cubicle, as most men know once you break the seal you can't stop. The *pissoirs* would be used often before we headed off.

The video screen would have to do. The singing was the same wherever you were and at least you could move here. We assumed our position, I saved our spec, and the lads went to get chips as they were starving, Charlie's croissant was a long time past and Kev's coach trip didn't afford the luxury of a Parisian breakfast. Me, I went to the *pissoir* a couple of times. I think I might get one installed in the Isle of Man.

As the main man came on, the crowd perked up and Jamie smashed through the matchday tunes, from Virgil van Dijk being as calm as you like, through Si Señor and giving Bobby the ball to score, and obviously we were all so glad that Jürgen was a Red! That was enough to convince us it was our day and send us off to the Stade de France with a real skip in our step.

With the final bars ringing in our ears, we were off to the metro to beat the crowds. It was obvious that many in the fan zone would be staying there for the night but those of us lucky to have tickets were turning and making our way north. As always, the police made it as hard as possible to get to the metro. Seemingly whichever entrance we wanted to use was the wrong one. Down one of the side streets we could see the water cannon and a line of riot vans, waiting for trouble. The fact they never got any must have really irked them, but they'd be taking it out on us for the rest of the night, though.

Eventually we found a way into the metro and headed down the steps looking for the RER line to take us north to Gare du Nord to meet the lads. Accompanied by a rousing chorus of 'Bring on yer Internazionale …' a song that shouts out that we fear no one in Europe, we were on our way. As the train pulled into the crowded platform there was a feeling of excitement and expectation. The train filled up quickly and the Reds were on the move en masse (as the French say), all heading early to the ground. We knew the score for a European Cup Final – you don't hang around. Seeing how packed the train was, I said to Charlie and Kev that there was no point getting off at Gare du Nord as we probably wouldn't get back on another train, and there was no point delaying getting to the ground. I messaged Zil and Mongoose saying that we would either meet them up at the ground or after the match. As it turned out this was to be a very good decision. What was to come next could have gone badly if it wasn't for me saying that it wasn't worth a quick pint.

As the train drew into Gare du Nord it was obvious that those on the platform had little chance of getting on this train. Good luck with getting on anything coming from Place de la Nation after the fan park emptied out. As the train pulled out of the station, I sat there knowing my decision was the right one. Within five minutes and as the clock was hitting 6pm, we were at Saint Denis station, and as the doors opened, the Reds poured off the train.

Echoes of the Past

AS THE wave of red headed up the ramps to the exits at Saint Denis, the songs burst into life. After breathing the stale and sweaty air of the baking train carriage, the songs had stopped briefly, and as we breathed fresh air again the excitement started to build. Thousands of fans were heading towards the stadium, many for the first time, unlike us. As we exited the station it felt different to the Friday afternoon. We headed down Avenue François Mitterrand, but within 200 yards we were being directed down a side street to the left and away from the main boulevard to the stadium (our route on Friday). The authorities had decided this was a better way to go for so many fans.

Initially there didn't seem anything wrong as we passed a couple of bars, with fans outside catching a last drink in the sunshine before the game, but within minutes we started to sense the danger that was coming our way. We were within yards of an underpass (that you couldn't see) and the world dropped away beneath our feet. Without warning we were forced down the underpass, taking us under the A1 motorway. Barely wide enough for four people side by side, it was a natural bottleneck and created the first danger on the way to the stadium. From a wide boulevard to a narrow underpass without warning, it was with great relief that we came out the other side on to a wide pavement, but within 100 yards we were greeted by another blockage.

This time it was deliberately caused by two police vans that had been parked nose to nose underneath a bridge, blocking the whole pavement. There was a narrow gap between the bonnets of the vans through which we were forced to walk, and by 6.25pm the crowd had ground to a halt. The police were kettling the fans and the mood of the crowd had changed, from jovial to fearful. Those with kids, me included, brought them in closer and we looked after one another. That's what you do, making sure the vulnerable in our presence were looked after. Personally, at this point I wasn't fearful for our safety, although it was becoming uncomfortable, but I was fearful of what would happen in the next few hours. While we weren't the first at the ground, the majority of fans, thousands upon thousands, were behind us and police had created the blockage, which was a ridiculous thing to do. The attitude of the police left a lot to be desired. They weren't here to look after our safety, that was for certain. As we inched our way through the narrow gap between the two police vans, I said to Charlie and Kev to stay close, keep together and don't give the police any reason to reach for the batons.

I gave the same advice to others close by who were becoming irate. I'd seen the French police at the PSG game in 2018, and they didn't need a good reason to crack heads, only the slightest encouragement.

There were many in this crowd who won't have been abroad before to watch Liverpool. Foreign police forces behave differently, and with the language barrier the riot sticks are generally used to influence crowds. It's how they police their own inhabitants, so why should we be any different? Keep your mouth shut, don't give them a reason to attack you. Once through the gap it was apparent that they'd done it that way as there was a ticket check ahead. In my opinion the thinking was flawed. They'd tried to stem the flow of fans, but only created a mass of people who they couldn't process quickly enough. We'd been told to get there early, and that's exactly what we did, but they weren't ready for us. The crowd was, thankfully, orderly and well behaved. There was enough evidence of that, but the ticket check was chaotic.

As we neared the barriers I looked to my right and saw a line of police standing watching, alongside a group of, I assumed, local youths. They weren't our fans, that was for sure, and they were all eyeing the crowds, seemingly looking for opportunities. The police showed no interest in them. What were they doing around the checkpoints with no tickets? I said to the lads to keep their phones close and their hands in their pockets. As I got to the ticket check, I had Charlie right behind me. I showed my digital ticket on my phone and then Charlie's physical ticket that I had tightly grasped in my hand. The steward had a magic pen to validate it as a real ticket. Even though I showed him two tickets they only let me through, and they were holding Charlie back. The steward certainly wasn't the sharpest tool in the box. I appealed to the policeman next to him and he nodded to let Charlie through. The phone and ticket went straight back into my shorts pocket and were zipped up immediately, as this was a pickpocket's paradise. Once through the check we stopped and looked back at the path we'd taken. We moved less than 200 yards in 30 minutes, and now there were thousands beneath the bridge, and thousands beyond them. It was gone 7pm local time, still some two hours to kick-off. I'll say it again, we were here in plenty of time!

As we headed up the ramp towards the turnstiles, we took the obligatory stadium photos and decided it was best getting in the ground while the turnstile queues were small; no point hanging around. We knew what was behind us, so getting in safe and sound was our priority. As I had a digital ticket on the official UEFA app on my phone and the lads had paper tickets, we had to go to separate gates. I entered through gate X and the lads entered through gate Z; the plan was to meet up inside. I wandered through lines of crowd control barriers behind about 20 people. There wasn't long to wait. The phone was firmly in my pocket until I got close enough to the gate. The ticket was worth over £400, and there was no way I was giving anyone a chance of snatching it. I opened the app and scanned the ticket, expecting a green light, and the light went red! I tried again, and it went red again, so I presented it to the steward to scan it himself. The technology didn't work, but he shrugged and ushered me through. I now know that, ten minutes later, I wouldn't have been ushered through. I probably would have been denied entry and faced all that came with being left outside the stadium. At least the lads didn't have to deal with dodgy technology with the paper tickets direct from Liverpool. Relieved to get in, I headed inside and went towards gate Z to meet the lads, only to be faced with a huge fence blocking my way. At least Charlie was with Our Kev, I knew he'd be okay.

I was hungry now. That croissant in the pavement café this morning was a distant memory. There were no queues for food, it was all relatively quiet, even though the time was ticking by towards kick-off. I bought a drink and paid €10 for a barely edible ham and cheese baguette and then settled down on the steps facing the stadium, blissfully unaware of the chaos ensuing outside the ground. My calm before the storm. It was still eerily quiet as I made my way to my seat on the back row, high up in the corner of the giant bowl. I could see Kev and Charlie high up behind the goal. We'd looked at the stadium app on numerous occasions in our excitement, so I knew roughly where they were seated. It was easy to spot them as the crowd was sparse. There was virtually no one in my section.

I took a wander down to the front of my section where the BT Sports gantry was. Steven Gerrard, Peter Crouch and Michael Owen were supporting Liverpool, and Rio Ferdinand as always was supporting anyone Liverpool were playing, while Jake Humphrey checked his teeth and his hair. The BT Sports crew were in and out of the concourse constantly, so you can't tell me none of them knew what was going on. At 8pm, and even though it was an hour before kick-off, our end was empty, and as Liverpool came out to warm up my mind was taken off the empty seats as I focused on the boys on the pitch.

They announced in the stadium, via the big screen, that there was going to be a 15-minute delay due to the late arrival of fans. That was absolute bollocks! No one arrived late. They failed to get everyone in, there's a real difference. Thousands had arrived between 6pm and 7pm and were met with dreadful organisation. I knew something was wrong in our end. I was looking straight across and saw thousands of empty seats ... how could that be? Everyone was here and trying to get in hours ago, so where were they all?

I headed outside to see what was going on. Once outside you could see for yourself, chaos reigned. From a balcony at the back of the second tier I was looking over gates Y and Z, and I had a perfect view of what was going on. Nobody was coming in through either of the gates now. A Scouse lad came and joined me, and he said, 'You know we'll get the blame for this, don't you.' There was nothing truer, it had already started. The 'late arrival of fans' and soon there would be 'fans stormed the gates' and then 'ticketless fans', does that sound familiar? It's all out of the Hillsborough playbook. They didn't account for the fact that all those statements could be disproved with the number of phones available to record the true version of events. It didn't stop them trying, though. I always said that if we'd had smartphones at Hillsborough, we wouldn't be still fighting 33 years on, the authorities wouldn't have got away with it.

Here in Paris in 2022, UEFA and the French police were wholly complicit in the shitshow in front of my eyes. Yes, there were people charging at the gates, and there were people without tickets, but seemingly all locals, doing a mass bunk-in. The riot police were on site, and they were using everything in their armoury, but they were using it against thousands of innocent football fans, who from my vantage point were desperately trying to avoid the volleys of tear gas, riot police batons and the indiscriminate releases of pepper spray aimed in their direction. Locals were using real fans as a smokescreen to create chaos. A stream of young men evaded the police and headed into our end, and none of them were Liverpool fans, they weren't wearing our colours or any match-going gear, I can say that hand on heart.

I felt sick to the pit of my stomach. I wasn't sure where all my mates were now as we were all seated in different parts of the stadium. Everyone tried to contact each other, or even those at home, to let them know we were in the ground and okay.

In this modern age, people at home would be able to see what was going on. After my previous experience at Hillsborough and Heysel I always try to make sure people know I'm safe. As soon as we had got in the ground, and I'd seen Charlie and Our Kev, I'd let Nikki know we were safely in. Imagine watching those scenes and not knowing that. I know lots of people were asking how we were, as they'd been following our journey since we got on the plane on Thursday evening, which seemed such a long time ago now. One by one, photos popped up on our

WhatsApp group showing that the lads were, thankfully, all in the ground.

It took me back to 1989. It had all the elements it needed for a disaster. UEFA and the French authorities were extremely lucky that there were no fatalities. I couldn't believe what I was seeing in front of my eyes as I was looking at the back of gate Y, until I saw the actions of a policewoman. I know it was a woman as she'd been wandering around only yards below me. She pulled her balaclava down over her face and walked over to the turnstiles. There were fans coming through one at a time now, and a young fella reached into his pocket and got his wallet out to retrieve his ticket. The policewoman, arm outstretched, pulled the trigger of the pepper spray gun and squirted it right into the young lad's face. She turned and walked away, leaving him and anyone close to him (even the stewards and police) coughing their guts up. As she walked away to the side, she high-fived a colleague: 'Good job!' The lad did nothing to deserve it, and that vision will stay with me forever. Thanks to a fan's video, that incident went viral over the next month or so, but live and in the flesh, I can't erase that.

People wonder why our support wasn't up to its usual standards in Paris. It's because half our end was traumatised getting into the Champions League Final. It shouldn't be like this. The greatest thing for us was that the mainstream media got caught up in the middle of it all, not that it was great for them, but it meant they were able to tell the truth right away, they didn't go with the lies. Kaveh Solhekol of Sky News was straightaway on our side with some great reporting. The bastards weren't getting away with it this time, although they'd try their hardest, even in the face of overwhelming evidence that showed what actually happened. It was all going to be our fault. '40,000 ticketless Liverpool fans causing a riot' obviously sounds better than 'we couldn't organise a piss up in a brewery'. I couldn't watch any more of what was happening outside, it was triggering all manner of feelings, so I returned to my seat. If I hadn't received counselling, where would that have gone? I could deal with it better than some, and I now know of many who couldn't, and ultimately what happened in Paris has caused at least two lads to commit suicide.

The game kicked off 35 minutes late, still with hundreds of seats empty, and an air of disbelief hanging over our end. In my section, with tickets from the UEFA ballot, I'm not sure where all these people came from, but there were few real fans of either club in my section. Imagine going through all that outside and it's not even your team. UEFA will be getting it in the ear from these ticketholders. To be fair, many may have even given up, as there were so many empty seats around me. I found some comfort in being alongside a Scouse lad and his young son, who'd been terrified outside. We tried to support the lads in red, but it was hard going in a block of people who seemingly didn't care. 'Benzema scored for Real, we got beat 1-0', but it was a night when football didn't matter. All that build-up for a match report that consists of eight words. There's nothing else I can remember or say, and I couldn't even watch the highlights. Don't get me wrong, we roared them on to get an equaliser as best we could, but it wasn't to be.

It was now about getting back to our hotel safely and dissecting what happened. I gave the Reds a quick clap and headed to the exit. They'd given us everything this season, so it was such a sad way for things to end. No one was talking about the match, everyone was more interested in meeting up with their friends and getting to their accommodation or transport.

We'd arranged to meet up at one of the UEFA merchandise marquees, tucked to one side on the main concourse. As I was waiting for Our Kev and Charlie, I was eagerly scanning the crowd to see them, and I caught sight of Kaveh Solhekol and his Sky News team interviewing fans caught up in the pre-match chaos. Their stories sounded terrible. We'd dodged the worst of things, that was for sure. With relief I caught sight of Charlie and Kev and within seconds of meeting we were quickly on our way. Charlie was keen to ensure I was okay. He was worried about what we'd been caught up in or seen before kick-off and he wanted to know I was alright. He knew the Hillsborough triggers would be firing, but yes, I was alright. I was relieved that he'd been with Our Kev. Initially my plan was that if I was ticketless (which I was for quite some time) I'd let him go in the ground alone and I'd wait outside. I was glad that plan was never needed, as I'm not sure what I'd have done if I was outside seeing all that go on, being totally helpless. Your worst nightmare.

We heard stories of people having their phones and wallets robbed before the game, so the plan was to stay close and not get split up. We retraced our steps to the RER station, under the bridge, through the underpass and through the dimly lit streets back to where the evening had started in a joyous mood in bright sunlight. It was now touching midnight and, even with an uneventful walk back to the station, there was an air of unease. Stories started circulating about people who were out the ground first being attacked and robbed. More and more of those stories would come to light over the next few days, but we were lucky. There was a strange atmosphere on the train down to the Gare de Lyon with Our Kev, who needed to get back to his coach parked at Place de la Nation. I didn't want to leave him on his own, we still needed safety in numbers. As we got off at Gare de Lyon it was time to say goodbye. He had a long journey ahead of him. At least we could get a night's sleep and make sense of it all before we started the long journey home on the Sunday afternoon.

I arranged to meet Zil and Mongoose in a bar we knew from the PSG night, Le Sully, a cracking little bar on Rue du Faubourg. It had a bohemian feel to it and an eclectic clientele, and the beer was the cheapest in Paris, by far. Charlie and I jumped on the metro a few stops and by 1am I was at the bar waiting for Zil and Mongoose to arrive. The Rue du Faubourg was still busy, but this wasn't a football crowd, this was your normal Saturday night crowd, a mix of students and hipsters, smoking Gauloises and putting the world to rights at the pavement tables on what was still a balmy evening. It was a million miles away from what we'd left behind in Saint Denis. I made sure

I messaged those at home to say we were fine and close to our hotel.

The lads arrived and with a pint in front of us we shared our experiences from the evening. As the lads shared their videos and stories it was even more apparent that our decision not to jump off at Gare du Nord before the game was the right one. They were caught up in the mayhem beforehand, climbing walls to escape the crush, and these lads are in their 50s. Even then, stewards were trying to force them back into the crowd. We'd all fared well after the game and were lucky to get away from the stadium unharmed, but there were loads who weren't so fortunate, stories of muggings and beatings abounded. Many fans, including vulnerable children and disabled fans, were victims of assaults and thefts. All while the French police stood by and did nothing. The barman decided it was time for him to go home and he quickly set about closing the bar down. That was fine as we didn't have the energy to carry on, Charlie and I, that is, Mongoose was up for more. For us it was time to head for the safety of the hotel. I felt that Paris tonight wasn't going to be safe until the sun came up. Zil tottered off to his gaff, Mongoose stumbled off for another pint and Charlie and I looked for kebabs.

The kebab search was fruitless, even though we ended up in a kebab shop 100 yards from our hotel, but it was full of drunks and arguments kicking off, so this wasn't a place to be. I'd rather starve than get caught in someone else's mayhem. 'Le Burger King' was shut, but a couple of doors down the road was an Italian pizzeria, and while I wasn't up for sitting in to eat, in my perfect French I found out they did takeaway, so I ordered a large margherita, with a promise of 'not long'. While it wasn't too long, and the restaurant was safe, outside looked anything but. Like any big city, the seedier side of life survives around the major railway stations. There were groups of young lads cruising the streets. This wasn't a place to be caught alone.

The piping-hot pizza came straight out the wood-fired oven, was slid into the box and cut into eight pieces. I gave them €10, and we were out the door, with the instruction for Charlie to keep walking and stay by my side. As soon as we were out the door the inhabitants of the doorways stirred and started shouting in our direction. 'Keep going, mate, ignore them.' Within seconds we were at our hotel door pressing the buzzer with the pack of hyenas behind us looking for their next prey. Thankfully the receptionist wasn't having a burst for a change, and we were inside and into our room swiftly. I could relax now, and with a cursory look at Twitter I was right to have been worried. Reds had been picked off all over Paris, whether at the ground or at the fan park. Loads of people had been robbed and assaulted. Even though no one back home would be awake, or truly aware of how shady Paris was, I dropped a message to all those who needed to know as Charlie tucked into the best-tasting pizza in Paris. This had been one of my worst nights following the Reds. As the clocked ticked past 3am the day was done and so were we, sleep would come soon.

* * *

Daylight came bursting through the window, it was 9am and time to start moving. A long sweaty day meant you needed a shower to wash the dirt and the stench from yesterday away. Zil and Mongoose were on the move already and had their first pint of the day in front of them, while we'd be heading back to yesterday's pavement café for a Parisian breakfast. We needed something to set us up for the day, it was going to be a long one. The next 24 hours meant a drive from Paris, boat across the English Channel, dropped off at Gatwick, have a night in a Premier Inn, fly home and get Charlie into school for as near to 9am as possible.

The sun was out, Paris was back to normal, and all the rats had gone back to where they came from. A croissant, fresh French bread, café au lait and orange juice in the sunshine was just what the doctor ordered. Zil and Mongoose joined us and, as always, you find others you know. Haddock and Glen from the Isle of Man happened to be walking by. Even stranger, Glen actually now lives in Austin, Texas, and had a much longer journey home than us, at least in miles travelled, as there was every chance he'd be home before us. We all tried to make sense of the previous night and catch up with what happened to each other. It wasn't all good, and even the sunshine couldn't make it better.

Several of us agreed that we were now done with following the Reds in Europe. Last night was more severe than normal, but I was fed up with being treated like shit by riot police for just following our team. While others (Frankfurt, Marseille, Napoli) rampage their way around Europe, Liverpool didn't have a single arrest during the

European campaign, and Merseyside police were glowing in their praise of fans on their travels. The hooligan tag still applied to us, but we were policed like they police their own ultras. They didn't account for the good behaviour of Liverpool or Real Madrid fans.

After a couple of hours' relaxation, it was time to go. Charlie didn't want to see any more of the sights, his energy reserves were low. We said our fond farewells to the lads, who were heading home via Charleroi and Birmingham, respectively. None of us were getting home anytime on the Sunday. 'Safe travels lads, see you next year. I'm never coming back to Paris,' was my parting shot. Charlie was already trying to convince me to not give in. He'd seen his future following the Reds, with his amazing trips to Munich and Madrid, but if your future is like Paris, I'd rather he didn't bother. Maybe I'll mellow over time, let's see (I did eventually).

Back to Gare de l'Est to jump on the metro back down to Villejuif Louis Aragon to meet Aki and Harry at 3pm, but we got on the wrong train, having to retrace our steps a couple of stops so we could get the right train. From having plenty of time we were now cutting it fine. Instead of making the 20-minute walk back to their hotel, I called my chauffeur – we are in France – to pick us up at the metro station. Aki found his way back to the Peripherique, which was already busy, and we crawled out of Paris, it was the start of the long journey home.

We caught up with each other's experiences from the Saturday night, us and Aki and Harry. They'd started watching the match in the fan park but decided to leave at half-time to find a bar, as it was getting moody. It wasn't only at the ground that people had bad experiences, it was all over Paris.

Thanks to Aki's driving skills, after a slow start leaving Paris we hit Calais in plenty of time and by midnight he was dropping us off at North Terminal at Gatwick Airport. Bless him, he still had hours ahead of him to get home, and while we were getting a comfortable bed for five or six hours, he'd be getting an hour or two in some godforsaken service station near Oxford. I've got to say a massive thank you to him, what a star, driving all that way, and not even getting into the ground to watch the match, but we'll always have that Friday night by the Moulin Rouge with our lads. Cheers mate.

The fallout from Paris will last a long time, and for some it will last forever, as it triggered many people who were at Hillsborough. All for a football match, where once again normal everyday people were let down by people who are responsible for their safety. As we've seen before, the authorities tried to wriggle off the hook but, with social media, first-hand accounts and evidence, they can't get away with it forever. Although they still try. I'm never going back to Paris, which is a real shame. A terrible way to end a glorious season that delivered much but ended on such a sour note. I hope it will be remembered for all the right reasons. Even writing this chapter has helped me focus on the good things that happened in Paris. Wonderful times with great people and sharing the adventure with Charlie and Our Kev. I can look at the picture from before the game and think happy thoughts.

The Long Goodbye

I BET you thought the story was over. I certainly did, but that's the thing with a life story, it's never over until they close your box. I couldn't leave it there on a sour note because the story of what came next needs to be told.

Friday, 26 January 2024, 10.30am, and an announcement that rocked our world. The club announced that Jürgen Klopp would be leaving Liverpool at the end of the season.

This was our 'Shankly moment'. 'Ya what? Yer havin me on, aren't ya?' (If you're old enough to remember.) I was in a meeting and my phone started vibrating like mad as messages started to flood through. It wasn't until 11am that I started to digest the news, reading my phone and the messages from a confused and upset group of friends.

But why? Why's he going? Why now? An accompanying video allowed Jürgen to give his reasons. Forget the conspiracy theories, he gave his reasons in his words:

> It is that I am, how can I say it, running out of energy. I have no problem now, obviously, I knew it

> already for longer that I will have to announce it at one point, but I am absolutely fine now. I know that I cannot do the job again, and again, and again, and again. After the years we had together and after all the time we spent together, and after all the things we went through together, the respect grew for you, the love grew for you and the least I owe you is the truth – and that is the truth.

I get it. Jürgen's only two years younger than me, and I know that I've had enough of working for a living. If I could retire right now, I would, as there's loads of things I want to do with Nikki and the kids. The energy's gone and that's happened over the last couple of years. Jürgen could see it coming, but he didn't want to be like me. He wanted to go out when he could still give his best. Ask anyone approaching 60 now and I'd say the majority will understand, no conspiracy, it's an age thing. Add into the mix that he had to be the best of the best every day of the week and keep millions of us happy with every decision he made, could you do it? Imagine the stress of that.

The strangest thing was that he'd looked the happiest he had in ages. He'd built a new team who were flying in all competitions, top of the league, and only 36 hours earlier the Reds had booked a place in the Carabao Cup Final at the end of February. I was at Craven Cottage on the Wednesday night as we booked our place and celebrated a return to Wembley. There was no sign of what was to come. As we headed back up the rail tracks from Euston to Lancaster and the ferry home, we must have talked about Liverpool for hours and not once was there any suggestion of what was to come, it was about more years, not fewer.

Charlie was devastated, like I was when Dalglish left in 1990. I'm a lot older and understand the decision. I've seen managers and players who we admire and love come and go, but for Charlie in real terms it's all been about Jürgen. The man has given him the greatest times in his young life, what was he going to do?

If this was to be the start of the long goodbye, let's leave the boss with the greatest memories to take away from his time with us. There's no doubt that he turned 'doubters into believers', he gave us belief, a sense of belonging and success, but most of all he gave us the feeling we all belong to Liverpool FC. The love for this man will live for ever. Now we needed to go out and win stuff, this was going to be emotional. The things that he has given us over his time here are beyond my wildest dreams. You've read my stories here and most of them don't happen without this man, so, Jürgen, thanks for everything. Liverpool fans, and Anfield in particular, were going to show the man how loved he was. Thanks Jürgen, getting tickets now became ten times harder.

Where shall I start with what comes next? Why not an amazing four days at the end of February, culminating in what could possibly be one of the greatest moments of my football life.

It started with Luton Town taking a shock lead against a depleted Liverpool. Injuries had hit us hard: no Ali, no Trent, no Salah, no Núñez, and no Jota. If you knew half the boys on our bench, you were better than me. The bench was populated with kids, five of them under 19, one only 16, and as we all know, 'you don't win anything with kids'. But these are Jürgen's kids; with a super-powered hug before you step across that white line, they can do anything.

Charlie and I were sitting together, tucked up on row 74 of the Kop (block 305), a mythical land that has its own ecosystem. While those at the front of the Kop were dressed for climbing the Eiger or Everest, those at the back were dressed for the beach, it was T-shirt weather up there, and the odd bikini or pair of budgie smugglers were rumoured to be on show. By half-time we were still one down, and while we'd played well enough, the final ball or shot on target wasn't good enough. Anfield had become a fortress, don't tell me a team in the bottom three was going to ruin the title charge.

As the second half started, Liverpool were on the offensive immediately, and within minutes could have had a penalty, a wayward Luton arm altering the course of the ball. Unbelievably the referee (and VAR) just carried on. We were livid, and as one the stadium rose and the crescendo of noise scared the living daylights out of Luton. Within minutes Virgil scored with his first momentous header of the week. Within two minutes, 2-1, as Gakpo headed in the fiercest cross you've ever seen from Mac Allister. The ground went wild. Every time the Reds flooded forwards, the ground, as one, roared them on, the crowd was feral. Rob Edwards admitted that the power of Anfield was in full effect: 'I think we made them angry … we saw Anfield, we saw Liverpool's full-throttle football, their counter-pressing was incredible, suffocated us, fans were amazing.' Funny that, 'Barry from Stourbridge' on Twitter always says it's a myth.

Díaz with his ninth shot of the game finally made it 3-1, and Harvey Elliott scored the fourth in the 90th minute. We, the crowd, made a real difference, and we need to keep doing that. We bounced out of Anfield that night top of the league and we were letting everyone know about it. Could we take that feral crowd atmosphere down to Wembley for the Carabao Cup Final?

* * *

I knew from an early stage that I was good for tickets for me and Charlie, thanks to a mysterious benefactor who could help me out. When I got locked out a couple of years ago he said he wished he'd known as he could have sorted me out. That's all words, isn't it? No, it isn't, he was as good as his word, the promise was made and gladly accepted. Weekends away in London for cup finals are well and truly behind me now, and the car was pushed into action again. You know the drill, evening ferry, a good sleep in Liverpool and then drive to the big smoke. Our Kev and the lads had been lucky in ballots and, once he knew I was driving, he asked if they could jump in. Of course, and by 8am we were on the M57 heading to London.

The club in its infinite wisdom had decided we should all have digital tickets, not like anything ever goes wrong with them is it? As evidence, I give you experiences in Paris and Anfield (every other week); there was every chance things could go wrong, so once in London, getting to the ground as early as possible was the order of the day.

We made great time down the motorway, and by 11.30am we were sitting in McDonald's in Stanmore. Suitably refreshed, and not looking for a pint, we were on Wembley Way by 1pm and heading to the turnstiles. Everyone, it seemed, had the same idea. There were more stewards stopping you on Wembley Way looking for bags than helping you if you had ticket problems. Even being early it still took 15 minutes to get in, as tickets were rejected at every turnstile, so you were sweating that your ticket would work. Being in early allowed us catch up with some great people, Daz Love, my favourite Twitter stalker, and Keifer now 'the man from the *Liverpool Echo*', which was great. Before you knew it kick-off was upon us and the teams were on the way to a cacophony of noise from the red end of the stadium. The Kop had travelled south and brought its A game. The team announced before kick-off was patched together, lots of stars missing and a bench full of kids, so the Reds would need our support. We're at our best when the chips are down and today was our day to step up, and we did.

The history books will show at 90 minutes for the third cup final in a row against Chelsea the score was 0-0, and we were heading for extra time and penalties again. It was far from boring, though, for a neutral it must have been great, but for us it was nerve-wracking. We thought we'd won it when Virgil powered a header in, then out of nowhere VAR decided there was some sort of infringement. In the ground you certainly didn't have a clue why, and even at 1am the following morning watching the highlights I still couldn't fathom why it was disallowed. I wouldn't mind but I'd called 'goal' as the corner was taken. I said we'd score, and I had a track record, forecasting goals from corners at both Arsenal and Forest in cup ties. Charlie thought I was magic – maybe I was!

In extra time the Reds really needed the travelling Kop, and as one we stood up and sung them home. There's a moment in extra time and the boys were running on empty, but the spine-tingling rendition of 'Allez, Allez, Allez' gave them an extra spring in their step. Then my next bit of magic came three minutes from time as Liverpool won a corner. Once again I said, 'Virgil will score here,' and much to everyone's surprise, especially mine, he got ahead of the defender and the ball flew across the keeper and into the corner of the net. Our end went mental, people were flying down the stairs and Charlie and I hugged, and hugged tightly, as tight as we ever had, and that's the moment, the moment I'll remember forever!

Don't get me wrong, as the whistle blew just three minutes later, we hugged, but it wasn't the same. That moment was one of relief, the first was of delirious joy, the moment you score the biggest goal of the year. Don't try to replicate it, you can't.

* * *

'Dreams turn to dust'. You all know what happened next, yeah, the Reds fell off a cliff! From a quadruple dream, we were left with holding just the Carabao Cup. I say just, but many would swap places with us. 'It's the hope that kills you.' We'd been saying it for weeks and unfortunately the damage was done by our two biggest rivals. Manchester United, with probably the worst team you've seen since the 80s, somehow managed to knock us out the FA Cup (in the final 30 seconds of extra time) and then dent our title hopes with a 2-2 draw. Both games saw us batter them but not finish our chances. At moments the gap between the teams was embarrassing, but if you don't take your chances that's what happens. Jürgen's glorious ending fell to pieces and the bastards ruined another book. Why can't you just leave me with a glorious chapter.

Oh yeah, and the final nail in the coffin was hammered in across Stanley Park by Everton, a team who until only ten days before hadn't won since the middle of December (and we were in mid-April). A team that was beaten 6-0 by Chelsea a week earlier, but a team who wanted it far more than us. That's the truth, we were second-best on the night and got what we deserved. I never even mentioned getting torn to bits by Atalanta at Anfield in the Europa League quarter-finals, which cancelled thousands of hotel bookings in Dublin, and had the touts, pubs and travel companies crying into their Guinness.

If you told us in August that we'd finish in the top four and win a cup we'd have taken that, but to go deep in all competitions, especially the league, in charge of our own destiny for once, it was hugely disappointing. Running on empty, whatever you want to call it, we weren't up to the job. Mentality? Big injuries catching up with us in key areas? This isn't the time for recriminations, it's a time to be thankful for what Jürgen brought us over his nine years. He won everything and he has given me, and more importantly Charlie, memories that will last a lifetime.

We travelled around Europe, watching the Mighty Reds with our mates (mine are his now), those wonderful memories of Munich, Madrid, Toulouse (most recently) and even Paris (it wasn't all horrendous). Charlie has learned some valuable lessons, such as you can't win everything, but you can have a great time, you meet the most amazing people doing what we do, and you'll always belong if you follow them the right way. It's fine to be upset, but see what happens when you believe and get behind people. Be a believer, not a doubter, Jürgen taught us that.

And do you know what? I'll treasure Wembley 2024 as much, if not more, than anything we ever won, because I was with Charlie and our bond was never as strong. I hope he has that as his go-to memory when I'm long gone. Mine was Wembley 1982 with my dad, as Ronnie Whelan curled one in the top corner to win us the Milk Cup against Tottenham.

* * *

And then before you knew it, the final game of Jürgen's reign was here. It was going to be emotional. I was okay with it, I understood his decision, I got it, I respected it, but the things this fella had given us, these words will never truly do it justice. He's one of us, just watch him rock up in an away end somewhere one day soon. I might approach him and say thank you, but then again I might leave him be. Never meet your heroes, but then again I might make an exception for the big fella.

The long goodbye had reached a crescendo during the week before the Wolves game, Jürgen's last, nine years in the blink of an eye. Charlie was with me as we headed up the Mersey and home, one last time. Jürgen is pretty much all he has known in his love affair with Liverpool. He loves them more than you'll ever know, Liverpool is the thing that makes him happy. Saying goodbye was going to be tough. As the weeks counted down to days the emotions ran deep and, as with everything to do with our club, it brings the echoes of the past. The journeys of those who went before us, my own journeys, and now Charlie's journeys, I find it hard to believe they could be any better than what we've seen over the last nine years.

The week had seen a whole range of interviews, most notably Jürgen speaking to *The Anfield Wrap*, where the conversation was more about him than the football. That should always be remembered, while as a manager he has been fantastic, as a human being he's exceptional. Stories from the Liverpool Disabled Supporters' Association, stories of Sean Cox and the bond between the two men, the Hillsborough families and then the average Joe in the street who Jürgen was good to, we're going to miss the man as much as the manager. He said he'll come running if the city of Liverpool needs him at any time, and that's no empty promise, you know he means it.

With every video, people were saying, 'I'm in bits,' or 'I won't be able to cope on Sunday.' You can laugh if you want but that's what it meant to people, as he gave us all a reason to believe, a sense of purpose and a real sense of belonging. Belonging to the community of Liverpool Football Club, and that's where our power lies, that community looking after each other. Wherever we go we'll be as one, we belong to each other and we'll look after each other, it's what we do, and Jürgen gets that. He knows what it means to be a Scouser, be it red or blue, he gets the fight in each and every one of us, fight for what's right, what we believe in, and never give in. Remember, we climbed the hill our own way!

The history books show that Liverpool beat Wolves 2-0 in Jürgen's last game, but the score didn't matter. A carnival atmosphere inside (and outside) the ground with a huge mosaic reading 'Danke Jürgen YNWA' (with a big German heart in the middle of it) stretching across three sides of the ground (exception being the Main Stand). The game was played out and his name was shouted until we were hoarse. He got the send-off he deserved. The last ten minutes heard all four sides of the ground singing his name incessantly, ten minutes of 'I'm so glad that Jürgen is a Red, I'm so glad he delivered what he said.' And he did! There were fewer tears than expected, it was as if it was right, it was the natural end to his tenure.

The presentations went on for ages, as everyone was thanked and allowed a golden goodbye before the gaffer, exactly what he wanted. It was never just about him, he'd said that often enough. One last run to the Kop (he didn't forget the other stands either) and his legendary fist-pumps and he was gone into Liverpool Football Club history.

As Jürgen bids farewell so will I. I hope you enjoyed my journey. This isn't the end, and it's a new beginning for Charlie. I'm far richer for having Jürgen in my life. These have been the best of times. Could we have won more trophies? Yeah, probably. I didn't even tell you he made us champions of the whole world, did I. Do you know what though? Everything we won was hard-earned and every bit has been cherished, but it's the moments with our friends, my Liverpool, that will remain in my heart forever.

* * *

I was lucky to follow in some fabulous footsteps, those of my dad, my uncles, Lenny and Dave, and my grandad, and now I've passed on the baton to Charlie. What amazing footsteps he follows in, and he can now take the path himself and go and explore the world, following the Mighty Reds. Some tips for him to help him on his travels:

> Don't make it everything in your life; leave space for love.
>
> Don't make it all-consuming, at least not forever.
>
> Make room for others.
>
> You'll find amazing people come into your life because of your passion.
>
> It's not only about football, it's about life and love. Now go and do more than I did.
>
> You've had a great education, more than any school can give you, so use that education wisely.

> Make yourself proud and follow the Reds in the right way, with love, passion, hope and belief, and remember …
>
> 'You'll Never Walk Alone'.

In the footsteps of our fathers, thanks to Bob, Bobby, Robert Salmon, my dad, for giving me the gift. Charlie, from your dad to you, this is my gift, it's all yours now mate.

And to you, the reader, thanks for following my journey. I hope it's made you laugh and helped you understand me and the life I've lived. I've tried to be the best version of myself: be good, honest, faithful and helpful. Fingers crossed I managed it.

Lastly, to my fellow travellers (those on these pages and those who aren't), thanks for letting me tell our story together. They've been the best of times and it wouldn't have been the same without any of you. Up the Reds!

Miss you Dad. I'll meet you by the wall!